Taunton's
CARPENTRY
COMPLETE

EXPERT ADVICE FROM START TO FINISH

The Taunton Press

Text by Andy Engel, © 2011 by The Taunton Press, Inc.
Photographs © 2011 by The Taunton Press, Inc., except as noted.
Illustrations © 2011 by The Taunton Press, Inc.
All rights reserved.

The Taunton Press, Inc.,
63 South Main Street, PO Box 5506,
Newtown, CT 06470-5506
e-mail: tp@taunton.com

Editors: Martin Miller, Alex Giannini
Copy editor: Seth Reichgott
Technical editor: Kevin Ireton
Indexer: Jay Kreider
Cover design: Kimberly Adis
Interior design: Kimberly Adis
Layout: Martin Miller, Cathy Cassidy
Illustrator: Christopher Mills
Front cover photographer: Randy O'Rourke
Photographers: Andy Engel and Patricia Steed, except where noted

Library of Congress Cataloging-in-Publication Data
Engel, Andy.
  Taunton's carpentry complete : expert advice from start to finish / Andy Engel.
    p. cm.
  Includes index.
  ISBN 978-1-60085-146-9
  1. Carpentry. 2. House construction. I. Title. II. Title: Carpentry complete, expert advice from start to finish.
  TH5606.E28 2011
  694--dc23
                    2011032770

Printed in the United States of America
10 9 8 7 6 5 4 3 2

No book is the work of one person, but rather a sum of knowledge and effort channeled through the author. In thanking people, I have to start with Patricia Steed, my wife and the center of my world. Pat took most of the photos for this book, many while hobbling around construction sites on a broken ankle. My sons Kevin and Duncan also pitched in. I was proud to see them working like men. I don't know how this book would have come to life without Kevin Ireton, who worked alongside me for months out of friendship and on my promise to return the favor. Others who helped include Brent Benner, Chris Green, Brian Rogers, Joe Cichowski, Bill Georgia, Dave Easter, Jim Larrabee, Strother Purdy, Mark Propsner, Mike Guertin, Greg Burnet, Glenn Mathewson, and Rob Arnold. This book would not have seen the light of day without the confidence of Helen Albert and Peter Chapman at The Taunton Press, nor without the layout and editing skills of Marty Miller. If I've forgotten anyone, I apologize. Thank you all.

I owe thanks to more than just the good people mentioned above. I owe them also to those who wrote down their knowledge in the magazines and books that fill my shelves, particularly those early *Fine Homebuilding* authors whose words were water in the desert to a young carpenter. And I do not forget the carpenters I learned from, veterans of WWII and Korea who are now mostly gone. In building new, we can't help but touch the past.

contents

>> >> >> >>

TOOLS AND MATERIALS

YOU CAN'T BE A CARPENTER without tools. Do you need a lot of them? No. The men I learned from began careers framing houses with a tape measure, a square, a chalkline, a plumb bob and a 4 ft. level, a handsaw, a knife, and a hammer. Trimwork added a hand miter box, a coping saw, nail sets, chisels, a brace and bits, two planes, and a couple of screwdrivers. A toolbelt back then was a canvas nail apron that the lumberyards gave away.

You'll find most of those same tools in my kit today, along with circular saws, power miter saws, electric drills–both corded and cordless–impact drivers, and a whole range of pneumatic tools that make carpentry more efficient and easier on the carpenter's body.

Carpentry is dangerous. Think about safety consequences. If something feels unsafe, stop and look for another way– there is always another way.

HAND TOOLS AND SAFETY

POWER SAWS

DRILLS AND DRIVERS

COMPRESSORS AND NAILERS

KEEPING THINGS IN LINE

SUPPORTS AND MATERIALS

TOOLBELT ESSENTIALS

The toolbelt adds considerably to a carpenter's efficiency by keeping the most frequently used tools and fasteners ready at hand. Inexpensive toolbelts can be fine for the occasional carpenter, although most pros use heavier-duty, better-designed models. A good one should last a decade or more—mine is by Occidental Leather®.

Don't be lured in by the promise of more and more compartments. Think about the tools you use every day, and be sure they have homes. In this day of nail guns, you might not need the voluminous nail pockets found in a lot of framer-style toolbelts. Consider how many fasteners you're likely to carry with you, and don't plan on carrying more. Bigger toolbelts mean heavier toolbelts, and you'll feel that at the end of the day.

Hammers

Hammers come in a range of sizes, from 16-oz. trim hammers to long-handled 28-oz. framing hammers. Worry less about size than about what feels good in your hand. Today, I drive most nails with compressed air, so I've replaced my specialty hammers with one Stiletto® 12-oz. titanium hammer for both framing and trim. It cost a ridiculous amount of money, but I love its balance, and its light weight leaves me a little less tired at the end of the day.

Toolbelts increase production by keeping your most-used tools ready at hand.

The chief characteristic of a good hammer is that it feels right in your hand.

A good utility knife is sturdy and comfortable and holds a readily accessible supply of blades.

BUY THE BEST TOOLS YOU CAN AFFORD

You don't need them all at once, though. Start out with a good toolbelt and a set of sturdy hand tools, including high-quality levels. If you're framing, get a good circular saw. For trimming, buy a miter saw that's big enough to handle the materials you expect to use. Cordless drills have become a practical necessity, and impact drivers put them to shame for setting screws and lags. Rent tools you use infrequently—scaffolding, ladders, and wall jacks, for example, and miter saws, circular saws, and nail guns as well.

Pullers

If you drive nails, you'll need to pull nails. Pull framing nails with a cat's paw. Hit it with a hammer to drive the claws under the nail head, then lever out the nail. When framing, there's one in my toolbelt, and I always carry a small Japanese-style prybar by Shark®. It weighs little, and is useful for everything from scraping ice to gently shifting trim into place. A flat bar is useful for prying boards apart. A crowbar is for heavy prying, and for levering out nails with heads driven above the surface.

Accessories

I keep a ¹⁄₃₂-in. nailset and a ³⁄₃₂-in. nailset in my toolbelt. These punches are useful for driving finish nails below the surface, setting under-driven framing nails, removing hinge pins, and a host of other purposes. Also in my toolbelt is a utility knife. Look for a sturdy feel, blade storage, and tool-less blade changing.

Cat's paws are driven into the wood around a nail head, then used to lever out the nail.

Toolbelt-sized prybars are handy for both framing and trim.

Nailsets do exactly as their name suggests—set nails below the surface.

Pulling sideways on a flat bar levers apart a header.

Use a crowbar, not a hammer, for pulling nails.

WARNING

I've hurt myself more frequently with hand tools than with power tools. Don't cut or chisel toward yourself. And wear safety glasses to protect your eyes from nails propelled either by a nail puller or an errant hammer blow. When hammering, you'll eventually hit your fingernail. The best protection is to pay attention. When I hit a fingernail, I find ice helps. See your doctor if it's too painful or shows signs of infection or a broken bone.

MEASURING AND LAYOUT TOOLS

Carpenters need accurate measurements and layout marks, and for those tasks, precision equipment is a must.

Tape measures

I carry a 25-ft. tape, although a 16-footer is fine for trimwork. (I think of tapes as throwaway items—it's rare to get more than a year out of one in daily use—but I still buy good ones, either Stanley® FatMax® or one of Tajima®'s offerings. The FatMax extends 11 ft. or so, unsupported, which is very handy, but the smooth action of Tajima's tapes is simply a pleasure.

Squares

Squares are another important tool. In my belt there is a Swanson® Speed® Square, or one of its clones. Handy for marking cut lines, it can also be used for laying out rafters. With rafter layout, though, I'm old school and prefer an aluminum Stanley framing square. This square is useful for both rafter and stair layout, and the aluminum doesn't overheat in the sun the way a dark-colored square does. For trimwork, I carry a Starrett® combination square—pricey, but dead accurate.

Chalklines

There are a bunch of decent chalklines on the market, some with a gear drive that speeds up reeling in the string. I use a Tajima chalkline, which I like because of its thin, strong string and smooth action.

Levels

I own Stabila® levels in various lengths: 18 in. for tight spots, 32 in. for checking door heads, 48 in. for everyday use, and 78 in. for door jambs. I also own a Bosch® laser level for kitchens, siding, and tile work, and a DeWalt® laser plumb bob that's remarkably handy for work under an existing ceiling.

Pencils

I use carpenter's pencils for marking most framing because they stand up to the rough lumber. Good lumberyards still give them away, which tickles my Yankee frugality. For trimwork, I use regular old #2 pencils, just like in grammar school, because I can whittle a fine point on them.

Look for smooth operation and good blade extension when buying tape measures.

Layout squares fit in the toolbelt. They mark cuts, rafter layouts, and a range of angles.

Use a framing square when you're laying out stairs, as well as rafters.

MAKING YOUR OWN BOLT MARKER

Grind a notch in the center of the blade of a combination square so a ½-in. bolt centers on the end of the blade. Then drill a hole at 5½ in. for your pencil mark. Reassemble the square.

Marking reveals is one of many jobs for a combination square.

A good chalkline reels in smoothly, is easy to fill, and minimizes chalk leakage.

Laser levels and laser plumb bobs have a far greater range than any bubble level.

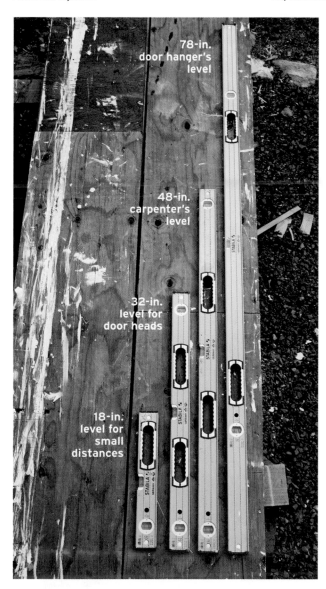

78-in. door hanger's level

48-in. carpenter's level

32-in. level for door heads

18-in. level for small distances

Every carpenter needs high-quality levels in a range of lengths.

THE CONSTRUCTION MASTER CALCULATOR

I own a Construction Master® calculator that's pushing 20 years old. It gets used on nearly every building project. Unlike most calculators, it works in the same units carpenters do—feet, inches, and fractions of inches. It's also designed to ease working with right triangles, the foundation of nearly all construction math.

The Construction Master allows you to enter the length of any two sides of a right triangle, and it finds the third—great for rafters, stairs, and laying walls out square to each other. Or you can enter the length of one side and the pitch of the triangle (as in roof pitch, say 4 in 12), and it will figure the length of either remaining side. I'm told the newer versions do even more, with functions like cumulative rise for stairs or cumulative spacing for balusters—all at the push of a button.

CUTTING WITH HAND TOOLS

Although there seems to be a power tool for every purpose, I still use a lot of old-fashioned tools to cut and finish edges.

Saws

One of my favorite saws is a Disston™ 12-tooth-per-in. (tpi) handsaw that was my father's—it's great for finishing cuts in rafters and stair stringers and for the odd occasion when you need a fine-toothed handsaw.

To keep from wearing out an heirloom, I use two new handsaws, both Japanese-style (they cut on the pull stroke, not the push). One is a Silky® Gomboy folding saw. Originally intended for arborists, the fine-toothed version folds up to fit in my toolbelt. It weighs little and sees a surprising amount of use. The other saw is a Tajima trim carpenter's saw. It's easy to swap crosscut and rip blades, it slides quickly into its tool pouch, and it takes up little space in my toolbox. Both the Gomboy and the Tajima have incredibly sharp blades because the teeth are hardened. When they dull, they can't be sharpened, but they last a long time between replacement blades.

When trimming, I use a coping saw every day. Mine is an old pre-Stanley Trojan® #20 whose frame is a lot more rigid than the new ones. That helps to keep the blade tensioned, making it easier to cut accurately. I bought it at a carpenter's estate sale for a couple of bucks 20 years ago. The main thing with coping saws is to use a fine-toothed blade—20 tpi. They cut slower, but more accurately.

Handsaws are often the fastest method for finish cuts. They don't require any setup.

This folding saw fits neatly in a toolbelt pouch.

Sharpening Handsaws If your father didn't leave you an estate with a vintage handsaw, you can probably pick one up cheaply at a flea market or tag sale. The trick is finding someone to sharpen it the old-fashioned way. Most saw sharpening today is done by completely shearing off the old teeth and grinding new ones in their place, drastically shortening the life of the saw. Try to find a sharpener who simply sharpens and sets the existing teeth or learn to do it yourself.

Planes

I regularly keep one of two different planes in my toolbelt. One is an old no-name standard-angle block plane from a tag sale that's great for trimming the edges of cedar shingles. Adjust the blade in by tapping it with a hammer and out by tapping the butt of the plane. The other is an amazingly good and amazingly expensive Lie-Nielson® low-angle, adjustable-throat block plane that can't be beat for shaving miters.

Chisels

In my toolbelt, there is always a ¾-in. chisel. It's particularly handy with trimwork when I just need to shave a little bit of wood (for example, to flush up a head jamb with its leg), but it also sees use when I'm framing. Chisels and planes, however, won't do their job if they're not sharp—a skill you can learn with a little practice.

ADJUSTING A STANDARD BLOCK PLANE

To set the blade deeper in an old-style block plane, gently tap the heel of the blade forward.

To retract the blade, gently tap the back of the plane body with your hammer.

Japanese-style saws are hard to beat for sharpness and clean cuts. They cut on the pull stroke, making cutting easier and more accurate.

A coping saw cuts curves.

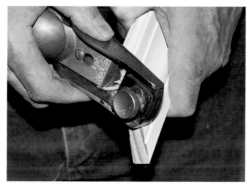

Low-angle block planes are the tool for fine-tuning miter cuts.

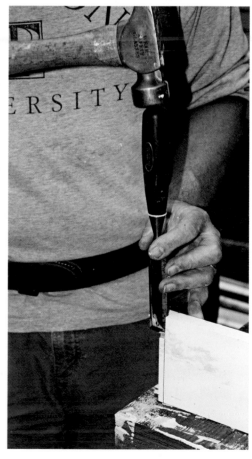

Keep a sharp chisel around and you're guaranteed to find uses for it.

PERSONAL SAFETY GEAR

Carpentry is dangerous, but safety gear can make it less so. Working safely, however, is also about attitude, vigilance, and knowing your limits. There are techniques I show in this book that may be safe for me and not for you. Each of us is responsible for our own safety. If it feels dangerous, you owe it to yourself and your family to find another way. Unfortunately, jobsite culture can often be stupidly macho—take responsibility and don't allow yourself to be pressured into an unsafe act. Now, to the gear.

Safety glasses

You can buy prescription safety glasses through your eye doctor. Prescription or not, safety glasses must meet the ANSI Z87.1 standard, and this will be printed somewhere on the glasses. The cheap ones tend to be uncomfortable. Spend a few bucks for comfort. If you work outdoors, get Z87.1 sunglasses with UV protection.

Hearing protection

Hearing protection doesn't have to be uncomfortable or inconvenient. In general, I hate wearing earplugs, but I don't mind Howard Leight's QB2 ear plugs. They're on a springy plastic neckband that makes them easy to remove when I don't need them, but leaves them handy when I do. For shop work, I use Peltor™ ear muffs—quiet and comfortable, even over glasses.

Lung protection

All sorts of things on the job are bad for your lungs. Wood dust is listed as a human carcinogen. Dust from old houses can be laden with lead. Paints and finishes contain VOCs. When working in a dusty environment, wear a mask, or better, a respirator. The cheap masks aren't good for much except nuisance dust, but a quality respirator will keep you from breathing in stuff such as lead from old paint.

Respirator filter standards are set by NIOSH. The standard designations have both a letter and number. The letters are

Look for the ANSI Z87.1 stamp on safety glasses, which will assure you the glasses provide proper impact resistance.

N (not oil resistant), R (oil resistant), and P (oil proof). The numbers refer to the percentage of 0.3 micrometer and larger particles filtered out: 95, 99, and 100 (the 100 series really gets only 99.97 percent of those particles, but who's counting?). An N95 filter is allowable for wood dust. But if you're around asbestos or lead paint, you want an N100 series mask.

Hardhats and other gear

Pros are required to wear hardhats on construction sites. Enforcement varies regionally. I've never seen hardhats on residential construction in the East, but they're common in the West.

Other personal gear that makes sense includes steel-toed boots and workgloves. Steel-toed boots can be particularly helpful when framing because of the weight of the objects being slung around. Work gloves have come a long way. The new ones are thinner, so you can grasp nails and tools. They're still hot in the summer, but they're a big help in the winter. And they reduce the number of splinters you get.

WARNING

Carbon monoxide can be deadly. Be smart—run fuel-powered equipment, such as generators or compressors, outside. If you use an unvented temporary heater, open some windows and keep a battery-powered CO alarm on the job.

Every year I read about a construction worker being electrocuted. Usually it's because a ladder contacted an overhead powerline. If you have to work around overhead powerlines, watch the top of your ladder and call the power company for a temporary shutoff or an insulation pad.

Shocks from electrical tools are common. Make sure your cords and tools are properly grounded. Use a GFCI-protected power strip to run all your tools.

Ear muffs provide the greatest hearing protection.

Respirators with replaceable filters work for a variety of breathing hazards.

Hardhats protect you from injuries caused by falling objects.

Ear plugs on neckbands are always there when needed. You can pop them in or out as you wish.

New fabrics make work gloves light and strong, and they offer improved tactile sensation.

First aid Cuts and bruises are part of carpentry. Mostly they're minor, but it's important to take care of minor cuts to prevent infection and to be able to recognize the difference between something you can treat with a bandage or some ice and something that needs a trip to the ER or a 911 call.

Take a first-aid class, and follow the advice about what should be in your jobsite first-aid kit. Know how to use those items. My kit contains adhesive bandages, gauze pads, tape, chemical cold packs, antiseptic ointment, cortisone cream, wet wipes, sharp tweezers, sterile eye wash, ibuprofen, antihistamines, and moleskin. Perhaps the most important first-aid item I own, though, is a cell phone.

POWER SAWS

The first power tool to come out on most jobsites is a 7¼-in. circular saw. There are two basic types—worm drives are favorites in the West and sidewinders rule in the East. Worm drives are heavier, and most are configured with the motor on the right and the blade on the left. Right-handed carpenters like this because it's easy to see where the blade is cutting.

Most sidewinders are configured with the motor on the left and the blade on the right, so it's a little harder to see the cut. Right-handed carpenters like the configuration of sidewinders because the weight of the motor ends up over the side of the workpiece that's supported on sawhorses or the lumber pile.

See the dilemma? As an East Coaster, I've almost always used sidewinders. Compensating for the lesser visibility is second nature, and I like the lighter weight. As an experiment, I once framed a house using a worm drive. By the end of the job, my right elbow was throbbing with bursitis because of the heavier saw. Each saw costs about the same, so pick what you like.

Blades

There is a huge selection of blades available for circular saws. The more teeth on a blade, the finer the cut. I have a heavy, expensive, 40-tooth finish blade for working with hardwood, but that doesn't come out often. Like most carpenters, my daily-users are the thin, cheap, 18-tooth carbide framing blades that lumberyards have sitting on the counter. When they dull, I throw them in recycling.

Tablesaws

Although jobsite tablesaws have become popular and accurate, I still don't own one. Instead, I do my ripping using a circular saw with a rip guide or bring the stock home and rip it on my shop saw.

Reciprocating saws and jigsaws

The two other hand-held power saws I use are a reciprocating saw and a jigsaw. The common name for a reciprocating saw is "Sawzall®," which is the Milwaukee Electric Tool Corporation® trade name. They made the first one, and my 25-year-old version still chugs along just fine. Reciprocating saws are used for demolition work and for other rough tasks. Jigsaws are finer tools, although they work in a similar manner. The Festool® jigsaw I own is one of the best I've ever used for making smooth cuts and for keeping its blade square to the tool when cutting thick stock.

Powerful worm-drive saws are favored in the western U.S. Their weight can make them a chore to use in a prolonged project.

Sidewinders are lighter and more common in the eastern U.S., but the location of the motor can make the cut harder to see.

Carbide-tipped circular saw blades are cheap and easily replaced when they dull.

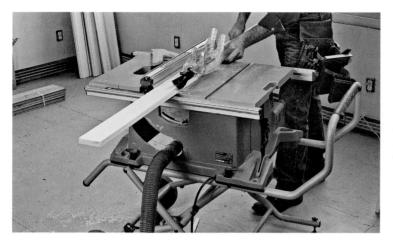

Jobsite tablesaws provide nearly the power and accuracy of some shop saws. (Photo by Charles Miller)

Reciprocating saws make cuts no other saw can handle. Blades are available for heavy demolition work, including cutting through fasteners.

Jigsaws can make rough curved cuts in framing, and with a finer blade, smooth, decorative cuts to embellish trim.

WARNING

Circular saws have killed carpenters. They can kick back from the workpiece, severing arteries and fingers. Support your work, and keep your fingers out of the path of the blade.

MAKING CLEAN CUTS

A circular saw with a rip guide can handle most rip cuts on the jobsite (right). But for cutting accurate and splinter-free crosscuts with a circular saw, I use a homemade shooting board. It's a piece of 1/4-in. plywood with a 1/2-in.- or 3/4-in.-thick fence screwed to it (far right). Make the 1/4-in. base so it projects beyond the base of the saw.

The first time you use it, the excess is trimmed off exactly where the inside of the blade falls. For subsequent cuts, all you need to do is align the edge of the shooting board where you want the cut and clamp it in place.

MITER SAWS

One of the first pro tools I bought 30 years ago was a Makita® 10-in. miter saw. I still own and use it. When I first trimmed houses, they all got a 3-in. base and a 2¼-in. casing. If there was crown, it was only 3½ in. wide. A 10-in. miter saw (chop saw, chop box) handled them with ease.

Today, it's rare to see a house that doesn't have a 5¼-in. base, which my 10-in. saw can't handle. That's why I bought a bigger miter saw—popular trim sizes increased.

I upgraded to a DeWalt 12-in. compound miter saw, which handled the bigger moldings and allowed me to miter 8-in. stock. That did the job for a few years, but I eventually upgraded again to a Bosch 12-in. sliding compound miter saw. It's heavy, and no fun to cart around, but it will miter any molding I use, as well as crosscut 12-in. stock, such as stair treads.

Blades

Unlike circular saw blades, I buy decent blades for my miter saws. For the 12-in. saw, I use an 80-tooth trim blade, and for the 10 in., a 60-tooth.

WARNING

A miter saw can amputate fingers in a heartbeat. Never put any body parts in the line of the cut. Don't try to hold small pieces of stock with your hand while cutting them—if the saw grabs the workpiece, your hand can be dragged into the blade. Be particularly careful if you're doing a bunch of repetitive cuts. Boredom can lead to lack of focus, and that's one time accidents are likely to happen.

A standard 10-in. miter saw **handles smaller trim, and its size and light weight make it conveniently portable.**

A tilting 12-in. miter saw will cut larger trim and boards—up to 8-in. molding stock.

A 12-in. sliding compound miter saw handles nearly any conventional lumber or trim.

Higher-quality miter saw blades yield cleaner cuts. Because of the precision required for many joints, these blades are worth the investment.

The versatile Jawhorse, with its miter saw accessories, sets up into a compact miter saw stand.

Stands

For most of my career, I used a couple of saw-horses and a 2×12 as a miter saw bench. I'd stick a couple of blocks of wood at the end of the 2×12 to serve as outfeed supports. The setup was crude, cheap, and ugly enough that I never worried about anyone stealing it, but it worked pretty good. I've upgraded that now, too. For the 10-in. saw, I use a Jawhorse™ with miter-stand accessories. It's a simple, compact setup, and the Jawhorse is useful for a host of other purposes as well.

My 12-in. miter saw lives on a stand made by the now defunct and much mourned company, American Design and Engineering. Although you can't buy that stand anymore, there are a lot of choices on the market.

Several manufacturers make sturdy, reliable miter saw stands that stand up to the rigors of jobsite work.

CORDLESS DRILLS AND DRIVERS

No one had cordless drills when I started out. I bought my first one, a tiny 7.2v Makita, in 1986. My helper laughed when I showed it off that morning. After work, he bought his own. Today, there's a host of manufacturers and battery sizes and types available.

The industry seems to have settled into 18v as the most common battery platform, but look around before buying. If you want more cordless tools than just drills and drivers, choose a manufacturer that makes the range of tools you like, and stick with that maker and that battery size. It's handy to be able to swap batteries between tools.

Today, I use three cordless tools. I have an 18v Bosch drill, which has plenty of guts for most drilling I encounter. This particular drill has a hammer function for drilling masonry as well, and of course, you can chuck a screwdriver bit in it, too.

My go-to tool for driving screws and lags is an 18v Makita impact driver. Nothing drives screws like an impact driver. Significantly lighter than drills of the same voltage, they have an internal hammer that kicks in

An 18v cordless drill handles most day-to-day tasks.

Battery use
Cordless-tool batteries are expensive, they last just two to three years, and you can shorten that by abusing them. Heat kills batteries. If you're using a battery hard, or it's hot out, or both, give it a break every so often. Do something else, or swap out the battery with a cool one.

Charging a battery when it's too hot or too cold shortens its life, too. Most modern chargers have a sensor that detects this and won't allow charging. Still, it's a good idea to find a warm place to charge cold batteries, and a cool place to charge warm ones.

No battery—lithium ion or nickel metal hydride—works its best in the cold. Always keep a spare in a warm place if you're working in the cold.

You may hear about batteries having a memory—that is, if you consistently recharge them before they become fully discharged, eventually they'll accept only a partial charge. That was true in the past, but with today's batteries and chargers, it's poppycock.

Impact drivers are far superior to any drill at driving screws, including lag screws.

Many drills and drivers **feature an LED headlight**, a handy feature that makes it easier to work in dark corners.

to add more rotational power when the going gets tough. I have driven 5-in. lag screws with this tool, so 2½-in. screws aren't even a challenge.

Impact drivers accept only hex-shanked bits, which limits them for drilling holes. This particular model, as well as most coming on the market today, comes equipped with an LED headlight, something I appreciate more and more with middle age.

Corded or cordless tools?

The current generation of cordless tools includes circular saws, jigsaws, and reciprocating saws. Manufacturers often sell kits with several tools and batteries at an attractive price. And the cordless saws I've tried have plenty of power.

However, the only cordless tools I own are drills and drivers. That's because I expect at least 10 years out of a corded tool, and I'm rarely disappointed. A cordless might last that long, but its batteries won't. And given that it usually costs about the same to buy a new tool in a kit with a charger and batteries as it does to buy two new batteries alone, I think corded tools win here.

CORDED DRILLS

Cordless drills still don't match up to corded models in terms of longevity or power. For example, when I do railing work, I might have to drill 100 ¾-in. holes into hardwood for the balusters on a balcony. That heavy, continuous use is hard on batteries. And in general, a corded tool is significantly cheaper than its cordless equivalent, particularly when you consider that the cordless drill will need new batteries within three years. The drill I reach for most often is a DeWalt ⅜-in. variable-speed model with an old-fashioned keyed chuck. Mine is about 15 years old, and it works as well as the day I bought it. >> >> >>

Extension cords Here's what you need to know. Don't be cheap. Buy 12-gauge cords, not the lighter 14 gauge, or God forbid, 16 gauge. The heavier wire reduces voltage drop, giving tools the power they need to work well and last a long time.

Corded drills still have their place because they have more torque and unlimited run time.

CORDED DRILLS (CONTINUED)

The next drill I look for is my ½-in. Bosch hammer drill. Carpenters end up drilling into masonry on a regular basis, and this is the fastest tool for the job. Hammer drills have both an aggressive hammer setting for drilling masonry, as well as a normal rotary setting for drilling holes in other materials. On its hammer setting, this tool calls for hearing protection.

For really heavy duty work, I'll use a rotary hammer. These tools work like big hammer drills for making large-diameter holes in concrete. Larger ones than shown here also have a straight hammer setting that turns them into mini-jackhammers. That's really useful with a chisel-shaped bit for tearing up old ceramic tile. Big and loud, this occasional-use tool requires hearing protection, too.

Finally, on the odd occasion when I need a lot of torque (for example, when using a large-diameter hole saw or drilling bolt holes in steel), I pull out my Milwaukee ⅝-in. drill. This low-speed drill has an incredible amount of torque and requires careful use.

⚠ WARNING

Drills seem to be about the safest power tools around, but they aren't without risk. Friction can make the bits hot enough to burn flesh. And with a high-torque machine like my ⅝-in. drill, if the bit binds and you aren't prepared, the drill itself can rotate. I have sprained my thumb with this tool. Another time it got completely away from me, the auxiliary handle came around and clocked me on the jaw, literally knocking me to the ground. I'm glad I wasn't on a ladder.

If you have long hair, secure it under a hat while using a drill. I know one man who was partially scalped when his ponytail got bound up in a drill.

Hammer drills make for fast drilling in masonry. A switch changes the action between straight drilling and hammer-drilling.

Rotary hammers are heavier-duty versions of hammer drills. Use them when you need to drill larger holes in masonry.

For holes that require higher torque, turn to a ⅝-in.-chuck heavy-duty drill.

DRILL BITS

The most common bits are twist bits, available in sizes from tiny to huge. They'll drill wood, metal, and plastic. For holes in wood up to 1½ in., I use inexpensive spade bits. When I need a larger-diameter hole in wood, I use a hole saw or a self-feeding bit. Masonry bits occupy their own category. If you're using a hammer drill, buy bits rated for the drill. Rotary hammers take special, splined bits, which can be rented with the tool.

Twist bits are used for smaller-diameter holes in wood, metal, and plastic.

Spade bits handle ¼-in. to 1½-in. holes in wood.

Hole saws and self-feeding bits bore larger-diameter holes in wood.

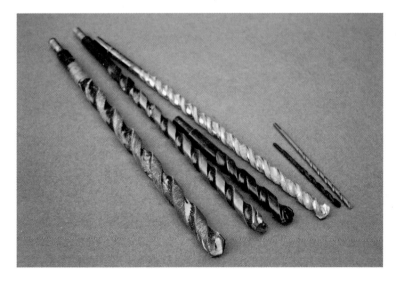

Concrete, brick, and stone require carbide-tipped masonry bits.

Heavy-duty spline-shanked bits are used in rotary hammers.

AIR COMPRESSORS AND HOSES

There's a reason nail guns have become ubiquitous on job sites—no other tool does more to increase your efficiency. From nailing studs and sheathing to roofing, siding, and trim, there's a nailer for every circumstance. And it's not just efficiency—nailers save wear and tear on the body. Nearly every carpenter from pre-nailgun days had some form of bursitis, tendonitis, or carpal tunnel syndrome by age 40. Nail guns can still bring on some issues from repetitive use, but it's nothing like it used to be. With a few specialty exceptions—models that use a small internal-combustion engine and battery-powered units—all nail guns require compressed air.

I own two compressors, a 2-hp Senco® with twin tanks—whose capacity I need for running multiple framing guns—and a smaller Bostich™ that's easier to carry around and will run one framing gun or a couple of trim guns. When buying a compressor, consider what you'll use it for and don't buy bigger than you need. Compressors are heavy and awkward.

You'll need heavy, large-capacity compressors to run multiple framing nailers.

For one framing gun, or a couple of trim guns, lighter compressors work fine.

TRADE SECRET

If the job is some distance from the electricity source, it's better to make the distance up with more hoses than with more extension cords. Longer cords mean more voltage drop, which is tough on high-drawing compressor motors.

Other air tools

You can buy an air-powered version of any electrical tool on the market, and it's common to see these tools—drills, sanders, saws, and grinders—in automotive shops. They're often quieter and faster than their electric counterparts, but you don't see them on construction sites. That's because they use a lot of air—more than any job-site compressor can produce.

Hoses

In addition to the compressor, you'll need hoses. The more expensive rubber hoses tangle less, but the urethane hoses are cheap and indestructible. Take your pick.

Hoses also come in two internal diameters, $\frac{3}{8}$ in. and $\frac{1}{4}$ in. If you're running multiple guns off a splitter, be sure the hose from the compressor to the splitter is $\frac{3}{8}$ in. so your tools are getting maximum volume. The hoses on the "outlet" side of the splitter can be either diameter. The splitter shown here is a commercially made model, and many like it are available.

Fittings

In addition to hoses and compressors, you'll need fittings to join everything together. Air-tool chucks are of the quick-release type, so changing between tools is a breeze. They come in several configurations and in two sizes: $\frac{3}{8}$ in. and $\frac{1}{4}$ in. Some larger framing guns need the flow from the bigger fittings, while the small fittings are less bulky on trim tools. In any event, choose one standard size and configuration for all your tools.

Rubber hoses cost more and tangle less than hoses made from other materials, such as vinyl.

Although they are inexpensive and durable, urethane hoses tend to tangle and kink.

With a splitter you can run multiple guns. A supply hose (right) comes from the compressor; multiple lines (left) run to several tools.

Hoses, compressors, and air tools all have either a chuck or a nipple to connect them.

WARNING

Compressors rarely pose hazards, but occasionally you'll hear of a tank blowing up, with catastrophic results. That's almost always because of corrosion.

When air is compressed, there's less space between the molecules, and water is literally squeezed out. It accumulates in the bottom of tanks, rusting them. Every compressor tank should have a drain cock on its bottom. Open it every work day to drain water.

Another hazard is from uncapped air hoses. A functioning chuck at the end of a hose will not let air out. But if you should pressurize an uncapped hose, the air will jet from it, whipping the end of the hose every which way. Never pressurize a hose with an open end.

Also, be careful of air hoses when working on a roof—stepping on one is a lot like stepping on a roller and can lead to a fall.

FRAMING, ROOFING, AND SIDING NAILERS

Ask a carpenter about nailers, and framing nailers probably come to mind first.

Some framing guns and all siding guns use coil nails. Coil nailers are great when you want the largest volume of nails in the gun's magazine. Those times are when you'll be using one-size nails for a lot of fastening–say, roofing, siding, and sheathing. It's a little harder to change sizes of nails in a coil nailer than in a stick nailer. And, because they hold a lot more nails, coil nailers run a little heavier than stick nailers. Finally, because of their drum magazines, coil nailers are bulkier than stick nailers. For prefinished siding, prepainted nails are available.

Other framing nailers are used for fastening metal framing connectors, something you should never try with a nailer not designed for that purpose. My regular Bostitch framer has a replacement tip that allows it to be used with metal connectors. A probe on the tip is inserted in the nail hole, and the nail follows the probe. Several manufacturers make dedicated metal-connector nailers that shoot 1½-in. to 2½-in. connector nails.

Finally come palm nailers. These tools have no magazine and will drive any nail you care to use. Place the nose of the nailer over the nail head and press down. This activates a fast hammer action that's great for driving nails that are hard to reach.

High magazine-capacity framing and siding guns use coiled nails.

Because of the large number of nails it takes to shingle a roof, roofing guns use coil nails.

Some metal-connector nailers locate the nail precisely in the hole by way of a probe.

Dedicated metal-connector nailers are usually limited to 1½-in. and 2½-in. nails. (Photo courtesy Mike Guertin)

Low-profile palm nailers make quick work of nailing in tight spots.

Metal-connector nailers

A special category of nail guns are those designed for attaching framing hardware such as joist hangers. First a word of caution–don't try this with a regular nailer. I already did that for you, when I was young and foolish. It doesn't work, and nails will ricochet unpredictably.

Metal-connector guns have special, pointed tips that locate the nail precisely in the hole. Some of these guns are limited in the size of nail they'll handle. These tools are extremely handy if you're nailing on a lot of framing hardware, but they're by no means a necessity for most DIYers.

NAILS FOR NAILERS

Most framing guns use nails collated together in a stick and bound with either plastic or paper at an angle of about 21 degrees, like my Bostitch, or about 30 degrees, like my Campbell Hausfeld®.

Nails for the 30-degree guns are usually held together with wire that's welded right to the nails, or with glued-on paper. Such nails actually contact each other in the stick, fitting the greatest number of nails in the magazine. It used to be, however, that these nails were only available with half-moon shaped "clipped heads." Clipped-head nails don't always meet code requirements. To allow full round-head nails (like the common nails you drive with a hammer), a lower magazine angle was adapted and the nails are collated with plastic strips that hold the nails farther apart. There are two downsides to that. First, you can't fit as many nails in the magazine. Second, little bits of plastic collation fly all over the place, making a mess and occasionally stinging when they hit skin. Some clever person figured out that by placing the head off center, full round-head nails could be made that feed in a gun designed for clipped-head nails, and these are readily available now. Take your pick—either format is way faster than hand-nailing.

The full round-head nails for lower-angle framing guns are collated with plastic.

The more tightly packed nails used in steeper-angle nailers are joined with welded wire.

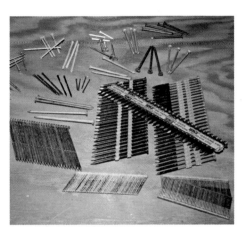

POWDER-ACTUATED FASTENERS

Carpenters often have to fasten wood to concrete. You can do this with hand-driven masonry nails, but they often move the wood or break partway in.

Powder-actuated fasteners are much faster and better. They work like a firearm, using a trigger-actuated system to ignite a powder charge to drive a piston that drives a special hardened nail. They require the same caution as a gun—mainly, never point the muzzle at anything you don't want to shoot and always wear safety glasses and hearing protection when using one.

These tools are pricey for most DIYers, but they can be rented in most areas. You'll probably have to watch a short safety video and pass a test before they let you out the door, though.

FINISH NAILERS

Finish nailers come in several sizes. The one I reach for most for general trimwork is a Bostitch 15-gauge angled gun. Most shoot nails from 1½ in. to 2½ in., which handles nearly all trim needs. The nails are thin enough that they usually don't split the trim, but thick enough to use when nailing in a door frame that you don't want to move.

Brad guns shoot even smaller nails—typically 18 gauge, in a range of lengths between ⅝ in. and 2 in. They're handy for smaller trim or, with the shorter brads, nailing thin plywood panels to cabinet sides.

Headless pinners shoot the smallest nails—23 gauge, in lengths between ½ in. and 1⅜ in. These are great for use with prefinished hardwood, since the nail holes are so small they don't require filling.

Another category of nailer is really a stapler. I use a Porter-Cable® ½-in. crown stapler for utility tasks such as joining drawer sides or putting down ¼-in. underlayment. I also use it for assembling jigs and fixtures in my shop. My Arrow® tacker operates entirely manually but gets even more use than the pneumatic stapler, mostly using thin, ¼-in. staples to fasten tar paper or housewrap.

One final category of nailer is the airless gun. This category was developed by Paslode®, whose guns are driven with a small internal-combustion motor, which runs off a flammable gas and a battery to provide the spark. They're pricey, the cycle time is slower than with a pneumatic tool, and you have to buy gas and replace batteries occasionally, but they're very handy in places you'd rather not have a hose. For example, an airless nailer is nice to have for nailing roof sheathing, where an air hose is a trip hazard. They're great for punch-list work, where you just have odds and ends to do, and setting up a compressor and hoses would take up a disproportionate amount of time.

An angled 15-gauge finish nailer **holds a range of nail lengths, handling most trimwork.**

For spots where shorter and thinner nails are required, an 18-gauge brad gun is the answer.

WARNING

Nailers are available with both bounce and sequential firing modes. All nailers that I'm aware of require a two-step process to fire. First, depress the nose. Second, pull the trigger. That's sequential fire, and all nailers do it. Bounce-firing means that you can hold the trigger down and fire the nailer by bouncing the nose on the work surface. Not all nailers can do this, but those that can are faster for repetitive nailing such as sheathing. The trouble is, if you don't remember to take your finger off the trigger, it's easy to fire the nailer by brushing it up against anything, including body parts. Most, if not all, currently made nailers can be switched between modes. I never set mine on bounce fire.

Never use a regular nailer for metal connectors. The nails will miss the holes in the connector, and they will ricochet off in unpredictable directions—eventually, someone could lose an eye.

Always wear safety glasses when using nailers and never have any body part in line with the nail. You should also wear hearing protection, particularly indoors where the sound is contained. Perhaps surprisingly, I wear a dust mask when using a trim gun for base molding. It's difficult to sweep or vacuum all the drywall dust from plywood floors, and my trim nailer stirs up a considerable amount of the stuff.

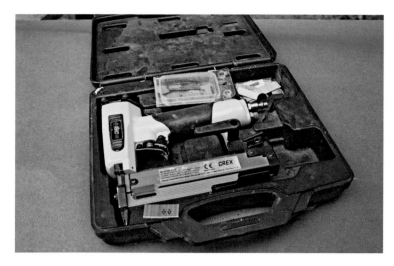

Headless pinners shoot 23-gauge brads and leave unnoticeable holes–great for small moldings.

Small staplers come in handy for a variety of utility tasks, such as assembling drawers or putting down thin subfloor material.

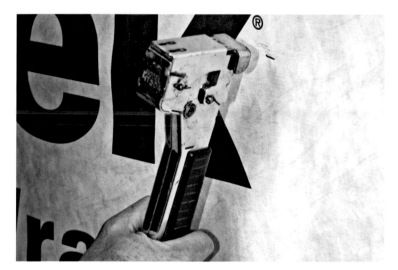

Tackers drive light-duty staples, securing housewrap, tar paper, and the like.

Airless nailers cost more but come in handy for small tasks and for situations where an air hose is unwanted.

Nail stats The
British penny symbol, "d," describes nail size; for example, 4d nails are 1½ in. long, 16d nails are 3½ in. For framing, common nails have heads and thick shanks. Drive finish-nail heads below the surface. Box nails, sinkers, and coolers have heads and thin shanks for attaching sheet goods. "Deformed shank" nails resist withdrawal with ringed or screw-like shanks. Most nails are steel. Galvanized steel resists corrosion. Use hot-dipped galvanized in treated lumber, stainless steel where severe corrosion is likely. Use copper or aluminum nails with those materials.

CLAMPS, JACKS, AND PULLERS

People tend to think of clamps as more of a woodworker's tool for glue-ups than something found on a rough-and-tumble job site. Clamps are good for glue-ups without a doubt, but that's not all I use them for. Clamps can be pricey—I'll bet I have a thousand dollars worth of them, bought over the years. However, you can save a bunch of money by shopping tag sales and flea markets for clamps—nearly every one I've ever been to has a couple of clamps, for only a couple of bucks. If they're rusty, buy 'em anyway. A couple of shots of penetrating oil and they'll be fine for framing.

C-clamps and small bar clamps

C-clamps and small bar clamps are great for holding material in place while you're routing or sawing it. They're also ideal for holding adjoining cabinet stiles together prior to fastening them. Tightened down on a sheet of plywood, you can use C-clamps as a handle.

Pipe clamps

Pipe clamps have as long a reach as you have iron pipe and come in handy for pulling work together for nailing. Pipe clamps come sized for both ¾-in. and ½-in. pipe. I find the ½-in. pipe ones plenty strong.

Spring clamps

Spring clamps don't cost much, and they're extremely useful for light-duty work such as clamping a guide to a square.

Cabinetmaker's and miter clamps

Bessey® parallel-jaw cabinetmaker's clamps are pricey, but they excel at forcing framing members into position. For clamping mitered trim until the glue sets, I use miter clamps by the Collins Tool Co. These are two types of clamps I've never seen at a tag sale, but I don't regret paying retail for either.

Wall jacks and pullers

The older I get, the less I like to lift things. About 6 years ago, I bought a set of Qual-Craft® wall jacks for raising framed walls and my back has thanked me ever since. The ones I have are relatively inexpensive and climb about 6 in. up a 2×4 with each pump of the handle. And once you get the wall raised, sometimes it ends up not quite where you want it. Another company, Proctor, makes wall jacks that use a cable winch and an aluminum mast. These seem like a nicer choice, but I've never used them. They're also a lot more expensive. Trojan's Wall Puller is an inexpensive and extremely handy tool for moving wall plates.

Use C-clamps or small bar clamps to draw tight work you'll be screwing together.

Pipe clamps have a long reach. You'll find a variety of uses for them, including drawing framing members together for nailing.

Spring clamps are simply handy—to clamp a square to a jig or a work light to a stud, or to keep a cord out of your way.

With their deep clamping faces, parallel-jaw clamps flush up uneven surfaces prior to nailing.

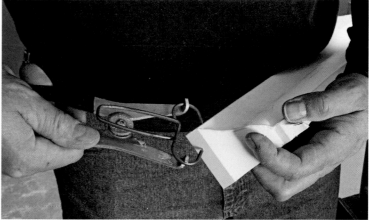

Spread apart with special pliers, miter clamps join miters until the glue sets.

Use jacks that climb 2×4 poles to raise walls with a mechanical advantage, not your back.

A wall puller based on the design of a logger's peavey brings a bottom plate to its line before nailing.

Alternative clamps Sometimes I find myself needing a clamp, and all of mine are back in my shop, 20 miles away. Lots of readily available items can work as clamps. For example, tie-down straps used to secure loads to a roof rack work great. For pulling posts or beams closer to each other, use a Spanish windlass. That's a fancy phrase for a rope looped around the objects and wound tight with a stick. I've cut wedges from framing lumber and driven them together as an ersatz clamp. A 2×4 wedged between the ceiling and the floor or a bench is a great clamp. You can use drywall screws to draw a stick down over an object.

Sometimes you need to push things apart a little. It's amazing what you can do by sledge-hammering a 2× that's cut a little long between two opposing surfaces. Alternatively, cut two 2×s that together add up to a little longer than the space you want to open, and push them together. Do be careful with all these techniques, though. They generate a surprising amount of force and can spring back at you if you're not prepared.

LADDERS

I own seven ladders, yet I still find myself renting or borrowing one on occasion. Usually, that's a 40-ft. extension ladder, and frankly, I'd rather not own something that big and heavy. I do own two other extension ladders, though.

All of my ladders but one are made by Werner®. One is an aluminum 32-ft. Type IA, which is pretty heavy, but I like its rigidity when I'm 25 ft. in the air. The extension ladder that sees the most use with me is an aluminum 28-ft. Type II. It's fairly light, and rigid enough for me to be comfortable at all but the fullest extension.

I also own a couple of fiberglass Type II stepladders in 5-ft. and 7-ft. heights. Home centers sell these commodity ladders dirt cheap, and they're extremely useful.

Recently, I bought a Little Giant® 22-ft. ladder. I don't quite know how to classify it. It's an extension ladder. It's a stepladder whose sides are adjustable so it can be set up on stairs or sloping ground. It comes apart and reassembles into two sections that can support a low scaffold. This thing is so useful I'm not sure why I waited so long to buy one.

Another useful item is a ladder standoff. Often, you don't want the ladder to rest on the surface you're working on—for example, a window. Standoffs also provide space to work around the top of the ladder itself, and their nonslip rubber feet add some stability.

Ladder ratings Ladders are rated as Type I, Type II, or Type III. Type III models are light-duty affairs with no real place on a construction site. Most of my ladders are Type II, which are rated at 225 lb.—sturdy enough for most work while still relatively light enough to move easily. Type I ladders are rated for 250 lb., and the "above-category" Type IA ladders allow a 300-lb. load.

Type I ladders weigh a lot, but their rigidity is a big plus high in the air.

Type II ladders are lighter weight and heavy duty enough for loads up to 225 lb.

Stepladders are probably the most-used way to reach high places up on the job site.

Little Giant ladders are extremely versatile.

Use a standoff to gain working space at the top of a ladder, or to get it past the eaves without damaging shingles.

Aluminum or fiberglass?

Most electricians use fiberglass ladders because they're non-conductive. That is, unless they're wet. So you have to be careful around wires, even with fiberglass ladders. Fiberglass ladders feel more rigid than their aluminum counter-parts, but they're heavier. They also cost more. My extension ladders are aluminum, because the lighter weight is an advan-tage when moving them.

⚠ WARNING

Ladders all come with safety warnings on them. Read them and follow them—it's really that simple. Here's a summary of safety prac-tices that apply to all ladders:

- Always provide a ladder with a firm footing so it won't slide out at the bottom. I've gone as far as driving stakes in the ground to secure the base of a ladder.
- Set extension ladders up at about a 15-degree incline.
- Never reach from a ladder.
- Don't walk on the non-rung side of stepladders.
- And perhaps most important, never bring a lad-der in contact with overhead powerlines.

SCAFFOLDING AND HORSES

One of the facts of a carpenter's life is that sometimes you work in high places. That can be downright terrifying, or as comfortable as a walk in the park–well, maybe in a park with cliffs. Anyway, comfort and safety depend on having the right scaffolding and using it properly.

When you buy or rent scaffolding, read and follow the instructions to the letter. You're planning to be high in the air. You don't want to take the quick way down. Like ladders, scaffold poles conduct electricity. Don't work with them around live overhead powerlines.

Pump jacks

Most carpenters use what are called pump jacks to support their scaffolding. A foot-operated lever makes them climb their poles. I own a set of old-school pump jacks that climb posts made from 2×4s nailed together. The new ones with aluminum poles by Alum-A-Pole® are a lot better–lighter, more rigid, and capable of carrying heavier loads. These are what you want to buy or rent.

Planks and supports

The jacks are just part of the game. You also need scaffolding planks, also known as staging or picks. Again, the best are made from aluminum, and they can span up to 16 ft. If you're using wooden planks, they need to be specially rated for this use and can usually span only 10 ft.

To comply with OSHA requirements, scaffolding must be at least 18 in. wide, which is a fairly comfortable working width. There must also be a guardrail across the open side of the scaffolding. Often, that's set up as a work surface. Additionally, there must be some sort of guard at the end of the plank to prevent people from walking off, although that requirement is honored more in the breach than the observance on most residential sites. There's a lot more to say about proper scaffold setup than there's room for here. You can find the rest of the information at www.osha.gov.

For lower scaffolding that I'll want to move frequently, I use a pair of homemade A-frames to support the planks. They're like big stepladders, and they fold flat for storage. Pipe scaffold is another option. Easily found in rental shops and fairly cheap to buy, pipe scaffold can be stacked to considerable heights with the proper bracing. On roofs, I set up staging boards supported by roof jacks.

Pump jacks support scaffolding and climb their poles when more height is needed.

Wood scaffold planks are thicker than regular lumber, knot free (or with tight knots), unfinished, and roughsawn for traction.

Homemade A-frames set up quickly to support a scaffold and are useful for lower work.

Another homemade item I use is a sawhorse. While you can buy some great steel horses, I like the wide top surface of my home-builts and I like the stacking design. And the traditionalist in me believes that carpenters should build their own horses—it's an opportunity to show off your skills and to produce horses that fit your particular needs.

That said, I do have a set of Rockwell® Jawhorses, which are folding steel sawhorses with a built-in clamp. They're great for use as a miter saw stand, my sheet metal brake fits in them, and they're very useful for temporarily bracing posts.

Pipe scaffolding can be stacked for greater height, but bracing may be required.

Roof jacks support boards to provide standing room on roofs. Nails placed below the upper shingle fit in elongated slots to hold the jacks.

The clamping action of Jawhorses can be used to support temporary poles.

Sawhorses can be used to support workpieces and low scaffolding. A stacking design limits the space they take up.

STRUCTURAL LUMBER

Framing lumber, for the most part, consists of solid wood sawn directly from trees. It is sometimes called dimensional lumber or solid sawn lumber. You can readily spot its origins in the knots where a branch grew from the main trunk, growth rings that document how the tree added girth throughout its life, pitch pockets filled with sticky, aromatic resin from sap, and wane, which is the round edge of a tree trunk where the wood stopped and the bark began.

All of these characteristics of the living tree are considered lumber defects, and defects are important because they affect the grade of a board, as well as its strength, its appearance, and where it can be used.

Defects and grades

Lumber is graded depending on how many defects it has and where those defects are located on the board. Most construction lumber is graded either number 1, with almost no defects, or number 2, with a greater number of defects allowed. Number 3 material is sometimes available, but it's not used structurally.

The distance a piece of dimensional lumber can span is determined in part by its grade. The lumber will be grade-stamped, and it's likely not to be allowed for structural use without that stamp.

Most framing is done with number 1 and 2 lumber being used interchangeably. Occasionally, the use of number 1 lumber will be specified for a

beam or the lumber for a floor that's pushing the span limits of a certain dimension of lumber. That's pretty rare today, with the availability of engineered lumber. Stud-grade lumber is of lower quality than number 2 stock and shouldn't be used in most weight-bearing horizontal applications.

Size

Size is another obvious characteristic of lumber. Typical dimensional lumber is sold in a nominal 2-in. thickness, and in even widths between 4 in. and 12 in. For example, you might buy a 2×4 or a 2×12. Some widths are also available in nominal 4-in., 6-in., and even 8-in. thicknesses, but these are harder to find except for treated 4×4s and 6×6s made for deck posts. Nominal sizes are not actual sizes.

Nominal size originally referred to roughsawn lumber, which is planed smooth before being sold as dimensional lumber. Planed lumber is safer to handle because you get fewer splinters, but more important, smooth lumber doesn't catch fire as readily as roughsawn lumber.

The actual size of nominal dimensions up to 6 in. will be about 1/2 in. smaller than nominal. A 2×4 actually measures about 1 1/2 in. by 3 1/2 in. Dimensions of larger nominal sizes are about 3/4 in. smaller: a 2×8 measures about 1 1/2 in. by 7 1/4 in. All of these dimensions will vary with changing humidity.

4x4
2x4
2x6
2x12
5/8-in. CDX plywood
3/4-in. plywood subflooring
1/2-in. OSB

STUD STOCK

Stud-grade lumber is cheap stuff, and can't be used in horizontal load-bearing applications, such as joists. Studs move, twist, and bow more than number 2-and-better lumber.

The choice of stud species available to you largely depends on where you live. Douglas fir, hem-fir, and SPF (spruce-pine-fir) studs are common in my area. Although they're cheaper, I avoid SPF studs. They split easily and tend to be about as straight as an eel.

Southern pine studs aren't available where I live, but one Texas carpenter told me he nails them in place as soon as he gets them, or they'll "crawl off the job."

Finger-joint studs seem promising—the worst knots and defects are cut out before manufacture, but I can't find them locally.

Best when straightness counts (behind a kitchen countertop) or when lateral strength is needed (tall gable walls that resist big wind loads) are LVL studs. LVL studs are expensive, and they're very heavy.

WOOD ISN'T STRAIGHT—CHOOSE LUMBER CAREFULLY

Lumber defects can make a board difficult to work with, even dangerous. Except for boards that are slightly crowned, it's best not to use lumber with defects. Crowned lumber, however, can often be brought into line by applying pressure before you fasten it.

Bow   Cup   Twist   Crook

(Photo by Craig Wester)

TRADE SECRET

Whether you use dry or green lumber probably depends on what's available regionally. Where I work, it usually rains or snows at least weekly. Paying extra for dry framing lumber is a waste of money. No matter how dry the lumber is when delivered, it will get wet during construction.

Green versus dried

Dimensional lumber may be either green or kiln dried. Green lumber can be so wet it splashes when hit with a hammer. Green lumber doesn't split as readily from nails, but it's much heavier than dried lumber and will shrink considerably as it dries. Whether you buy dry or green lumber will probably be determined by what your local lumberyards sell.

Species

The final factor in determining wood strength is species, and it will be called out on building plans and marked on the lumber. The two strongest common softwood lumber species are Douglas fir and southern pine, with hem/fir (a mix of hemlock and fir species) coming in next. SPF (spruce-pine-fir) is generally last on the list. Of these, I find Douglas fir the best to work with by

far—it splits and twists less than the other species.

Sheet stock

Plywood and oriented strand board (OSB) are sold in 4×8 sheets (and sometimes longer) and commonly used for sheathing floors, walls, and roofs. Plywood is composed of layers of veneer glued together at right angles. OSB is made from fast-growing aspen, which is shredded into strands and flakes, then oriented in opposing layers with an exterior glue, and pressed into panels. These products stiffen the structure against wind and seismic loads.

The plywood grading system uses the letters A, B, C, and D to indicate the quality of a surface. An "A" surface has virtually no blemishes and is sanded smooth. A grade D surface typically contains the maximum number of blemishes allowed.

>> >> >>

I-JOISTS

I-joists are a manufactured replacement for solid lumber. They have upper and lower flanges of either LVL or sawn lumber, joined with a web of OSB. They're lighter than solid lumber, straight, available in lengths to 40 ft. or more, and have fewer problems from seasonal wood movement.

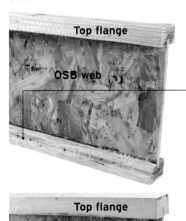

Top flange

OSB web

LVL-FLANGED I-JOIST

Bottom flange

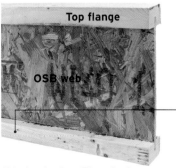

Top flange

OSB web

SAWN-LUMBER-FLANGED I-JOIST

Bottom flange

(Photos by Dan Thornton)

STRUCTURAL LUMBER (CONTINUED)

Letter grades come in pairs, with one letter grading the better side (the "face") and the other letter the reverse side. For example, the face of a sheet of A-C plywood will be smooth and virtually blemish free, with a relatively unfinished back. Thus, CDX plywood is great for structural use but not suited to be finish material. (C and D refer to the grades of veneer on the front and back of the sheet, and X refers to exterior glue.)

Structurally, CDX-grade plywood and OSB perform about the same. Both are available in nominal thicknesses of 1/2 in. and 3/4 in., with CDX also coming in 5/8 in. With plywood, veneers of fir or southern pine are laminated in layers laid at right angles to each other.

The number of layers varies with the quality of the plywood. The more layers for a given thickness, the better, because the panel will be more dimensionally stable. All structural plywood and OSB use water-resistant glue, so they can be left outside for a few months. The various thicknesses of sheet stock serve different purposes: 3/4-in. material is usually used for floor sheathing, 5/8 in. for roof sheathing, and 1/2 in. for wall sheathing.

BEAMS

Most main beams are built up from several layers of either 2× framing lumber or engineered lumber such as LVL (laminated veneer lumber) or PSL (parallel stranded lumber). LVL consists of layers of veneer, like plywood but with all layers oriented the same direction and glued together. PSL is commonly referred to by Trus Joist®'s trade name Parallam® and is made from wood fiber and resin. Either choice is stronger, more stable, and available in longer lengths than sawn lumber. LVL comes in planks a bit larger than standard sawn lumber. PSL can be had in planks as well, but is also commonly sold as heavy timbers, say 5½ in. by 14 in. I try to avoid these except for short beams because of their weight. For larger beams, it's a lot easier to lift individual planks into place and join them into a beam than it is to lift a beam weighing hundreds of pounds.

LVL beams come in sizes similar to sawn lumber. Several are typically joined to make a beam.

PSL beams are sold in full beam sizes. Rarely is it necessary to assemble several together into a beam. (Photo above courtesy iLevel by Weyerhaeuser®; inset photos by Daniel S. Morrison)

FINISH LUMBER

Finish lumber comes in the same widths as dimensional lumber, but it's generally thinner and smoother and has few if any waney edges. Like dimensional lumber, finish lumber's nominal dimension is not its actual dimension. Nominal 1× material is about ¾ in. thick. The other common trim lumber dimension is 5/4 (pronounced "five quarter"), and it measures about 1 in. thick.

Species and grade

Trim lumber is generally some sort of pine–eastern white, ponderosa, or radiata, or for exterior use, cedar or redwood. Sometimes it will be Engelmann spruce, which I try to avoid because it twists and splits like a gymnast. Trim lumber is graded number 1 (or "clear") and number 2, and is always dry. It's tough to paint number 2 without the knots bleeding through, but number 1 is very expensive.

In years past, number 2 pine was used strictly for utility grade purposes–the insides of closets, or basement trim. Number 1 was used for painted applications. From about the 1970s on, the cost difference caused number 2 pine to be used instead of number 1 in painted applications.

That can work (I used it on my house), but it takes an application of shellac and sealer before priming, and few builders were willing to pay for that. So, knots bled sap through the paint, and that created a market for finger-jointed boards, in which small pieces of clear lumber are glued together, sanded flat, and primed. It's a good compromise between number 1 and 2. Also, you can buy PVC lumber in the same dimensions as pine–it has no knots, works like wood for the most part, and doesn't rot, but it's pricey. For high-end interior work, you can buy hardwoods such as oak or maple.

Millwork

Millwork includes items such as doors and moldings. There is a staggering number of molding profiles on the market–literally hundreds if you go to specialty suppliers. Most lumberyards carry thirty or so profiles and sizes of trim, in both clear pine and primed finger-joint pine. The same profiles can be had in hardwood, with red oak being commonly stocked. Other species will probably be special order unless you're dealing with an exceptionally well-stocked lumberyard. And many profiles are available in PVC.

Putting trim in its place

Trim can be confusing, with names such as casing, base, crown, shoe, quarter-round, chair rail, and stool, all of which come in several sizes. For the most part, their names hint at their uses.

Keep your eyes open when visiting other people's homes; you can come up with a pretty good idea of which molding goes where. In fact, putting a little effort into developing an eye for what looks good and what doesn't is energy well spent. Pay particular attention to proportion–for example, use larger moldings in bigger rooms with high ceilings than you would in a small room.

Look to older homes for inspiration–long-dead carpenters and designers seemed to have a far better eye for trim than is common today.

FINISHED PLYWOOD

There are also finish grades of plywood, in the same nominal sizes as structural plywood, as well as thinner ones such as ¼ in. and ⅜ in. Finish plywood will have a smoother face, typically graded A or B.

You can also buy paper-faced medium density overlay (MDO) plywood, which paints very smoothly, hardwood veneered plywood, and a variety of types of particleboard.

Medium density fiberboard (MDF) has a smooth face that paints well. MDF is extremely dusty when cut, and heavy. A 4-in. by 8-in. by ¾-in. sheet weighs in at around 100 lb.

FRAMING FLOORS

WE THINK OF FLOORS as supporting walls, furniture, and people. It's the designer's or architect's job to make sure the structure will do these things. The carpenter's job is to put all the pieces together. Floors outline the shape of the building and set up everything above. Make the floor square and level or you'll fight mistakes all the way to the roof.

If the floor isn't square, the sheathing won't fit the framing. Walls follow the perimeter of the floor, and if the floor isn't square

the walls won't be either, and you'll have a hard time fitting rafters or roof trusses.

If a floor isn't level, walls built on it will be square or plumb, but not both. Out-of-whack floor framing makes it hard to fit everything from cabinets and countertops to tile and wallpaper.

Poor framing creates squeaks and can cause stone or tile floors to crack. Pay attention to the details in this chapter, and you'll frame square, level, and stout.

MUDSILLS

BEAMS

JOISTS

SUBFLOORING

ESTIMATING FLOOR-FRAMING STOCK

Although many lumberyards will develop a materials list if you give them a plan, I usually do this myself, noting on a spreadsheet the purpose for each stick of lumber and where it goes. That spreadsheet saves a lot of time when I'm trying to make sense of a truckload of lumber, and reviewing the plans in detail helps me understand the building.

Mudsills

For mudsill (and sill seal), just add the lineal feet required. Rough lumber varies in size due to milling differences and moisture content, and you'll want your materials to be as uniform as possible. To increase the odds of getting stock of consistent dimensions, order materials whose length isn't critical, such as mudsills, the same length, usually 12 ft. or 16 ft. This way, the wood will likely come from the same bunk of lumber, which was probably milled on the same machine.

Lumber comes in 2-ft. increments, so if your plans call for a 14-ft. 3-in. board, you'll need to order a 16-footer. Plan how you'll cut shorter lengths from longer ones to minimize waste.

Joists

Lumber joists typically span only half the foundation, so instead of 28-footers (assuming you could even find them), use two 14-footers and support them where they meet in the center on a beam or bearing wall.

TRADE SECRET

Order material a phase at a time—first-floor framing, then first-floor walls, second-floor framing, etc. Add about 5 percent to the total for mistakes and bad stock. Don't worry about over-ordering. Extras on hand reduce trips to the lumberyard. After the first load, factor in what's left that you can use. Most lumberyards will take back extras in good shape for credit, less a handling fee.

FLOOR-FRAMING ANATOMY

All loads on a house need an uninterrupted and adequate path to the ground, through the foundation. The most obvious loads on a floor are people, furniture, and the weight of the flooring materials. Less obvious loads are those of the wind and the earth, which might push a house sideways off its foundation. Those loads are borne by the framing and its nails and hardware to the mudsill, which transmits them to the foundation both through friction from the weight of the building and through the foundation bolts.

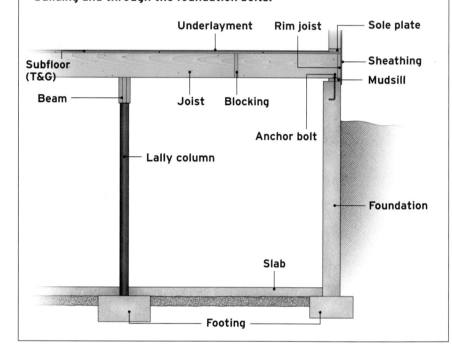

Making notes when estimating helps organize your building materials when sorting out the delivery of a truckload of lumber.

FLOOR-FRAMING ANATOMY

Using the dimensions specified in your plans, construct a materials list or "take off" to guide your material purchases. The list should specify the purpose of every piece of lumber. You can do this by hand, but using spreadsheet software makes it easier to adjust the list if, for example, you need to add a new length of lumber to an existing category.

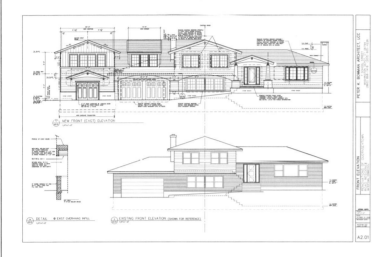

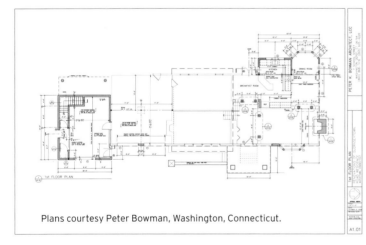

Plans courtesy Peter Bowman, Washington, Connecticut.

All lumber is Douglas fir, #2 and better. Studs may be stud grade. Purpose	2x6x8 precut	2x4 precut	2x4 x8	2x4x 10 pt	2x4x 12	2x6x 16	2x6x 14
Mud sill							
Garage wall studs	112						
Garage wall plates						12	15
Jacks							11
LVL to span 13/8, supporting 40 lb ll, 10 lb dl, 1/2 of 28 ft. wide floor above							
Column with plates							
Sheathing							
Nails for Bostitch Strip nailer							
Joists for landing							
Hangers							
Floor sheathing							
Bath floor				5			
Bath studs							
Headers							
Garage walls total	112	0	0	5		12	26
Floor joists							
Headers							
Floor sheathing							
Glue							
Hangers							
Second floor wall plates					9	24	15
Studs	24	24					20
Headers							
Rafters							
Ridge							
Brackets							
Roof sheathing							
Roof edge							
Ceiling joists						9	
Hood rafters			22				
Hood brackets							
Hood soffet							
Wall sheathing							

When working on 16-in. centers, find the number of joists by multiplying the length of the span by 0.75 and adding one. Then count materials for doubled joists, rim joists, and blocking. To maintain uniform stock widths, order rim joists the same length and from the same bunk as the floor joists.

I-joists

If you're working with I-joists, that's a different story. I-joists usually run the full width of the building, not half. With I-joist floors, order extra ¾-in. plywood for web stiffeners, and sufficient studs for cutting squash blocks.

➡ See "I-joists," p. 35.

Sheathing and fasteners

To figure the number of sheets of sheathing, divide the square footage of the floor by 32 (a 4×8 sheet is 32 sq. ft.). If you're using a nail gun, get a case of 2½-in. deformed-shank nails (spiral or ring-shanked) for the sheathing and a case each of 3-in. and 3½-in. spirals or ring shanks. For a house, you'll need at least a case of big tubes of subfloor adhesive per floor; for an addition, probably half of that. Don't forget framing connectors, such as joist hangers, as well as the special nails for them. If you're hand nailing, order nails by the 50-lb. box.

LAYING OUT MUDSILLS

Mudsills are the first component of floor framing, and they're what carpenters use to make a building square and level. Mudsills are the wood members that run along the top of the foundation, joining the first-floor joists to the foundation of the basement or crawlspace or the bottom plates of framed walls to the foundation. Mudsills are typically made from pressure-treated 2×6 stock, and they're bolted to the foundation. Your foundation contractor will have already set the anchor bolts in the foundation at the correct intervals.

To make sure the mudsills you install are square, you'll snap chalklines on top of the foundation, using the plan dimensions.

Check the foundation for square

Because mudsills have to be square around the entire foundation, the first task is to see if the foundation is the size stated on the plans and whether its corners are square. Rectangular foundations are simple to check—just measure the diagonals. They should be within 1 in. of each other. ❶ A perfectly squared and accurately sized foundation will result in mudsills that are flush with its outside face. Perfectly square foundations, however, generally don't exist. For foundations within 1 in. to 2 in. of square and the correct size, you can square the mudsills by adjusting their position on the foundation. Errors of larger than an inch or two can require consultation with the designer or calling the foundation contractor back.

Snap layout lines

At both ends of the longest wall, measure and, if you're using 2×6s, mark a point 5½ in. from the outside edge of the wall (3½ in. for 2×4 sills). Lumber sizes can vary slightly from "standard"–be sure to measure the stock you're using. Ignoring any bays, openings, or inward projections for now, snap a line on top of the wall between these points. Repeat this process on the wall opposite the longest wall. ❷ Measure the distance between the lines on both walls. If your measurements are the same along the entire length of the lines, they are parallel. If they are not parallel, split the difference of the measurement and move the lines on the last wall in or out to make them parallel. Sometimes, this will make the mudsill overhang the foundation. I don't sweat an overhang of ½ in. or less.

Next, go to the walls perpendicular to the first walls you marked and repeat the process, using the width of your mudsill to mark end points on the interior edge of these walls and snapping lines between them. ❸ Now measure the diagonals of the snapped lines to verify that the layout is square. If it's not square, move the lines on the perpendicular walls in or out by half the difference between the two diagonal measurements, and re-check. ❹ If you use a Construction Master calculator, you can find what the diagonal measurement should be in feet, inches, and fractions of inches. This information can speed things along if you need to tweak the mudsill layout square.

➡ See "The Construction Master Calculator," p. 9.

Refer to the illustration on pp. 44-45 for an "overhead" view of the layout process. >> >> >>

1 Measure the foundation diagonals; if they're equal, the foundation is square.

2 Snap lines on the inside edge of the longest and opposite walls. Adjust to make them parallel.

Line snapped on
perpendicular wall.

3 Repeat the measuring and marking process on the walls perpendicular to the long walls. Measure to check for parallel.

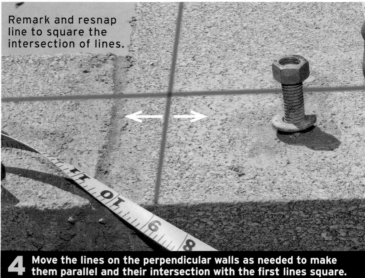

Remark and resnap line to square the intersection of lines.

4 Move the lines on the perpendicular walls as needed to make them parallel and their intersection with the first lines square.

When squaring mudsill lines on the largest rectangle in the foundation, ignore openings in the foundation when snapping lines.

When you've finally installed them, mudsills should ideally be flush with the foundation, but they can overhang or sit inward slightly of the edge.

COUNTING INCHES WHEN INCHES COUNT

Plans should have the important dimensions detailed on them by the designer. Most missing dimensions can be figured mathematically by comparing provided dimensions. Occasionally not though, and then you're left to scale the dimension. Most plans are drawn so that ¼ in. on the plan equals 1 ft. in the field, and you can harvest rough dimensions using a tape measure. To get down to inches on a plan, though, you need an architect's scale, which is a triangular rule that allows you to read feet and inches in scale. They cost a couple of bucks at office-supply stores.

LAYING OUT MUDSILLS (CONTINUED)

LAYING OUT A MUDSILL

In a perfect world, a perfectly square foundation will result in perfectly square and parallel mudsills, all nicely flush with the foundation's outside face. Perfectly square foundations, however, don't exist. What matters more is that they are close enough to square that they will allow you to snap square layout lines on the top of the foundation walls, adjusting the position of the lines so the mudsills themselves are square, even if the foundation isn't. Follow the steps illustrated here to square the layout of your mudsills.

1. Measure the diagonals of the largest rectangle on your foundation (use the 1' mark on your tape for a starting point, as shown in the inset, "Taking Accurate Measurements").

If the diagonal measurements are the same, your foundation is square.

If the measurements are within 2" of each other, that's close enough to work with.

If you have more than a 2" difference, however, call your concrete contractor.

3. Next, mark both corners of the opposite wall (C and D) 5½" from the outside edge. Now measure the distance between these corner marks and the line on the opposite wall. If your measurements are not the same, make another end mark at a distance that would make the lines parallel.

4. Snap line C-D at these points. Check to make sure this line is parallel to line A-B.

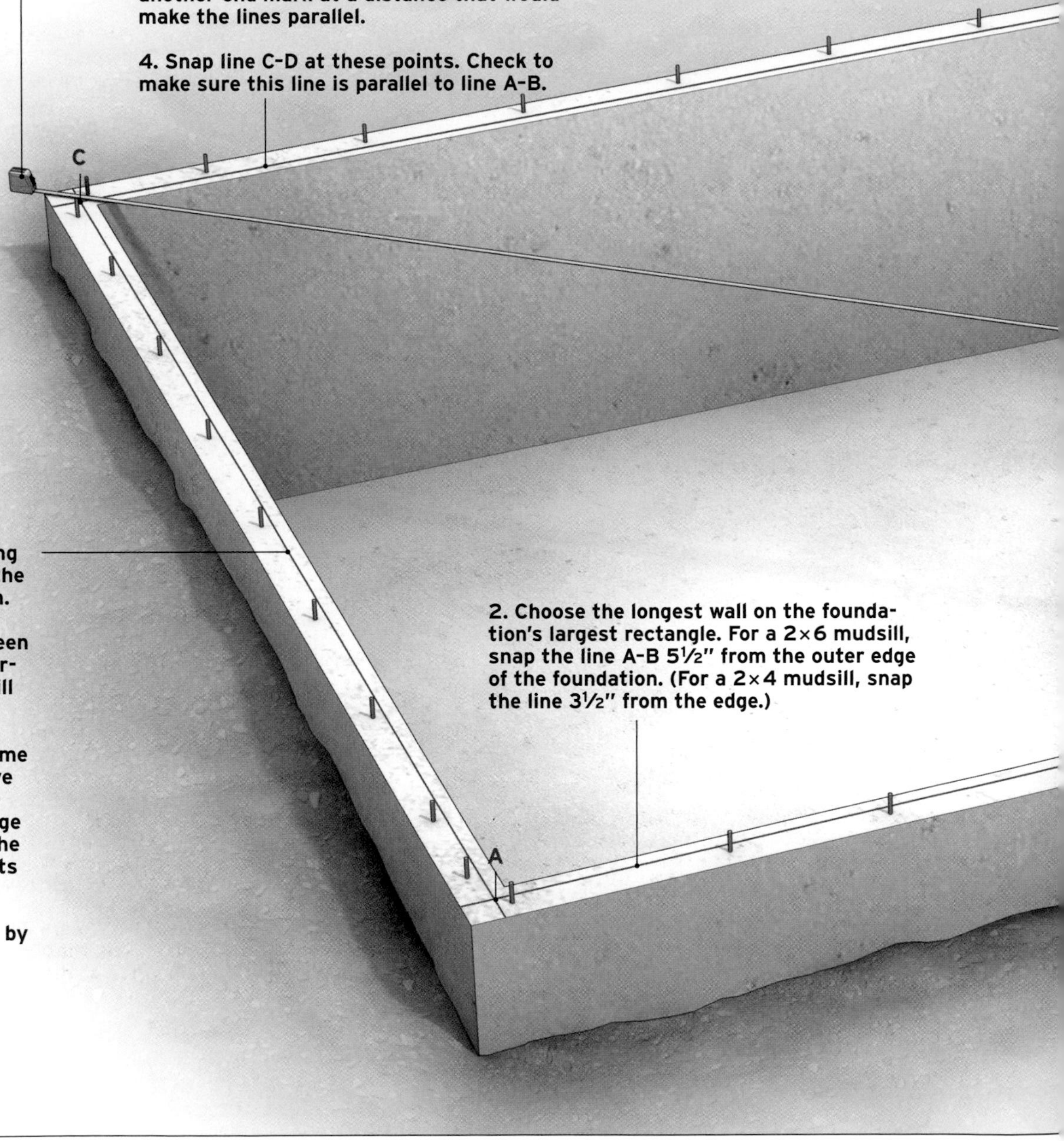

5. Repeat the process on the perpendicular walls by snapping lines C-A and D-B 5½" from the outside edge of the foundation.

6. Measure the distance between these new lines. If they are parallel to each other, your mudsill layout will be square.

7. If these lines are not the same distance from each other, move the end with the shorter measurement toward the outer edge of the wall by the amount of the difference in the measurements and resnap the line. This will mean your mudsill overhangs the foundation, but if it's only by ½", you'll be OK.

2. Choose the longest wall on the foundation's largest rectangle. For a 2×6 mudsill, snap the line A-B 5½" from the outer edge of the foundation. (For a 2×4 mudsill, snap the line 3½" from the edge.)

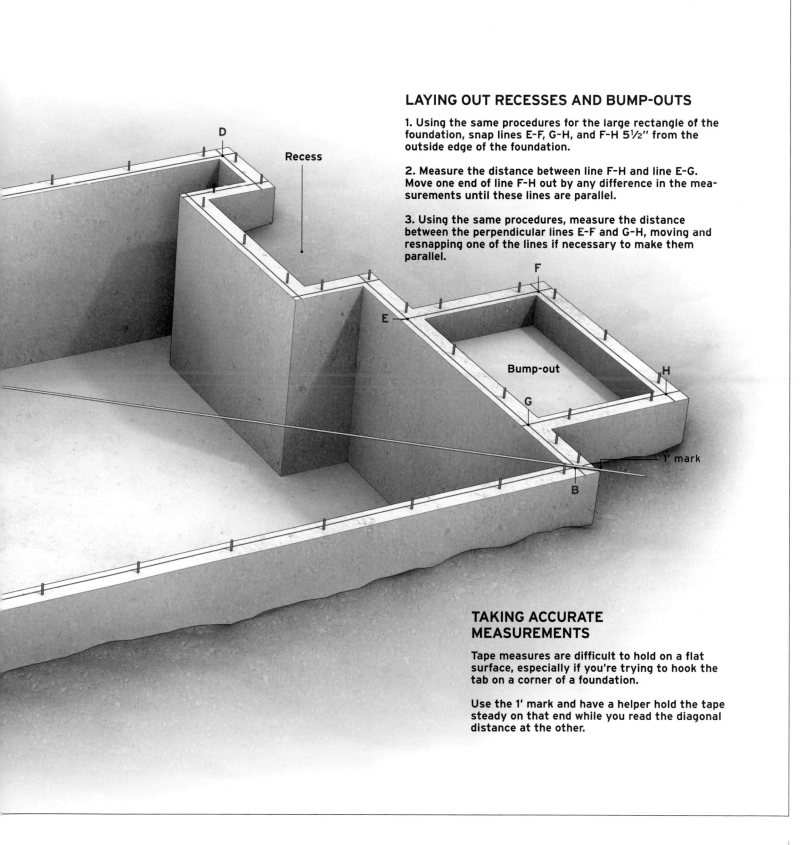

LAYING OUT RECESSES AND BUMP-OUTS

1. Using the same procedures for the large rectangle of the foundation, snap lines E-F, G-H, and F-H 5½" from the outside edge of the foundation.

2. Measure the distance between line F-H and line E-G. Move one end of line F-H out by any difference in the measurements until these lines are parallel.

3. Using the same procedures, measure the distance between the perpendicular lines E-F and G-H, moving and resnapping one of the lines if necessary to make them parallel.

TAKING ACCURATE MEASUREMENTS

Tape measures are difficult to hold on a flat surface, especially if you're trying to hook the tab on a corner of a foundation.

Use the 1' mark and have a helper hold the tape steady on that end while you read the diagonal distance at the other.

LAYING OUT MUDSILLS (CONTINUED)

1 Measure from an established line to locate the endpoints at both ends of the wall you will snap the new line on.

2 From the endpoints, snap a chalkline on the wall.

3 Mark short walls using a framing square.

C.H. Hanson®'s A-Square is a folding 3-4-5 triangle that measures 3 ft. by 4 ft. by 5 ft. It's extremely handy for laying out walls and decks, and folded up, it takes up almost no room at all.

Laying out bays and insets

After you've laid out the main rectangle, move on to any bays, ells, or insets. Have a helper hold the dumb end of the tape (the tabbed end) while you mark the endpoints of the lines and check lines for parallel. Don't forget that you're marking the location of the inside edge of the mudsill, not the outside edge.

With the lines on the main rectangle already parallel, use them to mark the inside edge of the mudsill on the walls of bays, ells, and insets. You can approach this several ways, depending on the depth of the inset or protruding wall. In any event, the first move is to measure from the main chalkline to establish endpoints and then strike the chalkline along the parallel foundation wall. **1**, **2**

Then mark and snap lines on the side walls. For side walls 2 ft. or shorter, use a framing square and a pencil to mark the foundation for the mudsill location. **3** If you have an A-Square, the range is 4 ft.

If it's a deep bay, you can accurately square the corner mathematically. See "Squaring a Mudsill Layout with a 3-4-5 Triangle," at right, and follow the directions for marking lines. This method works because if the legs of any triangle are 3 ft. and 4 ft. and the hypotenuse is 5 ft., the triangle is square and the legs are perpendicular to each other. This is the Pythagorean Theorem, and it looks like this: $a^2 + b^2 = c^2$, but you don't need to use the formula. Just mark the lines.

Furthermore, not only is any triangle measuring 3, 4, and 5 units a right triangle, so are triangles whose sides are multiples of those numbers. For example, 6, 8, and 10 or 9, 12, and 15 work just as well as 3, 4, and 5 (actually, larger numbers are more accurate), and you can work in feet, inches, or cubits, as long as you're consistent.

SQUARING A MUDSILL LAYOUT WITH A 3-4-5 TRIANGLE

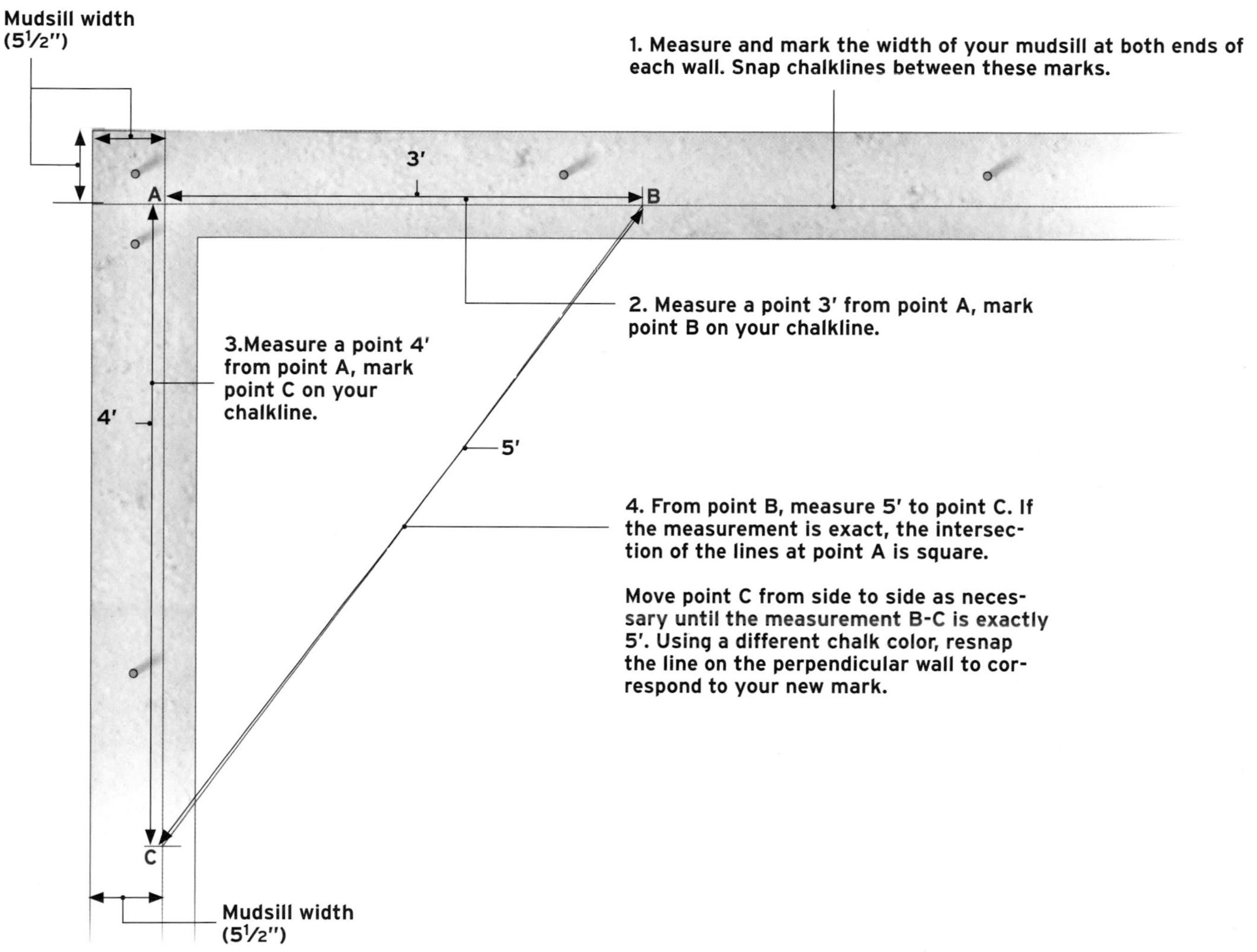

Mudsill width
(5½")

1. Measure and mark the width of your mudsill at both ends of each wall. Snap chalklines between these marks.

3'

A

B

2. Measure a point 3' from point A, mark point B on your chalkline.

3.Measure a point 4' from point A, mark point C on your chalkline.

4'

5'

4. From point B, measure 5' to point C. If the measurement is exact, the intersection of the lines at point A is square.

Move point C from side to side as necessary until the measurement B-C is exactly 5'. Using a different chalk color, resnap the line on the perpendicular wall to correspond to your new mark.

C

Mudsill width
(5½")

A 3-4-5 triangle is one way to establish a point for marking and snapping a perpendicular line. It's especially useful on walls longer than a framing square. Using any multiples of 3, 4, and 5 in a triangle (6 ,8, and 10, for example) will produce a right angle with legs perpendicular to each other.

INSTALLING MUDSILLS

Compared to layout, installing mudsills is easy. In most cases, you can mark the mudsill stock to length in place. At the corners, run one piece of mudsill stock past the perpendicular chalkline and butt the other at a right angle to it. If one leg is particularly short, make it the piece that runs long. You can alter the layout of the pieces if one arrangement will suit the bolt pattern better. At the end of runs without an adjoining wall, run the stock to the end of the wall beyond the last foundation bolt. ❶

Marking the sill

To mark the holes in a mudsill so they correspond with the location of the foundation bolts, lay the mudsill stock on the foundation. Align the ends to correspond with their location when installed, and make sure you have what will be the inside edge of the mudsill exactly on your chalkline.

At this point, you can draw lines across the mudsill square to the bolts and transfer the measurements from the edge of the mudsill to the center of the bolt to these lines—but it's much easier and more accurate to modify a cheap combination square to use as a bolt marker. Making a bolt marker is ten minutes well invested. ❷

➜ See "Making Your Own Bolt Marker," p. 8.

By code, mudsill bolt holes can be no more than 1/16 in. oversize, so for 1/2-in. bolts, drill 9/16-in. holes at all your marks. ❸ ≫ ≫ ≫

1 Mark mudsills in place, lined up on your chalk lines.

2 Locate holes in mudsills accurately and quickly with a homemade bolt marker.

3 Drill 9/16-in. holes for 1/2-in. bolts at each of the bolt locations you marked.

BOLTING MUDSILL JOINTS

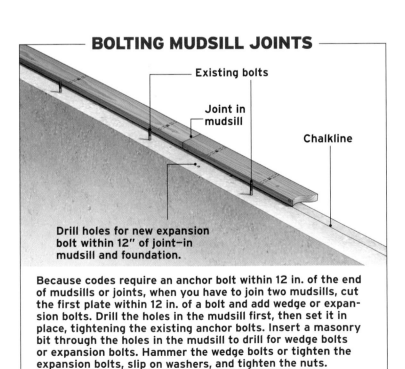

Existing bolts

Joint in mudsill

Chalkline

Drill holes for new expansion bolt within 12" of joint—in mudsill and foundation.

Because codes require an anchor bolt within 12 in. of the end of mudsills or joints, when you have to join two mudsills, cut the first plate within 12 in. of a bolt and add wedge or expansion bolts. Drill the holes in the mudsill first, then set it in place, tightening the existing anchor bolts. Insert a masonry bit through the holes in the mudsill to drill for wedge bolts or expansion bolts. Hammer the wedge bolts or tighten the expansion bolts, slip on washers, and tighten the nuts.

— FOUNDATION BOLT FIXES AND OPTIONS —

If foundation bolts aren't set plumb, it's difficult to mark and drill their holes. Slip a length of pipe over the bolt to lever it straight. Thread a nut on to protect the threads.

If bolts are badly placed or don't offer enough thread for the nut, there are alternatives—bolts that epoxy into the concrete, bolts that grip the concrete with steel wedges, and bolts that fit into holes drilled in the concrete.

Use an iron pipe to straighten bolts. Slip the nut on the threads first.

Wedge bolts are one way to add bolts to an existing foundation when needed.

Self-tapping bolts are an alternative to traditional anchor bolts.

Use an impact driver to set self-tapping bolts in predrilled holes.

It sometimes helps to nail mudsills before using other bolts.

WHAT CAN GO WRONG

If there are severe low spots in the foundation, 1/2 in. or more, level them before setting the mudsills. Use non-shrink grout, a mortar that retains its strength in thin applications. You'll probably have to buy this at a masonry supply house.

TRADE SECRET

Bolts are required at least every 6 ft., and within 12 in. of corners and joints, but no closer than 7 bolt diameters to the board end.

INSTALLING MUDSILLS (CONTINUED)

Align sill seal with the chalklines, and push it down over the bolts.
❹ Holding the mudsills as level as possible, set them in place, with the bolts through the holes. Slip washers on each bolt and snug down the nuts so they're tight, but not so tight as to crush the wood. ❺

Once the mudsills are snugged down and laid out for joists (see "Mudsills: Marking Joist Locations," below), check them for level with a builder's level or a laser level. ❻ The latter is more accurate and easy to use if you're working alone.

Set the beam a comfortable height above the foundation and check the elevation around the entire perimeter. I don't worry about elevation differences of ¼ in. or less. If the foundation is low in spots, place steel shims between the mudsill and the foundation. If the mudsill bows up, drive it down with masonry nails or concrete screws. If the concrete is high, remove some of the surface with an air chisel.

4 Push sill seal down over the bolts. Then set the sill in place with the bolts through the holes.

5 Slip washers on the bolts and snug down the nuts, but don't tighten them enough to crush the wood fibers.

MUDSILLS: MARKING JOIST LOCATIONS

Once you have fastened and leveled the mudsills, mark the edges of the joists on the sill. Indicate their position clearly with an "X".

16"

16"

16¾"

Joist location

Mudsill

Foundation

6 Check the mudsills for level. Shim low spots; chip high spots level with an air chisel.

Always drill bolt holes as straight as possible, to avoid the holes not lining up with the bolts. (Photo by Ron Ruscio)

SHIMMING MUDSILLS

Make quick work of shimming a mudsill after snugging the nuts on the bolts. First, if your plans call for increased headroom in the basement, nail a second 2×6 on the mudsill.

Then use a builder's level to measure the height of the corners and shim them within ¼ in. of the highest point. Mark joist, beam, and point loads on the mudsill. Then run a tight line from corner to corner and slip shims under the line in whatever amount will bring them level under it. Loosen the nuts slightly and slide the shims under the mudsill. Then retighten the nuts and check for level one last time.

Place shim at low spots on mudsill.

Tight string line from corner to corner

Doubled mudsill installed for added ceiling height

(Photo by Ron Ruscio)

HEAVY-DUTY FOUNDATION CONNECTIONS

If you're working in an area subject to high winds (all coastal areas in the East, South, and Alaska, as well as a surprising amount of inland area) or seismic activity (generally the West, Alaska, and Hawaii, but also some parts of the Midwest), you'll face code requirements beyond the scope of this book. To get a building permit in these areas, the plans will have to provide construction details and specifications for these severe loads.

There are four main ways in which wind and seismic loads act on buildings: racking, sliding, overturning, and uplift. In general, the building designer will figure out ways for all forces to be transferred through the structure into the foundation. Sometimes that's done through the wood-to-wood connections of the building's floor, wall, and roof sheathing, while other times specialty hardware is called for.

In terms of the floor system, in most cases wind and seismic loads transfer to the foundation through the attachment of the mudsill and joists. Mostly, that means properly fastening the mudsill to the foundation with bolts or other anchors. Sometimes plans will call for thicker foundation bolts or square (not round) washers under the foundation bolt nuts. The shape of the washer may seem a small detail, but square washers significantly increase the area over which the force of the nut is applied, thereby reducing the likelihood of the mudsill splitting. You may also be required

Special hardware may be required in wind or seismic zones. Here, metal straps will tie the floors to the walls, strengthening the structure against high winds.

to install metal straps that tie the floors to the walls. None of this is difficult, but the possible variations of each design are numerous.

Summing up what we carpenters need to know about seismic and wind-resistant construction is simple: Follow the plans, and when in doubt, check with a design professional or the hardware manufacturer.

INSTALLING BEAMS

Beam pockets are usually cast oversize because it's easier to shim the pocket than to enlarge it.

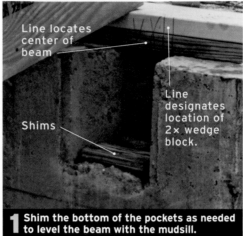

Line locates center of beam

Line designates location of 2× wedge block.

Shims

1 Shim the bottom of the pockets as needed to level the beam with the mudsill.

2 Cut the beam about 1 in. short to make it easy to handle. Lower it in place.

WHAT CAN GO WRONG

Concrete beam pockets aren't always molded correctly. Shim low ones with steel, pressure-treated 2× stock, or non-shrink grout. Adding a 2× to the top might bring a low beam flush with the mudsill or close enough to shim. Shallow pockets have to be enlarged, and missing pockets have to be installed. Both improvements require cutting the concrete, a job for the concrete contractor.

Pressure-treated 2× wedge

3 Cut a pressure-treated 2× block and wedge it next to the beam. The block tightens the beam in the pocket, preventing rotation.

In poured concrete or stem-wall installations, the ends of beams are usually supported in beam pockets cast into the foundation. Beams in stud walls are supported by steel or built-up wood posts in the wall framing. The posts carry the load down to a footing. Except for short beams, support the span with one or more steel Lally columns anchored to concrete footings.

➜ See "Setting Lally Columns," p. 56.

Installing beams in concrete

Before placing a beam in a beam pocket, make sure the location of the pocket corresponds with its location on the plans. Also check the depth of the pocket. Ideally, when installed, the top of a beam in a pocket will be flush with the top of the mudsill (but you

may need to notch the mudsill to accommodate the beam end). Mark the location of the center of the beam on the mudsill, as well as the position of the 2× wedge block you will install to keep the beam in place.

If you're using pressure-treated framing lumber for your beams, you can set them directly in the concrete pocket. However, other beams will require a piece of galvanized sheet metal (aluminum flashing can corrode) in the bottom of the pocket—LVL, PSL, or untreated lumber cannot contact concrete directly.

As necessary, shim the bottom of the pocket with a piece of pressure-treated scrap so the top of the beam will be level with the mudsill when the beam is in the pocket. **1** Cut the beam a little short so it

will be easier to maneuver—a 1/2-in. clearance from the back of the pockets will do. Then set the beam in the pockets. **2** Cut lengths of 2× block equal to the depth of the beam and wedge them between the beams and the sides of the pockets. This will prevent the beam from rotating. Fasten the wedge-blocks to the beams. **3**

Installing beams in stud walls

Everything about beams is heavy and awkward—all the more so when placing beams in stud walls because you're working overhead. Lacking a crane or all-terrain forklift, building them in place from individual members is my favorite approach. A-frames are a great help in supporting the members of the beam until you can anchor them permanently.

In wood framing, support beams with posts that provide a direct load to the foundation.

➡ See "Scaffolding and Horses," p. 32.

Set up the A-frames close to the ends of the beam and under any splices in the beam. Make the tops of the A-frames level with the beam pockets or support posts, and nail braces across the bottom of the frames so they don't open. ❶, ❷

Crown the beam stock, and to make sure all the crowns face up, mark them with an arrow, then walk one end of the beam onto an A-frame. ❸   >> >> >>

TRADE SECRET
Cut beam stock so that any splices will fall on the Lally columns or other supports. Don't splice all the members of a built-up beam at the same point— at least one member should be continuous across each support for lateral stability.

1 When setting up your A-frames, set each unit to the height you'll raise the beam,

2 When your A-frames are in position, tack a 2×6 to both bottom rungs of each frame to brace it and keep the legs from shifting.

3 Walk one end of the beam up one A-frame. Slide the beam forward until it can be set on the other A-frame.

INSTALLING BEAMS (CONTINUED)

When one end of the beam is on top of an A-frame, raise the other end to the top of the other A-frame. ❹ Turn the beam and set it upright in its pocket. ❺ Secure the ends of the beam by toenailing it into the framing. ❻ Repeat this process for each remaining beam member and fasten blocking between the edges of the beam and the pocket framing. ❼

Tack 2× scraps at both ends of the beam and anchor a tight string line across the face of each of the scrap blocks. ❽ This will give you a reference line to straighten the beam along its length. Your beam will be straight when its face in the center is the same distance off the string as it is on the 2× end blocks.

Use lumber braces to wedge the center of the beam straight and check it by slipping another scrap 2× between the beam and the string, adjusting the wedging as necessary. ❾

When you've got it right, clamp the beam members together, secure the beam with 2× braces attached to the walls perpendicular to it, and nail the beam together. ❿, ⓫ A typical nailing schedule is two 16d nails every 16 in., staggered top and bottom. More is fine. Leave the perpendicular braces that tie the beam to the tops of the walls in place until you set the Lally column.

4 Set the first end of the beam on top of the A-frame. Raise the other end of the beam to the top of the other A-frame.

Blocking installed to stabilize beam

7 At the ends of the beam, cut and install blocking on both sides (top and bottom) to prevent the beam from moving.

CONSIDER STEEL BEAMS

Steel I-beams handle greater spans than wood, so require fewer columns. They don't dry out and change dimensions. Best of all, the supplier measures, delivers, and sets them. Be sure the beam is flush with the foundation or on a second floor, at either the top of the studs or the bottom of the double top plate. That way, fastening one or two layers of 2× to the steel beam brings the plates to the proper level for joists. To attach lumber to steel, bolt the wood down through holes drilled by the supplier. (Don't volunteer to drill holes in steel beams. They're incredibly hard.)

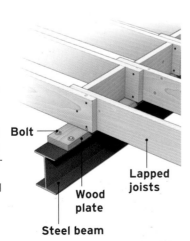

Bolt

Lapped joists

Wood plate

Steel beam

BEAM NAILING PATTERN

Typically, you will fasten the members of the beam to each other with 16d nails, driven from both sides, and at a minimum, in the pattern shown below. More fasteners than shown here, of course, are permitted.

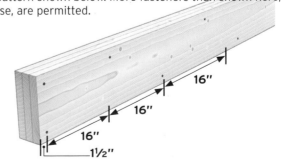

16"

16"

16"

16"

1½"

5 Roll the beam upright in place and set it in the beam pocket over the posts.

6 Secure the end of the beam member by toenailing it to the framing in the pocket.

2× block tacked to beam to anchor string line

8 Space a string off the beam on 2× blocks at both ends. Use a center block to check the distance between the beam and the string.

9 Using a 2×4 wedged against the wall, push the beam until the line touches the 2× block. Then your beam is straight.

10 Nail the wedged 2×4 brace to the beam and add horizontal bracing as seen in the background.

11 With all the pieces of the beam in place and braced to the top of the opposite walls, clamp them and nail the members together.

SETTING LALLY COLUMNS

Lally columns are concrete-filled steel tubes (usually 4 in. diameter) sold in various lengths that you cut to fit on site. When installed they bear on steel plates lag-bolted to the beam and fastened to the footing with concrete fasteners. Raised tabs in the plates lock the column in place. In circumstances where additional lateral strength is required, saddle hardware will be specified instead of plates.

Level the beam

Before cutting a Lally, check the beam for level using a laser or a builder's level. Level the beam if need be, using a house jack or 2× stock wedged between the beam and a secure foundation (concrete block works well).

Then use a plumb bob or a vertical laser between the beam and footing centers to locate the plates. Install the plate, replumb the beam plate location, and install the top plate. ❶, ❷

Cut the column

Next, measure the distance between the plates. Using this measurement, cut the column with a column cutter (large ones can be rented). First score the column, then support it near the cut and whack the scrap end with a sledge. It should drop off. ❸, ❹ Level any excess concrete with a hammer or sledge and cold chisel.

Install the column

Raise the beam slightly so the Lally can clear the tabs on the plates, then lower the beam onto the column. ❺ Check the column for plumb at two spots about 90 degrees opposed. ❻ Some jurisdictions require welding the column to the plates, which is done on site after installation.

Saddle hardware adds lateral stability to the joint between column and beam.

CAPTURING A LALLY COLUMN

Another common way to set steel columns is to center them on a footing before pouring the surrounding slab.

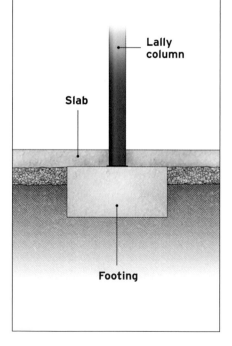

Lally column

Slab

Footing

Steel Lally columns support beams midspan.

WHAT CAN GO WRONG

If you cut a Lally column too short, shim up its base with additional plates. If you cut it too long, shorten it with a hand-held grinder. Remove any excess concrete with a cold chisel.

1 Positively connect a Lally's steel bearing plate to its footing. Locate the position of the top plate with a plumb bob or laser.

2 Fasten the top plate at the point indicated by the plumb bob or laser. Then measure the distance between the plates to find the post length.

3 Cut the post to length. Use a rented column cutter to score the steel tube.

4 Knock off the end of the scored column off and clean off any excess concrete.

5 Wedge a 2× to raise the beam as needed to provide clearance to slide the Lally in.

6 Lower the beam onto the column, then check the column for plumb.

WHAT CAN GO WRONG

Lally columns should stand as close to the center of their footing as possible. An off-center column loads its footing unevenly, which can cause the footing to rotate and the column to drop. Check with the designer before installing a column more than an inch or two off-center—the concrete contractor may have to replace the footing.

INSTALLING JOISTS

Joists (as well as studs and rafters) can be spaced at a number of different intervals—as long as those intervals allow the edges of the sheathing or subfloor to fall on the center of the framing member. That way, you have a surface you can nail the edges to.

Spacing options

Joist spacing is often specified at 16 in. on center, as well as 12 in., 24 in., and 19.2 in. (though this spacing works only for the 8-ft. dimension of the sheet). Of these, 16-in. intervals are common and provide plenty of structural stability. The layout illustrated on the opposite page uses intervals of 16 in. Most tape measures highlight multiples of 16 in red, and place a small black diamond at multiples of 19.2 in.

Marking the layout

Mark the joist layout for the first floor on the mudsill and any beams, and those for the second floor on the top plates of the walls.

The marks on the tape show centers, but you mark the location of the edge of a framing member when laying out. To do so, offset the layout mark by half the thickness of the member from the center dimension (typically 3/4 in.). For example, the edges of joists set on 16-in. centers can be marked at either 15 1/4 in. or 16 3/4 in. Pencil lines square at this mark, and indicate where the joist goes with an X.

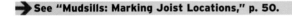

➡ See "Mudsills: Marking Joist Locations," p. 50.

Installing the joists

Install special joists first, such as doubled joists along fireplaces or stairwells. Sometimes such doubled joists fall close enough to the normal spacing that one of the joists functions as one-half of the pair.

Plans often specify the size of stairs or fireplaces, not the location of the joists that surround them. I frame stairways 2 in. wider than the finished stair to allow for wall finishes. Fireplaces and chimneys must be separated from combustible framing by at least 2 in., so I frame their openings 4 in. wide (2 in. on each side). Where joists lap a beam and are thus offset in the middle, you'll have to add nailers on the offset joist to support the subfloor.   >> >> >>

A proper joist layout will allow the edges of standard-sized subfloor panels to land in the center of the joists for nailing.

Lay out the edge of a framing member by marking beyond its center dimension by one half its width, here, 16 3/4 in.

Where they lap a beam or bearing wall, half of the joists will be offset, but adding nailers will support the subfloor over these joists.

LAYING OUT JOIST LOCATIONS

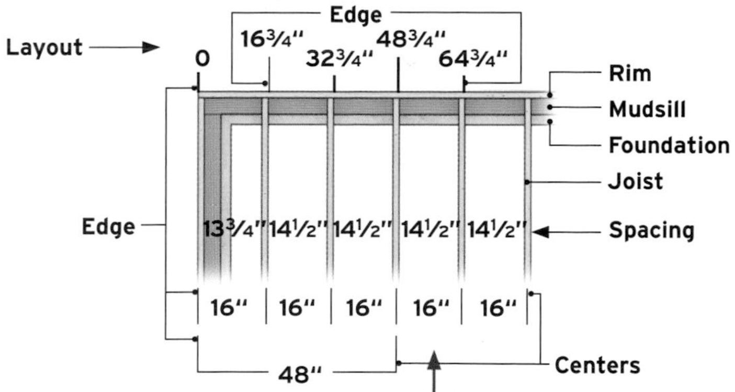

Layout →

Edge

0   16¾"   32¾"   48¾"   64¾"

Rim
Mudsill
Foundation
Joist

Edge   13¾" 14½" 14½" 14½" 14½"   Spacing

16" 16" 16" 16" 16"

48"   Centers

Mark the framing for the edges of the joists ¾ in. more than the center-to-center increment you're using. For example, if you're working with joists on 16-in. centers, the far edge of the first joist falls at 16¾ in. from the perimeter edge, the second at 32¾ in., and so on. That way, when the outside edge of the subfloor panel is laid on the outside edge of the framing, the interior edges of the panels will fall in the center of the joists. This also means the first joist bay will be ¾ in. narrower than the others.

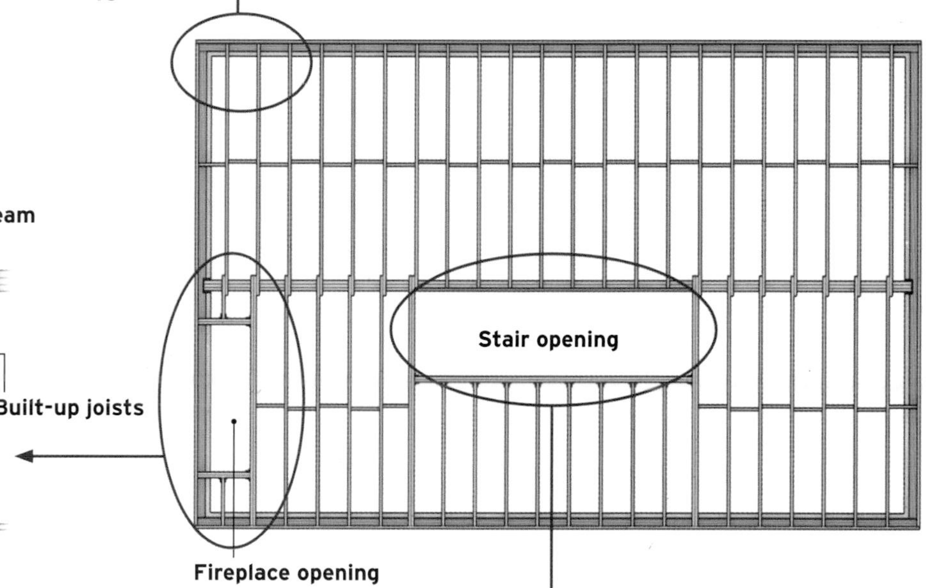

Foundation
Mudsill
Beam pocket
Beam

Built-up joists

Opening + 4"

+4"

Hangers

Stair opening

Fireplace opening

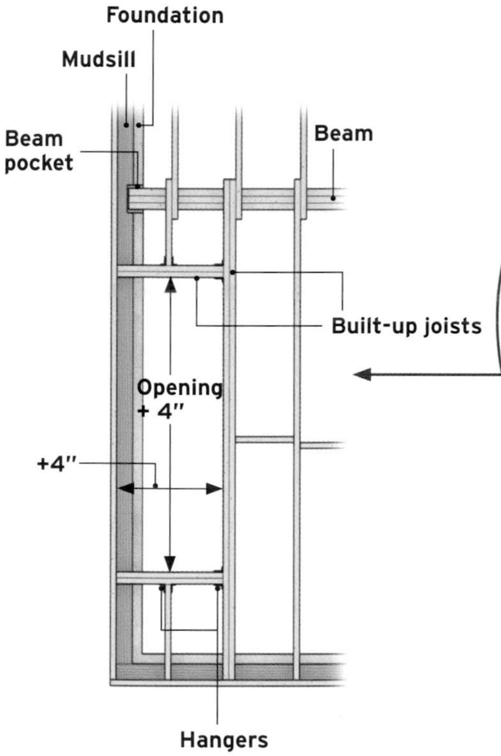

Frame openings for fireplaces so there's at least a 2-in. space between the framing and the masonry. Support the truncated joists on joist hangers nailed to double or triple joists around the opening.

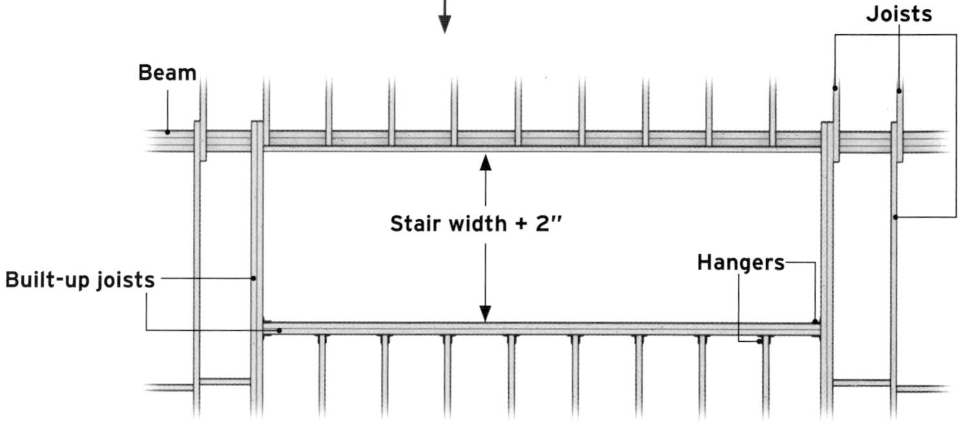

Joists
Beam

Stair width + 2"

Built-up joists

Hangers

Make stair openings 2 in. wider than the width of the stairs to allow for drywall and trim. As with fireplaces, create the opening with built-up joists that support the shortened ones.

INSTALLING JOISTS (CONTINUED)

Every floor gets a rim or band joist. It's the first one you install. This member runs perpendicular to the floor joists on top of the mudsill or wall plate, stabilizing the joists and keeping them from rolling over. Use straight stock for rim joists so they sit consistently on the mudsill or plate. To aid in setting the joists plumb, mark lines square up from the mudsill or plate on the face of the rim.

Locate the rim by snapping a line 1½ in. from the outside edge of the mudsill or wall plate, and toenail the rim joist down with one 8d nail every 6 in. ❶, ❷

Crown the joists as you take them off the pile, and mark the top of the arc with an arrow. Installed with the crown up, joists tend to straighten with time, and because the arcs all face the same way, the floor is less likely to have noticeable hills and valleys.

If you're building a ground floor, lay the outer ends of all the joists along the foundation. Then carry the interior end across the basement, up a ladder, and on to the beam. Lay the joists out flat with the crowns facing in one direction, then come back with a worker on each end, set them upright, and nail them.

Assemble double or triple joists before placing them. Pay attention to both the crown of the joists and any bow they might have. To make the assembled double joists straight, nail the joists together with the bows opposing each other. Use at least one 10d nail every 16 in., staggered top and bottom, and work from one end to the other. If the crowns go out of alignment, drive them back with a toenail. Once assembled, carry these joists to their location and fasten them. ❸

Fasten each joist through the rim with three 16d face nails, and toenail each joist to the mudsill or plate with three 8d nails. Where the joists lap at the beam or center bearing wall, join them with three 10d nails. Fasten them to the beam or wall plate with two 8d nails in each joist. ❹

Align, or stack, your framing to maintain a continuous load path from the top of the building to the foundation. A layout that places joists over studs, with studs (and later rafters) in the same vertical line, begins at the bottom. Start the layout of the floor, walls, and roof from the same end. ❺

When the joists run across in one length, the layouts on either side of the floor mirror each other. With wider floors, lumber joists will span half the width and lap each other on a beam or bearing wall, which offsets the joists. To account for the offset, lay out the joists on one side 1½ in. (one joist thickness) closer to the origin. So, if a layout mark on the first side is at 16¾ in., its counterpart on the second side would be at 15¼ in.

Joists that will lap a center beam can be left uncut—just let them run long over the beam. They have to lap the joists from the other side by 3 in. anyway. ❻ When you have the special joists set, continue placing the remainder. ❼

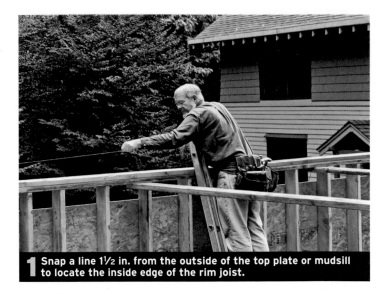

1 Snap a line 1½ in. from the outside of the top plate or mudsill to locate the inside edge of the rim joist.

4 Nail through the rim into each joist with three 16d nails and toenail the joists to the mudsill, top plate, or beam.

6 Lap joists by at least 3 in. at bearing points, and secure with three 10d nails.

2 Set the rim joist in place and toenail it to the top plate (or to the mudsill if working on a first-floor foundation).

3 Install double and triple joists first, so the other joists won't be in the way when you move these heavy members into place.

5 Lay out joists to stack over studs for a continuous load path. If there's a wall above, stack its studs on these joists, then rafters.

REMEMBER THE PLUMBER

Plumbers don't have much flexibility in setting toilet, tub, or shower drains, and most will cut joists in their way. Such joists won't pass inspection. Avoid this problem by moving joists that fall where a drain will be located. I avoid placing a joist within 3 in. of center of a toilet or tub drain, even if I end up with a joist bay a little wide. Add blocking or an additional joist to the far side of the drain if needed to avoid overspanning the subfloor.

7 Once the special joists are set, continue placing and nailing the common joists.

USING JOIST HANGERS

Joist hangers are sized for the lumber they'll support—a single 2×10, for example—as well as for double and triple joists. Wider hangers are made for engineered lumber.

Use the correct fastener

Be sure to fill every nail hole with the proper nail. The size to use is specified on the hanger, often 8d or 10d. That designation doesn't refer to length, but to shaft diameter. A 10d hanger nail for a 2× joist is only 1½ in. long, but it's a full 0.148 in. thick. If you can use a longer nail that diameter, it's OK. However, some inspectors will check the size stamped on the nail head—you may have to use nails supplied by the manufacturer.

Special nailers for hangers

It hasn't been long since framing hardware had to be hand nailed. While it's incredibly dangerous to nail hardware with a standard nailgun, specialty guns that locate the hanger nails precisely in their holes work great.

➜ See "Metal-Connector Nailers," p. 24.

It's usually easier to toenail a single joist in place, then install the hanger. Because of the weight of doubled or tripled joists, nail the hanger in place first. Hold a stub of joist scrap in the hanger to position it. Some hangers are made for diagonal nails, called "shear nails," which penetrate the hanger, the joist, and the beam. That nail is usually a full-length 10d or 16d.

Set a stub of joist material in a joist hanger to form it while nailing.

Support joists that are flush with their supporting beam using joist hangers.

Joist hangers are available for single joists and also for double and triple joists.

Drive full-length so-called shear nails at an angle through the joist hanger.

Some inspectors check for the proper nail size to be stamped on the nail head.

CORROSION-RESISTANT HANGERS

Most, if not all, joist hangers are lightly galvanized, which is fine for interior use with untreated lumber.

If you're using joist hangers outside, or with treated lumber, be sure the hanger is rated for that use. One common acceptable designation is G-185.

Outside in marine environments, use stainless-steel hangers and nails. And don't mix and match stainless and galvanized nails and hangers. Contrary to what you might expect, that leads to a fast corrosive reaction.

Galvanized hangers for use with pressure-treated lumber must be marked G-185.

BRIDGING

Bridging or blocking is usually cut from lengths of joist material. It's typically installed in a continuous offset line down the midspan of a run of joists. Bridging helps prevent the joists from twisting under loads. The International Residential Code (IRC) requires midspan bridging only for joists exceeding 12 in. nominal depth—a situation I've never encountered. Still, I think bridging stiffens floors, and I consider it standard in any floor framing installation.

Cutting bridging stock

Cutting bridging from joist stock helps use up scrap, and you should cut it 1⁹⁄₁₆ in. shorter than the joist spacing. This is ¹⁄₁₆ in. shorter than the nominal space between joists and allows for cupped joists, while still making for a tight fit.

Snap layout lines

Snap a line across the joists at midspan, and fasten the bridging between the joists on alternate sides of the line using 16d nails. Sight down the length of every third or fourth joist to be sure the bridging isn't bowing them. If that happens, custom-cut a piece of bridging to straighten the next joist. In addition, custom-cut bridging to fit special joist layouts. The first bay laid out in a floor will always be half a joist thickness narrower than the rest, and the last bay usually requires a custom cut.

Mind the plumbing and utilities

If bridging will interfere with drains or ducts, bridge the joist opening with a piece of 2×4 fastened on the flat at the bottom of the joists. Mechanical contractors can drill it for supply pipes or wires.

Solid blocking is required where a floor cantilevers beyond a wall and whenever there's a point load on a joist. The idea in both cases is to prevent the joists from rolling under load.

Stagger blocking on either side of a midspan chalkline to ease nailing. Periodically sight down the length of the joists to make sure they are not bowing.

Blocking nailed on the flat allows room for ducts or drain lines.

Block both sides of joists that carry a load from above to a beam.

CONTINUOUS STRAPPING

Another way to stiffen joists is to run continuous 1×3 strapping along their bottoms. In eastern New England carpenters often run such strapping on 2-ft. centers. The belief there is that this detail makes for flatter ceilings with fewer drywall nail pops.

Strapping run along a ceiling acts similar to blocking. (Photo by Roe A. Osborn)

INSTALLING I-JOISTS

There aren't many details in the International Residential Code (IRC) for I-joists because they're a manufactured product. Manufacturers provide instructions with delivery and on their websites, and building inspectors look for framing installations that follow these directions.

I-joists are always part of an engineered system, so it's crucial that you follow the plans exactly. The details shown here are typical to most I-joist systems, but always follow the manufacturer's instructions in case of differences, or in more complicated applications.

A variety of materials can be used for I-joist rim stock, including ¾-in. OSB. Because of OSB's limited compressive strength, 2× squash blocks must be used with ¾-in. OSB rims to support the wall above. Using 1⅛-in. rims eliminates the need for most squash blocks, although you still may need them under point loads, such as studs supporting a header over a window.

I-joist layout doesn't differ from that of lumber joists, except that most I-joists are at least 2½ in. wide, which will affect your layout measurements. Instead of moving the layout mark for joist spacing ¾ in. for each successive joist, with I-joists, you move it over 1¼ in.

Carrying and cutting

Like any material, I-joists are stronger across their depth than their thickness. When carrying them, particularly longer lengths, keep the joist on edge. Carrying them can flex and damage them. And because of their shape, cutting I-joists goes easier with a jig. (See "Making an I-Joist Cutting Jig," facing page.)

Flanges and stiffeners

If there's to be a deck or a porch, upgrade to 1¼-in. or 1½-in. rims to provide better attachment. Web stiffeners cut from ¾-in. plywood stabilize I-joists below point loads, where I-joists bear on a beam, or when joist hangers are used. They're fastened to both sides of the web with through nails. Bend over protruding nails.

Bracing

Brace I-joists as they're installed to prevent them rolling underfoot and breaking. Many manufacturers call for a continuous run of 1×4 bracing for every 8 ft. of I-joist, removed as the floor is sheathed.

I-joists are lighter and straighter than sawn lumber. Carry them on edge to avoid damaging them.

I-joists require special hangers. Not only do the wide flanges fit in them, but the hangers are built to prevent the joist rolling under load.

Install squash blocks wherever a point load will land on an I-joist.

Nail web stiffeners where I-joists sit in hangers, or when they cross a bearing member.

Use engineered rim board (rather than OSB) to avoid the need for squash blocks below each stud, and to provide solid deck attachment.

Nail I-joists to the sill through their flanges.

TRADE SECRET

Lumber joists are often deeper and stronger than needed to meet the IRC's maximum deflection standard of L/360, meaning that under its maximum design load plus a safety factor, the floor may deflect no more than its span divided by 360. To save money, I-joist floors are often engineered to just meet the L/360 standard, and they can be bouncier than we're used to. I-joists with a stiffer deflection, such as L/480, are a big improvement but may be deeper, have wider flanges, and will cost more.

MAKING AN I-JOIST CUTTING JIG

1 Begin by cutting a piece of rim board to fit snugly between the flanges.

2 Nail a straight piece of stock square to the piece of rim board to act as a fence.

3 The jig keeps the saw out of the web, and ensures a square cut at the same time.

LAYING SUBFLOOR

1 Don't count on the rim being straight. Snap a line 4 ft. from the end joists to align the subfloor.

2 Spread construction adhesive on the top edge of the joists, but don't spread more than a sheet will cover—it will start to set up, or you'll step in it and slip.

4 Butt new panels and drop into place. Start the second row with a half sheet.

5 Drive succeeding rows of T&G together with a sledge and a beater block.

6 Where joists are offset, add nailers to support the edges of the panel.

Plywood or OSB subfloor ties the structure together and provides a smooth base for finish floors. The vast majority of new construction uses ¾-in. tongue-and-groove (T&G) subfloor. Without the T&G edge, code requires blocking under unsupported edges to prevent them from sagging when stepped on—a lot of unnecessary work.

Keeping things straight

For T&G panels to fit snug across the entire floor, the first row must go on straight. To eliminate any influence from imperfect joist installations, measure 4 ft. in along the two end joists, and snap a line representing the leading edge of the first row of subfloor sheets. 1

Apply adhesive and fasten

Although not a code requirement, applying construction adhesive is good practice. It helps prevent floor squeaks. Clear the groove in the sheet of splinters or debris before you spread glue on the joists. Only spread glue on as many joists as you will cover with a sheet to prevent the adhesive skinning over, losing its grip. 2

Pay attention to the nailing schedule—use one 8d deformed-shank (ring or twist shank) nail at least every 6 in. along the edges and every 12 in. in the field. 3

Completing the installation

Start the second row of subfloor with a half sheet. 4 Doing so helps you to abide by the code, which says the end joints in subsequent rows of structural sheathing must be staggered by at least two joist bays. T&G subflooring usually needs to be sledge-hammered into place. If need be, have a helper hold down the joining edge by standing on it, and protect the edge of the driven piece with a scrap of lumber. 5

If the joists are offset over a beam, add a nailer to maintain the layout on the short side. Cut openings after nailing down the sheet. Measure to the framing below, and strike chalklines at the framing's edge. Set the saw to just cut through the subflooring. 6

3 Snap chalklines in line with the joists for accurate nailing, one 8d deformed-shank nail at least every 6 in. along the edges and every 12 in. in the field.

INSTALLING UNDERLAYMENT

Although technically part of the floor structure, underlayment is installed after the roof is on. Underlayment can beef up a floor for stone, tile, or strip flooring or provide a smooth surface under resilient materials. A layer of underlayment is often needed to reinforce an old board subfloor before installing a new finish floor.

The most common underlayment I've used is ½-in. underlayment-grade plywood. Often, a layer of cement or gypsum-based tile backer is also used to provide a substrate for setting tile (but it does not strengthen the floor).

Sweep thoroughly. Lay out underlayment so the joints do not fall on the joists—this allows the joists to move without disturbing the finish floor. Fasten the sheets to the subfloor on 6-in. centers with deformed-shank nails, such as ring shanks, or deck screws. The fasteners should fully penetrate the subfloor.

SUBFLOOR AND WATER

All subfloor should be rated at least "Exposure 1," meaning it should show no ill effects from a few months exposure to the weather during framing. Still, severe exposure can cause plywood to delaminate and OSB to swell (cheaper, commodity-grade OSB is more susceptible to swelling than brand-name boards).

To drain pooled water, drill holes through the subfloor. Use a hole saw that's about 1½ in. diameter. That makes a hole big enough it won't clog with leaves. Save the cutout. When the roof is on, screw a backerboard below the hole and glue the cutout back in place.

Fasten underlayment to the subfloor, keeping joints off of the joists, making sure the fasteners penetrate the subfloor. Gluing underlayment isn't a code requirement, but it is a good practice.

BUILDING WALLS

BUILDING WALLS gives you the first real sense of the shape of your creation. As mudsills establish the shape of a floor, plates (the horizontal members at top and bottom) establish the shape of the walls.

In addition to being square to each other, walls have to be plumb in both vertical directions. A wall that's out of plumb side-to-side will make the dimensions of intersecting walls inconsistent. Out-of-plumb walls will also make it hard to install windows, doors, cabinets, and tile later in the building process.

Walls carry loads from above to the structure below, with studs providing the load path, and headers above window and door openings carrying the horizontal loads to the studs alongside the opening.

Sheathing stiffens the structure and goes a long way in keeping out the wind. Last comes building paper or housewrap, whose primary job is to drain water that gets behind the siding.

LAYING OUT THE PLATES

BUILDING THE WALL

RAISING THE WALL

BUILDING OTHER WALLS

ESTIMATING WALL MATERIAL

Interior walls are usually framed from 2×4s, exterior walls, more often with 2×6s, to house thicker insulation. When you're building your take-off list, count one bottom and two top plates for each wall, and on slabs, make the bottom plate rot resistant.

➡ **See "Floor-Framing Anatomy," p. 41.**

Lumberyards stock plate lumber in lengths up to 20 ft. or 24 ft.– make all but the longest walls joint free. When you do need a joint, make the shortest plate section at least 8 ft. for strength.

Studs

Rather than tally individual studs plus extras for bracing and blocking, get an accurate count for every-thing by ordering one stud per foot of wall on 16-in. centers. For 24-in. centers, figure one stud per 18 in. Unless the wall is an odd height, order precut studs. Precuts fac-tor in the thickness of the plates: 8-ft. precuts are 92⅝ in. long (92¼ in. west of Denver). Together with three plates (an additional 4½ in.), that makes a wall about 8 ft. 1 in. Full 8-ft. studs and three plates would make a wall 4½ in. taller than standard drywall. (Pre-cuts are also available for 9-ft. and 10-ft. walls.)

Doors and windows

For walls with standard 6-ft. 8-in. doors and windows at the same height, order one 14-ft. 2× for each door and window—you'll cut it into two jack or trimmer studs to sup-port headers. Headers longer than 6 ft. require two jacks on each end, and rarely, three.

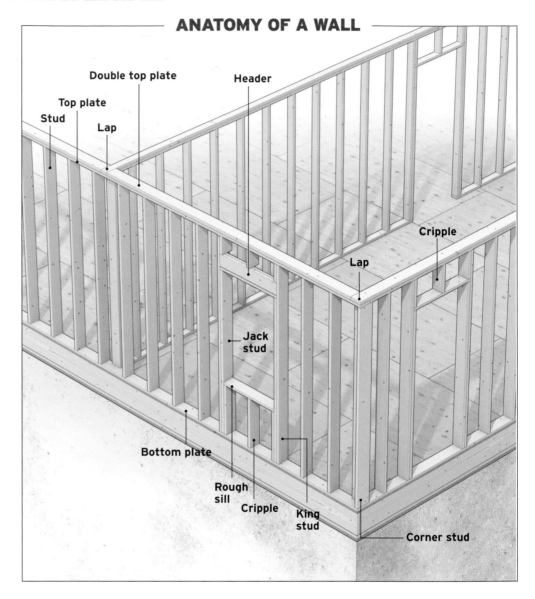

ANATOMY OF A WALL

Double top plate · Header · Top plate · Lap · Stud · Cripple · Lap · Jack stud · Bottom plate · Rough sill · Cripple · King stud · Corner stud

Exterior walls are often 2×6s instead of 2×4s to allow space for more insulation.

Short studs above headers or below sills are called cripples.

Headers

Most headers are doubled 2×12s, or doubled 2×10s with a 2×4 or 2×6 nailed flat to the bottom for a nailing surface flush with the studs.

Although stronger than needed for most openings, when held tight to the top plate in an 8-ft. wall such headers create a rough opening the perfect height for 6-ft. 8-in. doors. Smaller header stock may be specified to save lumber and allow for more insulation. Cripple studs make up the difference in height between the header and top plate. Headers can also be LVL or PSL. Cut header stock 3 in. or 6 in. longer than the rough opening to bear on the jack studs.

Nonbearing walls take less lumber, are lighter, and are easier to raise if you skip the header and continue the layout across the top of the opening with cripple studs. Without a header to shrink and expand, cracks in the drywall or trim joints are less likely.

Fasteners

Use 16d nails for the plate-to-stud connections and 10d nails to join headers and fasten the double top plate. Order masonry nails and sill seal when building on a slab.

To save wood, skip the headers when there's no load above other than the wall itself.

For each header, include in your materials list a 2×4 or 2×6 nailer.

CUSTOM STUDS

Carpenters hate this, but sometimes designers specify odd wall heights, and you have to custom-cut all the studs. You can cut each board individually with a miter saw and a stop, but that's time-consuming. For a fast, consistent method, cut the studs right on the pile they came in. Align the ends of a layer of studs, mark their length on the studs on each side, and snap a chalkline to guide your cut.

Gang cutting is a fast way to produce uniform studs if precuts aren't available.

ONE OR TWO TOP PLATES?

Most houses are built with double top plates. The upper plate laps intersecting walls, tying them together.

Single top plates are not in the IRC, but they require joining with steel straps—and almost no one does that.

With a single top plate, joists or rafters must be within 1½ in. of stacking on studs—not a requirement with double plates. You can't use standard precut studs, or the wall will be 1½ in. short. Cutting custom studs for double top plates takes time. No one hates wood waste more than I do, but what little is consumed by double top plates is a far more renewable resource than is my time.

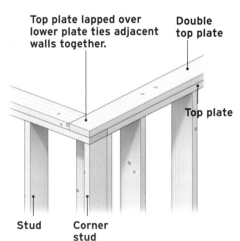

Top plate lapped over lower plate ties adjacent walls together.

Double top plate

Top plate

Stud

Corner stud

Double top plates tie the walls together and greatly increase the strength of the assembly.

Corner stud

Stud

LAYING OUT WALL PLATES

1 Mark the width of the bottom plate on the subfloor. This mark represents the inside edge of the plate when you install it.

2 Snap chalklines for the plates between your marks.

Layout can get confusing—keep your plan goof proof by marking which side of the line the bottom plate goes on.

TRADE SECRET

Some chalk colors are permanent. Blue and white are the only two that can be removed or washed away. Most of the time I prefer blue chalk because it shows up well and can be erased. When re-marking a line snapped in the wrong place, I'll use red chalk to avoid confusion. And when snapping lines in the wet, I use red or orange chalk so the lines don't wash away.

The first step in laying out walls is to reproduce the building plan on the subfloor of your structure, marking the edges of all the wall plates with chalklines. Before you do that, spend time with the plans, looking for dimensions that don't add up. Mentally follow load paths to verify they run continuously to the foundation, noting where extra blocking will be needed for attaching cabinets and hardware, such as handrail brackets. Note any other potential problems you need to be aware of before picking up the hammer.

Check and correct for square

Check the floor for square before snapping layout lines for the wall plates. This is done the same way you'd check a foundation—measure the diagonals of each rectangular section.

➡ See "Check the Foundation for Square," p. 42.

You can correct slight imperfections by overhanging the bottom plate slightly past the edge of the floor and adding shims before

sheathing. Verify the dimensions of the floor—sometimes it's a little big or small. An inch or so is usually no big deal, as long as you're careful in how you adjust the dimensions of affected parts of the house. For example, 1 in. makes little difference in a large living room, but it can make or break a small bath.

Mark layout lines

Assuming the floor is square, start your layout by penciling marks on the floor at each corner. Measure and mark the width of your bottom plate from the edge of the floor. These marks represent the inside edge of the wall plates. **1** Keep in mind outer walls might be 2×6, even if the interior walls are 2×4. Snap chalklines on these marks on the entire perimeter. **2** Then, using the dimensions from the plans, proceed across the floor, striking one chalkline for each wall, and marking which side of the line the wall goes on with Xs. When marking the position of interior walls, outlining both sides of each plate will help avoid mistakes.

After you snap the lines for the longest parallel walls, take a corner-to-corner measurement to make sure the corners are square. (Photo by Roe A. Osborn)

DON'T TRUST THE SUBFLOOR

If the floor is inset from the rim joist, use a level from which to measure the layout line.

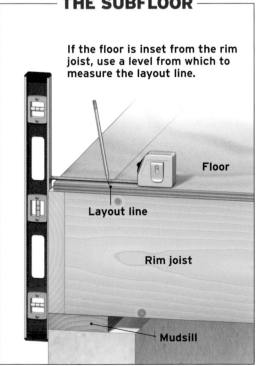

Floor

Layout line

Rim joist

Mudsill

PIPES IN A SLAB

When working on a slab, you'll work with a variety of pipes and conduit stubbed out of the concrete. These often aren't exactly where they're supposed to be, but moving a pipe cast in concrete costs a lot of time and money. If possible, adjust the walls to fit the plumbing. Often, just a small shift in a plate location, or changing a section of wall from 2×4 to 2×6, will bring the plumbing inside the wall. Make sure these little changes don't affect critical dimensions such as where cabinets, stairs, or plumbing fixtures must go.

ARRANGING THE PLATES

1 Cut and temporarily place the plates for the longest walls first. Butt the intersecting wall plates to the long plates.

2 Longer walls usually run past shorter ones. Cut and lay out the plates in a pattern that reflects their relationship to each other.

After snapping lines to locate the position of the wall plates, your next step is to cut and lay out the plates in their correct locations.

Cut and place the plates

Where two walls meet, determine which one will run past the other. I build and raise the longer walls first, then raise the perpendicular walls between them. With that in mind, cut the plates for the longest outside walls to length and lay them at the outside edge of the floor. **1** Butt intersecting walls to these. **2** Use the straightest stock for top plates. The bottom plates get nailed to the subfloor, and are easily straightened during installation.

When planning joints in plates in a long wall, make the joined sections 8 ft. or more for strength and locate the joint over headers or centered on studs so there's something to nail the ends to.

Mark the openings first

Once the top and bottom plates of a wall are placed (but not the double top plate yet), mark the framing for doors, windows, and intersecting walls. **3** Mark common studs with an X, jacks with an O, and cripples with a C. Wherever your plans call for a double or triple joist in the floor above, lay out the wall structure so a double or triple stud will fall immediately below the joist.

In walls perpendicular to the joists, lay out the common studs beginning at the same end of the house as the joist layout. Doing so stacks the studs atop the joists and ensures continuous load paths from the roof to the foundation. While not a code requirement with a double top plate except at point loads, stacking the framing provides clear paths for running pipes and ducts between floors.

Outside walls parallel to the joists are usually the shorter walls, and you'll build and raise

Plan plate joints to fall over headers or studs to give them a sound nailing surface. Offset joints in upper and lower plates by at least 8 ft.

them inside the longer walls. Sheathing on these walls will lap the end of the long walls. To avoid cutting each end piece of sheathing, begin the stud layout for these shorter walls measuring from the outside of the plate of the long wall. **4**

Make sure the inside edges of rough openings for windows and doors at corners are at least 3 in. from the intersecting wall

to provide room for trim. Moving the opening an inch or two means the trim carpenter won't have to scribe-fit a casing leg to the wall. Structurally, moving an opening slightly usually isn't a problem. Just make sure you do the same thing to any window that's above it so they lie in the same exact vertical plane.

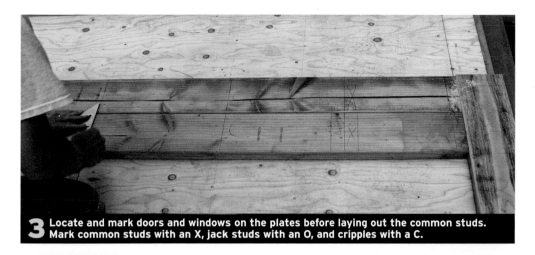

3 Locate and mark doors and windows on the plates before laying out the common studs. Mark common studs with an X, jack studs with an O, and cripples with a C.

TRADE SECRET
It's pretty common for plumbing vents to be centered behind bathroom sinks, and shower valves will be centered at the end of the bathtubs. If you put a stud in those spots, the plumber will rip it out. Either change the starting point of the layout to avoid this problem, or go off layout in these spots.

4 Lay out abutting walls so a full sheet of sheathing starts at the outside corner.

5 Partially cut openings before installing studs. Finish after the wall is nailed.

Lay out your wall structure so double or triple studs will fall under double or triple joists.

Precut door plates

The bottom plate runs through doorways and is cut after the wall is raised. Make a circular saw cut 1 in. deep at the sides of doorways before assembling the wall. This leaves enough meat to stabilize the wall during raising, and finishing the cut with a handsaw or reciprocating saw once the wall is up is quick and easy. **5**

ROUGH OPENINGS

Windows and doors fit in rough openings slightly larger than the dimension of the door or window. This extra space allows the unit to be shimmed plumb and level and provides space for insulation. Plans usually specify window and door size and make, not rough opening size. Carpenters use manufacturer-provided rough opening sizes for windows and exterior doors. For interior doors, rough openings are normally 2 in. wider and taller than the size of the door itself, not including its jamb. Standard headers may make the opening a little taller than this, but that height accounts for hardwood flooring or tile under the door frame.

ASSEMBLING THE COMPONENTS

There's a lot more to walls than studs and plates, and you'll assemble walls a lot more efficiently if you have all the components ready to go. Cut all headers, jack studs, corners, rough sills, and cripple studs before you nail a single stud to the plates. Follow the same staggered 16-in. nailing schedule for headers as for beams and double joists.

Nail jacks to studs and corner studs to each other, with two 10d nails about every 16 in. Look for straight studs for corners and stud/jack assemblies. Because the jacks are cut from 14-footers ordered specially for that purpose, there will probably be some bowed "bananas" you can't help using. In that case, nail these bowed jacks to bowed studs, but point the bows in opposite directions to straighten out both.

Using a story pole

To speed up preparing these components, as well as to increase your accuracy, make a story pole. A story pole is simply a length of wood on which you mark the lengths of all the wall components. Use one side for vertical members and the other side for horizontal ones. Once you've marked up the story pole, you won't need to pull out your tape and mark the correct dimension every time you go to cut a piece of wood.

Making efficient corners

Traditionally, outside corners were made by nailing together two studs spaced apart by scraps of other studs. That wastes time and material, provides no space for insulation, and makes a challenging spot for the electrician to drill for wires.

Instead, simply nail two studs together in an L shape. This provides nailing at the corner for wall sheathing, and nailing inside for drywall. It's easy to insulate, and the electrician may be happy enough to buy you coffee.

Where one wall meets the center of another, carpenters traditionally nail three studs together in a channel to provide drywall nailing. This is even more wasteful than traditional corners. Instead, use one stud, the next width up from the intersecting wall, on the flat. Duplicate the adjacent plate layout on headers and rough sills, so you know where to nail the cripples.

Straighten jack stud assemblies by nailing the king and jack studs together, with any bows opposing each other.

Mark the length of all the wall components on the story pole. Use it to speed layout and marking work to length.

Square off the mark from the story pole and cut all the cripples with a circular saw.

Nail corner studs in an L-shape to provide adequate nailing for sheathing, easier drilling for wiring, and space for full insulation.

Where two walls intersect, provide a nailing surface for drywall with one wider stud, such as the 2×6 on the flat behind the 2×4 stud shown here.

To mark layout on a sill or header, place it next to the plate and square the line with the layout on the plate.

Nail a 2×6 to the bottom of exterior wall headers to provide a nailing surface that will be flush with the studs.

TRADE SECRET

Carpenters commonly add a piece of 1/2-in. plywood to the face of a lumber header to make it the same thickness as a 2×4 wall. This wastes plywood and time. The plywood adds negligible strength, and provided that there's a 2×4 nailed to the bottom of the header, the bottom of the header is in plane with the wall to support the drywall.

ASSEMBLING THE WALLS

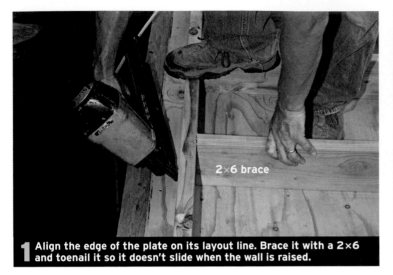

1 Align the edge of the plate on its layout line. Brace it with a 2×6 and toenail it so it doesn't slide when the wall is raised.

2×6 brace

2 With the top and bottom plates on the floor, nail in the studs and other components. Frame openings before common studs.

After layout and cutting, assembling the walls is almost anti-climactic. Build walls that bypass other walls first. Pick up and move out of your way any plates of perpendicular walls that will interfere with assembling the longest outside wall.

Anchor the bottom plate

Set the bottom plate on its edge, so what will be its bottom surface aligns with the layout chalkline you snapped. Brace the plate square and immobilize it with a 2×6. Toenail it in place every 4 ft. to 8 ft., nailing from the bottom of the plate into joists under the subfloor. Toenailing helps to keep the bottom plate from slipping while you're raising the wall. **①**

After you get the wall assembled and raised, these toenails may pull from the floor and stick out of the plate. Snip them off with diagonal cutters. With extremely heavy or tall walls, or garage walls that are raised directly on mudsills, secure the bottom plate by nailing straps made from lumber banding to the plate and the floor or sill.

Building the wall

Place the top plate on edge on the floor at a distance from the bottom plate roughly equal to the stud length. Begin filling in the wall with studs at the layout marks you made on the plates, driving nails through the face of the plates into the studs. Frame around the openings first. If you don't, you'll often find that there's a common stud in the way when you go to nail into the end of a header or rough sill. **②**

Crown the studs as you go, or the wall will have waves in it that are visible from the side. Place the crowned edges up, so the studs don't rock on the floor as you're trying to nail them to the plates.

Blocking provides nailing surface at a joint in the sheathing.

3 If the edges of the sheathing will need blocking for nailing, fasten the blocking on the flat to allow for insulation and mechanicals.

When working on a wall that will support cabinets, use the straightest studs you have.

There aren't a lot of tricks to nailing studs and plates together. Use two 16d commons through the plate into the ends of the studs (or three 8d common toenails). Keep the faces of the framing members flush at all the edges. Any double top plate that won't lap another wall can be nailed on now.

Install blocking

The plans may call for blocking between the studs to provide nailing for the horizontal edges of sheathing panels. You'll have to toenail one side of the blocking. Installing this blocking so its wide face contacts the sheathing leaves room for insulation and mechanicals. **③**

For heavy walls or garage walls, nail steel strapping to the plate and underlying framing to keep the wall from sliding when raised.

When the wall is raised and braced, cut any protruding nails flush.

BE WARY OF BOUNCE FIRE

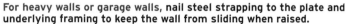

Many nail guns are capable of bounce fire, meaning you can hold the trigger and fire the gun repeatedly by pushing down on the gun's nose. This speeds sheathing work, but increases the danger of firing a nail unexpectedly. When shooting the upper nail through a plate into a stud, it's possible to catch the edge of the nosepiece on the plate, discharging the nail through the air. If you're holding the stud in place with your other hand, well, ouch. I once took a helper to the ER with a 10d nail shot through his index finger because of this situation. Not fun for either of us.

To minimize this danger, hold the stud on its line and fire in the bottom nail first. A surprise second shot in this location isn't likely to become airborne. (Keep the hand holding the stud far enough away from the plate so that if you miss the stud with the nail, your hand is clear.) Now, move the hand that was holding the stud out of the line of fire, and shoot in the top nail.

Move your free hand out of the line of fire in case of an accidental misfire when driving the upper nail.

SHEATHING EXTERIOR WALLS

Outside walls can be sheathed before or after raising them, although as a practical matter, a hybrid approach is usually required. I prefer to sheath the outside walls as much as possible before raising them, simply because it's a lot easier to nail sheathing panels to a wall lying flat on the floor than an upright one on the outside of a building.

Square the wall

Be sure the plates are straight (which you accomplish when you tack the bottom plate to the floor before assembly) and square before installing the sheathing. Just as you would check a foundation or floor, check the wall for square by measuring the diagonals and tapping on one free corner or the other till the measurements are equal. Once it's square, and to keep it there, tack the wall to the floor. ❶

Nail the sheathing

Locate the top of the first row of sheathing by measuring up from the bottom plate, allowing for the sheathing to hang below the bottom plate to lap the floor framing or to meet sheathing on a lower wall. Then snap a line across the face of the wall where you want the top of the sheathing. ❷, ❸ This adds an additional element that ties the wall to the floor framing. About the only sheathing you can't install while the wall is on the floor are the end pieces on walls that you must cut to fit between the ends of other walls.

The nailing schedule usually calls for one 6d ring- or spiral-shank nail every 6 in. along panel edges, and every 12 in. in the field. Do not overdrive the nails—the heads should just be flush with the sheathing. Take this seriously. The wall sheathing and its connection to the framing creates most of the shear strength needed to resist seismic and wind loads. Overdriving nails severely reduces their holding power, and the sheathing will not perform as designed. ❹ In seismic or high-wind zones, the plans may call for more nails, larger nails, and thicker sheathing. And if your mudsill is treated with CA or ACQ, the IRC requires hot-dipped galvanized or stainless-steel nails.

Tar paper and housewrap

Apply the tar paper or housewrap before raising the wall to keep out rain that gets past the siding (and it will—no siding is waterproof). ❺ Install the building paper from the bottom up—overlap lower pieces by 3 in. or so. Make vertical laps and corners about 12 in. Space staples or plastic-capped nails at 12 in. to 16 in. to secure the building paper. In windy areas or if your siding installation will be delayed, use plastic-capped nails.

Plastic housewraps install similarly, although different brands may have different requirements. Follow the instructions. Seams in housewrap are often taped, and that's a good practice. However, tape is not a substitute for proper lapping. Either housewrap or building paper will be integrated with window and door flashing later on.

1 When sheathing a wall, make sure its plates are straight and square to each other, then tack it to the floor.

2 Snap a reference line for the location of the top of the sheathing, then nail it to the studs.

3 Extend sheathing past the bottom plate so it laps either the bottom of the mudsill or the top of the sheathing on the wall below.

4 Drive nails so they're tight to the sheathing, without crushing its fibers. Crushed fibers reduce shear strength significantly.

5 It's much easier and faster to roll out and staple any tar paper or housewrap before raising a sheathed wall.

FOAM SHEATHING

Foam sheathing is common in cold areas, but it provides little shear strength so it's not useful in severe winds or seismic loads. It does, however, provide insulating qualities greater than its R-value suggests because it eliminates thermal bridging between the studs and interior walls.

However, siding nails set into studs can compress the foam, creating a wavy wall. And if the siding is lightweight, such as wood clapboard or vinyl, you can literally break into the house with a utility knife or a well-placed boot.

If installed, the first 4 ft. of the corners are sheathed with ½-in. plywood or OSB for shear strength. The rest of the walls get 1-in. foam, and ½-in. foam over the structural sheathing.

WHAT CAN GO WRONG

Houses can often survive hurricane-strength winds if they have sound wall and roof sheathing. Most times, if the sheathing stays put, the house will be standing when the skies clear. The failure of one piece of sheathing allows the wind inside the house, and that can level the building. At best, there will be significant water damage. Never skimp on proper sheathing.

Housewrap or tar paper?

Builders debate the virtues of housewrap over tar paper. Both keep out rain, but housewrap is touted as breathable—its high perm (permeability) rating allows interior water vapor to escape—a good thing. However, OSB sheathing's perm rating is less than 1, technically making it a vapor retarder. Since moisture has difficulty passing a vapor retarder, the value of the high permeability of housewrap fastened to OSB is for all practical purposes defeated.

Housewrap has other advantages—it's lighter, doesn't tear easily, comes in 9-ft.-wide rolls that speed installation, and has edges that are easily taped, making it a good air barrier. On the other hand, sheathing keeps out most air, tar paper costs less, and it's got a century-long track record. I'm comfortable with either.

The equation may change behind brick veneer. Because brick can hold tremendous amounts of water, sometimes the moisture drive behind it is inward, the opposite of the conditions most walls face. This is especially likely in warm, humid climates. To counter this, some building scientists recommend the use of lower-perm housewraps—between 5 and 10—behind brick.

RAISING WALLS BY HAND

1 Slide the hammer claw under the top plate and lever the plate off the floor.

2 Grip the bottom edge of the plate, bend your knees, and let your legs lift the wall.

Raising walls by hand requires more deliberation than it might seem. Any wall assembly is heavy, and moving heavy objects always requires forethought and careful planning.

To get the process started, lift the top plate with your hammer claw enough to get your fingers under it. **1** With your knees bent and your legs doing the work, come to an upright position. **2** Keeping your back straight, lift with your arms past shoulder height, then walk the wall upright, but not past vertical. **3** When you have the wall steadied, nail the bottom plate into the floor joists with two 16ds per connection. **4**

Plumb the wall in both directions, then nail it off to either intersecting walls **5** or a brace nailed to a block fastened through the subfloor into a joist. **6** Use 16d nails. To brace a wall plumb laterally, simply nail a 2× from plate to plate.

If the day isn't windy, you can use a minimal number of braces on most walls. At that, all but the shortest walls should receive at least three. At this point, the purpose of bracing is mainly safety—you don't want the walls to fall down. Walls raised on slabs require bracing from outside the perimeter.

➡ See "Building Walls on a Slab," p. 88.

As you build, raise, and brace interior walls, these in turn brace the sheathed exterior walls, taking the place of the temporary braces. Braces are also used to straighten walls, but more on that later. If I have to leave for the day and I haven't raised any interior partitions to tie in the outside walls, I'll double up the bracing. If it's windy, I won't leave until I've braced the exterior walls with interior walls.

You can build lighter walls by omitting headers, installing them after raising, or sheathing the walls once they're up. Long walls can be broken into shorter sections. That's pretty inefficient, though, and when walls get heavy, it's best to raise them with wall jacks.

➡ See "Raising Walls with Jacks," p. 84.

Lift safely

Like most construction accidents, those involving wall installation are almost always avoidable.

For example, it can be tempting to try to raise a wall that's too heavy. When you've raised the wall past waist level and are going for shoulder level, this is the point where people suddenly realize they've bitten off more than they can chew. They may start to give up, putting an unexpected burden on everyone else. The result can be a domino effect that gets people hurt.

If it's a windy day, think twice about raising sheathed walls. Particularly when working on the second floor, if the wall starts to topple to the outside, let it go. No one should fall trying to save a wall. You can always build a new one. You did make sure no one was working below, right? And that your truck isn't parked in the fall zone?

The most important piece of safety gear you have is your brain. Use it at all times.

3 Once the wall rises past your shoulders, walk it into position—not past vertical.

4 Steady the raised wall, then nail the plate down, making sure it aligns with the chalkline.

5 Plumb the wall at the corners, and nail it to any intersecting walls or roofs.

6 Fasten 2× blocks into the joists, and nail braces to the blocks.

Tips for teamwork

Generally, if it's not a strain to get a wall to knee height, things should be fine.

One person should be in charge of coordinating the lift and watching out for safety. If the crew is big enough, this person should be standing apart from the lift.

When the wall is vertical, some of the crew should continue steadying it, while others attend to the bracing and initial plumbing. Everyone needs to know their job before the lift begins.

RAISING WALLS WITH JACKS

I prefer to sheath outside walls and install the headers when the wall's on the floor—even though that can make a wall pretty heavy. So rather than do the job by hand, I use wall jacks to raise most outside walls—for safety and to minimize crew size. Jacks can be rented. The ones I own climb 2×4 masts as they're pumped. Another type of jack is an aluminum mast that raises the walls with a small cable winch. If using the first type, select knot-free, tight-grained material for your masts.

➡ See "Clamps, Jacks, and Pullers," p. 28.

The jacks I own can raise 1,000 lb. each. Make sure you use long enough 2×4s—it's pretty awkward to run out of 2×4 before running out of lift. Verify the mast length you need with the Pythagorean theorem, and assume both legs of the triangle are the height of the wall. Use the same formula ($a^2 + b^2 = c^2$) as you would if you were using a 3-4-5 triangle to square a foundation.

For an 8-ft. wall, you'll need 12-ft. 2×4s, and 9-ft. walls call for 14-ft. masts. Depending on how many headers and how tall the wall is, I allow 10 ft. to 20 ft. of wall length per jack. If you have any doubts, figure out the actual weight of the wall, or get an additional jack.

To use a climbing wall jack, first secure the wall's bottom plate to the floor if you haven't done so already. Nail a 2×4 block to the floor to spread out the weight from the jack.

➡ See "Anchor the Bottom Plate," p. 78.

Then, raise the top plate of the wall off the floor enough to fit the tongue of the jack under it. It helps to use temporary blocks, and with heavy walls, you may need to use crow bars for this initial lift. With the jack on its 2×4, place the tongue under the top plate. ❶ Nail a block to the floor behind the 2×4 so it can't slide out. ❷ Nail braces to the top ends of the wall with a single nail to swivel on so they follow the lift and are in place once the wall is raised. ❸

Place an iron-pipe handle in the jack and start pumping. Lift evenly. ❹ With taller walls, you'll have to finish the lift working from stepladders. ❺

The jacks lift the greatest weight at the beginning. As the wall goes up, more and more of its weight shifts to the bottom plate, and the lift gets easier. Pay attention at the top of the lift—the last bit is so easy that it's possible for the wall to fall outward.

Once the wall is raised, check the ends for plumb and nail off the braces. Nail the bottom plate with two 16d commons into each joist. Use a sledgehammer to drive the plate outward if need be, and a peavey to pull it in. ❻ Don't forget to nail off any sheathing that laps the floor framing.

1 Always set the mast on scrap so the weight of the wall doesn't push the mast through the floor.

Mechanical advantages
The taller the wall, the harder it is to lift. This isn't just a factor of weight—as a tall wall goes up, it reaches a point where its weight gets behind and above you and gains a mechanical advantage. If you're not using jacks, this is when you need a reserve crew to push up on the headers or the top plate with lengths of lumber. Eventually, you'll get past the balance point and the rest of the lift eases. Slow down near the top of the lift—the wall can gain enough momentum to continue past the apex and topple over.

Wall jacks eliminate all that. The climbing jacks I use can raise a 10-ft. 6-in.-high wall. Aluminum mast jacks can raise a 16-ft. wall. Anything bigger than that calls for diesel power. Rent an all-terrain forklift for a day or hire a crane. And once you have either of them on site, use it to move as much material as possible before you have to return it.

2 Nail a block behind the jack to keep it from sliding backwards during the lift.

3 Fix braces to the corners with one nail. As the wall rises, the braces will follow and be where you need them at the end of the lift.

4 Always raise walls evenly, keeping an eye on your partner's progress, or switching between jacks when working alone.

5 Most walls require you to finish the lift working from stepladders. This is where wall jacks especially come in handy.

6 Line the bottom plate up on the chalk line, driving it outward with a sledge. Pulling the bottom plate in takes a peavey.

TRADE SECRET

Climbing wall jacks can also be used to raise beams into place. Set the 2×4 plumb, and brace its top.

STRAIGHTENING WALLS, INSTALLING TOP PLATES

1 Tack blocks at each end of the wall and run a string between them. Use a third block to compare the wall's straightness to the string.

2 To straighten a wall from the outside, push it with a brace till the top plate is straight with the string, then nail the brace home.

5 Fire blocking slows the spread of fire from one cavity, such as that between the stringers, to another, in this case, the joist bay.

6 Blocking set between studs at the side of stairways provides a solid support for handrail brackets.

Once the outside walls are raised and nailed down, plumb the corners and nail the walls together through the corner studs. With the corners plumb, tack 2× blocks to each end and run a string along the wall's top plate. Use a third 2× block to check how close the wall is to the string. **1**

If you need to, it's pretty easy to use a brace to push a wall in from the outside or out from the inside. **2** Sometimes, however, you have to pull a wall in because there's nothing to push against. In that case, use a spring brace to pull on the wall. Make a spring brace by nailing a length of 2× to the top plate and to a block on the floor. Forcing a shorter length of 2× under its center will pull the wall in. **3**

Once the outside walls are straight and braced, build and install the interior walls. The final step is installing any double top plates that lap the adjoining wall.

➡ See "One or Two Top Plates?," p. 71.

Nail the double plate with two 10d commons over each stud. I try to avoid nailing in between studs. This is a courtesy to the plumber and the electrician, because they can now drill the plates for pipes and wires between studs with no fear of dulling their bit on a nail. **4**

Blocking and nailers

Once all the walls are up, go back and add blocking where needed. Any framing cavity that leads into another requires 2× fire blocking. Walls require fire blocking between the studs when the cavity is greater than 10 ft. in height. **5**

Additional blocking is what I call courtesy blocking. Other trades will appreciate finding it there, as it allows them to do a better job. For example, once you have installed the stairs, run blocking with its top 36 in. above the tread nosings near the top, bottom, and

3 Use a spring brace to pull walls in when needed. Anchor the bottom to the floor and the top to the top plate.

4 To create a double top plate, lap the upper plate on the lower one at the end of the wall and secure it with 10d nails.

7 Tubs, showers, and grab bars all will require strong supports behind the finish wall surface. Fasten blocking at these locations.

8 Without a horizontal surface on top, ceiling drywall has no anchor. Extend drywall nailers from the top plate by at least 1 in.

middle of stairs to provide an anchor for handrail brackets. On balconies, make sure there's a stud or some blocking centered at 36 in. from the floor where the handrail will hit the wall. **6**

The future edges of tiled showers and bathtubs, where a shower door will require anchoring, should get at least a 2×6 installed on the flat to provide a wide target for screws. Add a row of blocking centered at 36 in. around the perimeter of showers and baths for grab rails, and one along the top edge of the tub or shower pan to support the tile substrate. You can also block for towel bars and toilet paper holders, if you know where they're to go. **7**

Last, any wall that's parallel to the joists will require nailers for the ceiling drywall. These are pieces of 2× nailed to the top plate so they extend into the ceiling-joist bay. **8**

TRADE SECRET

A row of blocking just below the tops of future upper cabinets—usually about 7 ft. off the floor—and another row at about 34 in. off the floor for base cabinets will earn you points from the cabinet installer.

BUILDING WALLS ON A SLAB

When laying out the walls on a slab, you won't have the benefit of working on a wood floor that you built square. Check the slab for square and level as you would a foundation wall.

➜ See "Check the Foundation for Square," p. 42.

Slabs are sometimes stepped down to provide space for a brick ledge—that is, a surface to support brick veneer. If you need to adjust the walls to fit square on the slab, don't overhang this space. Brick facing needs a minimum 1-in. airspace between it and the wood framing, so make sure that there's enough space for the ledge to fully support the bricks and for the airspace.

When building on a slab or a stem wall, you'll need to notch the bottom plate to fit around pipes or conduits. ❶ Leave as much wood as you can, but be sure that the plate will fit around the pipe after the wall is raised. You don't want to find out a pipe interferes with placing the wall as you're raising it—you'll need to take the wall back down and re-cut. Sometimes it's best to completely notch the plate and reinforce it with a steel strap. ❷

The bottom plate of a wall bolts to the slab much the same way as a mudsill to a foundation wall. Use a bolt marker as you would for a mudsill, but drill the pencil hole at the width of the wall plate.

➜ See "Making Your Own Bolt Marker," p. 8.

One thing that's harder when raising a wall on a slab is that the walls must be lifted up and over the foundation bolts This can be tough with a heavy wall, and it may be better to sheathe walls after raising them, to reduce the weight. In the same vein, headers can be installed after the wall is up. Alternatively, bolt down a mudsill, get it inspected, then counterbore the bottom plate at the bolt locations and raise the wall atop with the counterbores aligned with the bolts. ❸

Depending on the seismic and wind zone of your building, all the walls may not need to be bolted down. Some interior partitions might simply be nailed down, with either hand-driven masonry nails or nails fired from a powder-actuated gun.

➜ See "Powder-Actuated Fasteners," p. 25.

That said, seismically prone and many high-wind areas also tend to be slab construction areas. If you build in these places, you'll encounter specialized hold-down hardware, which is beyond the scope of this book. However, you'll find detailed installation instructions on most manufacturers' websites.

When building on a slab, it's more convenient to brace to the outside. Drive stakes well into the ground, and fasten the braces to them.

1 Notch around pipes so the bottom plate can rotate into place as the wall is raised.

2 Reinforce notched plates with steel straps made for that purpose. The straps help maintain the structural integrity of the plates.

3 On slabs or garage walls, it's easiest to bolt the mudsill down and counterbore the wall's bottom plate to drop over the bolts.

SQUARING PLATES ON AN OUT-OF-SQUARE SLAB

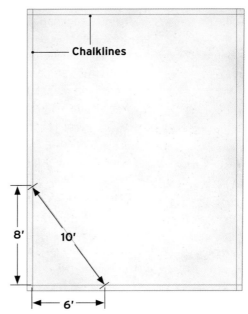

Chalklines

8' 10' 6'

Plates can be inset by the thickness of the sheathing or more with some sidings, to square the walls on the slab.

Plates can overhang the slab as much as 1 in.

With the marks for the bottom plate on the long walls parallel, square the layout of the perpendicular walls.

Slab floors don't offer any place to nail a brace block, so for walls on slabs, brace them to stakes driven into the ground.

SHEAR WALLS

Most sheathed walls are technically shear walls, in that they provide racking resistance against wind and seismic forces. In some cases, even interior walls are sheathed to add shear strength.

When shear walls are designated on the plans, don't deviate from the design. One area that's notoriously difficult to provide with sufficient shear resistance is garage walls around the doors. Often, there's just not enough wall to do the job with traditional stud framing. In these cases, the shear strength is often provided by prefabricated shear wall panels.

Manufactured shear panels are one way to gain the lateral strength needed from narrow walls such as those flanking garage doors. (Photo courtesy Simpson StrongTie)

ERECTING RAKE WALLS

Also known as a gable wall, a rake wall fills the gable of a building from the rafters down to the floor below. Often, this is an attic floor, or in the case of a Cape Cod structure, the floor of the second story. In any case, rake walls almost always go up after the rafters are installed.

➡ **See "Setting the Ridge and Rafters," p. 104.**

You can build and raise rake walls before framing the roof, but I rarely do that. It's too easy to frame the wall slightly different from the roof, which means you have to rebuild the wall, or change the roof pitch slightly, or find some other workaround. Instead, I frame the wall to the rafters. That way, I don't have to worry if the wall I build exactly matches the rafters. The only exception to this in my work is when the rake wall forms the ends of a cathedral ceiling and will support a beam.

➡ **See "Building a Wall for a Cathedral Ceiling," facing page.**

Start by installing and laying out the bottom plate. Nail plate stock to the end rafters. In the case of a Cape Cod-style roof, it makes sense to run a horizontal plate at the ceiling level to provide a stop for insula-tion. ❶ If it's an attic, then skip the horizontal plate and run the plate on the bottom of the rafter to the ridge.

To find the length of studs, hold stud stock plumb and on the layout mark, and mark them in place. ❷ Cut the studs with a saw set to the angle of the roof pitch (most layout squares have tables that convert rise and run to degrees). ❸

Toenail the bottom of the stud to the plate with three 8d commons. It's better to end-spike the top connection using a couple of 16ds. You can toenail the top, but doing so tends to wedge the rafter up. ❹

1 If a rake wall is to meet a finished ceiling, run a top plate at that level.

2 Install the bottom plate and lay out the stud locations, then mark the cut lines for rake wall studs in place.

3 Set your circular saw to the angle of the roof pitch and bevel-cut the ends of the rake wall studs.

4 Don't toenail the upper connection, or you might wedge the rafter out of plane. End-spike instead.

BUILDING A WALL FOR A CATHEDRAL CEILING

The one time I will build and raise the rake wall first is when there's a cathedral ceiling and the wall will support the beam carrying the rafters.

To lay out a rake wall, I use a combination of math and full-scale layout. Rake walls are framed so they fit between the side walls. Their top plate (a single top plate) angles at the roof pitch, and should meet the top of the side walls' double top plate.

The wall height at the sides will match that of the perpendicular walls. Figure the plate height at the center using this formula,

where x is the distance from the top plates of the side walls to the apex of the rake wall plate:

$$\frac{\text{Roof rise}}{12} = \frac{x}{\frac{1}{2}\text{ distance between walls in inches}}$$

Use this information to snap the outline of the wall on the floor right where you'll build it.

Rake walls are raised between the side walls, which are braced to the outside because interior bracing would get in the way.

1 Snap chalklines on the floor to mark the location of the wall top plates and the outline of the perimeter framing.

2 Cut the gable-wall top plates to length and tack them to the perimeter chalklines.

3 Assemble wall components as you would any side wall and frame and sheathe the gable wall.

4 Raise the gable wall, using push poles and a good-size crew. Be sure you stop the progress of the wall when it is vertical.

BUILDING A WALL BETWEEN A FLOOR AND CEILING

1 Nail blocking every 2 ft. to secure the top plate of a wall that falls between ceiling joists.

2 Plumb up from the bottom plate to locate the ends of the top plate. Mark the location of each end.

Some remodeling work, such as finishing a basement or an attic, requires that you build walls between an existing floor and ceiling.

If the wall will run parallel to the joists above, add 2×4 blocking every couple of feet to give yourself a nailing surface for the wall's top plate. **1**

Layout is no different than it would be for new construction, except that you'll need to transfer the layout from the floor to the ceiling framing. You can accomplish this with a plumb bob (I prefer a laser plumb bob) or a level and a straight piece of lumber that spans floor to ceiling. **2** Mark the edge of the upper plate at both ends of its location and snap a chalkline between the marks. **3** There are two ways to proceed from here.

Cutting the studs

Most carpenters fasten plates to the floor and the ceiling, then cut studs and toenail the studs between the plates. If you're lucky, the stud length will be consistent, and you can gang-cut the whole wall.

In basements, that rarely happens, however, because the concrete slab will vary in elevation. In that case, you'll have to fasten each stud in place, cut it, and toenail it home. These methods are accurate and create a wall that fits tightly in place, but there's an alternative.

Preassembling the wall

A faster method is to measure the floor to ceiling distance in a few spots, and build the wall flat on the floor, but ¼ in. shorter than the smallest height.

That ¼ in. is enough to allow you to stand the wall up without it jamming against the blocking. **A** Use a pair of cedar shingle shims every couple of feet at the top to wedge the wall in place, and nail or screw through the shims into the ceiling above. **B**

Rarely will a wall built between an existing floor and ceiling be a bearing wall. Don't use this method should you encounter an exception.

3 Snap a line between the marks to locate the top plate. Fasten the top and bottom plates and install the studs between the plates.

Building a wall perpendicular to the joists
If the wall will run perpendicular to the joists, the joists provide you with a nailing surface. You can proceed as described here, marking the location of the plates and either cutting each stud after fastening the top and bottom plates or pre-assembling the wall on the floor, raising it, and shimming the top plate tight against the ceiling joists.

BUILDING A WALL IN PLACE

A Assemble the wall on the floor with its height ¼ in. short of the distance from floor to blocking and raise it into place.

B Shim the ¼-in. gap between the plate and the blocking prior to nailing the top plate in place.

FRAMING ROOFS

ROOFS ARE THE QUINTESSENTIAL element of buildings—what's more important than keeping out the rain and snow? And there are few moments more satisfying than standing on a roof you built, taking in the view from a vantage no one before has ever had.

Yet people find roof framing intimidating. In part it's the height, but also the math and geometry. There's little reason for that. It's all basic stuff about triangles that most of us learned in high school. The math is easily done on a calculator. I'm also told you can use trig functions, which may help the math geeks. I don't. I aim to keep it visually and mathematically simple.

Roofing is not without its dangers. Any time you're more than 6 ft. above a lower surface, you should use a harness and rope or scaffolding at the roof edge.

LAYING OUT GABLE AND SHED RAFTERS

SHED-ROOF FRAMING

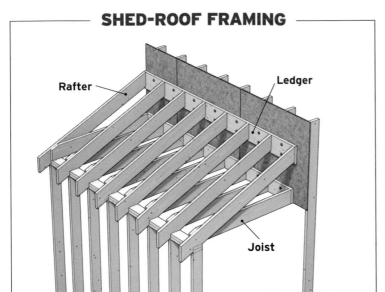

Rafter

Ledger

Joist

ANATOMY OF A GABLE ROOF

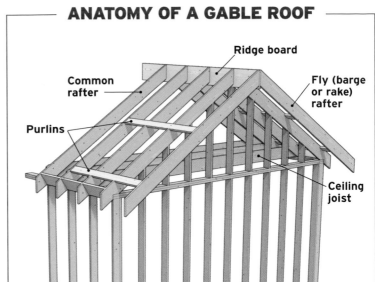

Ridge board

Common rafter

Fly (barge or rake) rafter

Purlins

Ceiling joist

GABLE-ROOF TRIANGLES

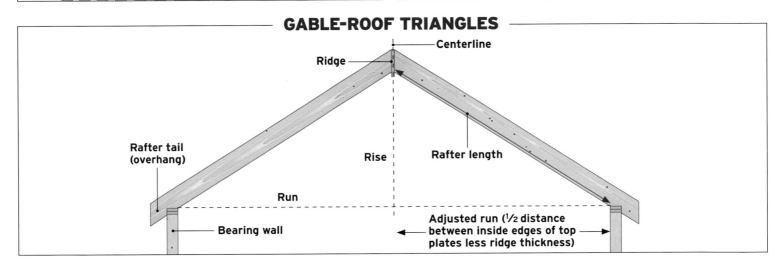

Centerline

Ridge

Rafter tail (overhang)

Rise

Rafter length

Run

Bearing wall

Adjusted run (½ distance between inside edges of top plates less ridge thickness)

Laying out rafters is a subject accompanied by as many methods and theories as there are publications and carpenters. Perhaps the simplest way to grasp the techniques of rafter layout is to start with this: a rafter is the hypotenuse of a right triangle whose vertical leg is called the rise, and the horizontal leg the run.

The simplest rafter form is found on a shed roof—it's a single triangle. The next step up is a gable roof. Think of a gable roof as two right triangles butted together at their common rise.

All three characteristics of a right triangle—rise, run, and rafter length—interact with each other, and since your

primary goal in laying out rafters is to get them cut correctly, you'll have a little math to manipulate, using your choice of any number of calculating tools.

Geometry: Theoretically speaking

First, familiarize yourself with the terminology of rafters (see "Coming to Terms with Rafters," facing page). Note what endpoints define the rise, run, and rafter length. One of the first terms to come to grips with is pitch.

The pitch, or slope, of your roof is a numerical statement describing how many units your roof rises for every horizontal units of run. Pitch will affect how fast your roof sheds rain or snow and also functions

as the main element of its appearance.

Pitch selection, which is usually called out on the plans, comes down largely to a matter of aesthetics, but it also carries practical consequences. For example, steep roofs are more difficult to work on and require longer rafters and more roofing material. If you're undecided, match the pitch of the roof on your house—it helps unify the architecture of the buildings in your landscape—but keep practicality in mind. When I have a choice, I prefer pitches lower than 8-in-12, as that's the steepest roof I can comfortably walk.

Roof pitch is expressed as a fraction of rise over run, and for common rafters, the run is always 12 (the run for hip-roof rafters is dif-

PROPORTIONAL SCALES

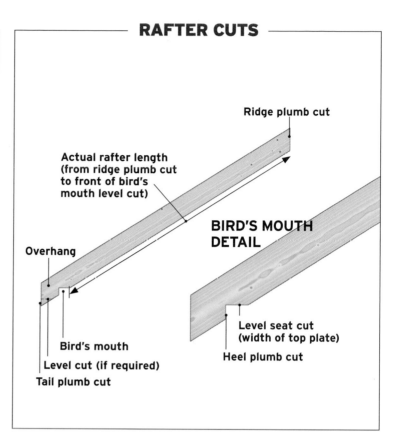

Tongue of framing square

Blade of framing square

8

12

8'

Plumb cut

12'

Level cut

It's the plumb cuts on a rafter that produce the angle of the roof, and a framing square simply scales the proportions of the roof down to inches, which allows you to lay out the correct angles.

The angle of the plumb cut on a roof with a 12-ft. run and an 8-ft. rise is exactly the same as the angle you get with the 12-in. and 8-in. marks on the square. Duplicating this scaled-down relationship on the rafter puts your cuts at the correct angle.

RAFTER CUTS

Ridge plumb cut

Actual rafter length (from ridge plumb cut to front of bird's mouth level cut)

BIRD'S MOUTH DETAIL

Overhang

Level seat cut (width of top plate)

Heel plumb cut

Bird's mouth

Level cut (if required)

Tail plumb cut

COMING TO TERMS WITH RAFTERS

Listed below are common definitions for terms associated with building roofs. You may find in actual practice that you need to adjust them slightly to make your rafter layout fit the particulars of your installation.

MEASUREMENTS

- **Pitch:** how much the rafter rises for each foot of its run. For example, a roof with a 6/12 (6-in-12) pitch rises 6 in. for every foot of run.
- **Rise:** the distance from the top of the top plate to the bottom edge of the rafter at the ridge board.
- **Run:** the distance from the midpoint of the ridge to the outside edge of the top plate—the heel cut of the bird's mouth.

RAFTER CUTS

- **Ridge plumb cut:** a cut made in the top end of the rafter, so it meets the ridge board at the proper pitch.
- **Bird's mouth:** a notch in the rafter where it meets the top plate of a wall. Its level seat cut and heel cut (a plumb cut at right angles to the level cut) allow the rafter to fit squarely on the wall top plate.
- **Rafter tail:** the end of the rafter that extends beyond the wall and terminates

in a tail plumb cut at the same angle as the ridge cut.
- **Rafter length (theoretical):** from midpoint of ridge to outside edge of the wall. The actual cut rafter length is short of the theoretical rafter length by one half the thickness of the ridge board.
- **Rafter length (actual):** from the ridge plumb cut to the front edge of the bird's mouth level seat cut.

ferent—more about that later). For example, an 8-pitch (or 8-in-12) roof would have a rise of 8 in. and a run of 12 in. One example of an 8-pitch roof would be a gable roof 24 ft. wide and 8 ft. high at the peak. Here the run of the roof is not 24 ft. but half that distance, or

12 feet. There is also an adjusted run, which you'll use laying out rafters.

The main layout tool you need is a rafter square, and although no rafter square extends to 8 ft. and 12 ft., the 8-in. and 12-in. marks on the square are in the same proportion and will give you accurate rafter

angles. Holding the square along an edge of the rafter with the 8-in. and 12-in. marks on the outside edge of the tongue and blade intersecting the rafter edge will produce the angles for the plumb and level cuts required for an 8-pitch rafter. >> >> >>

LAYING OUT GABLE AND SHED RAFTERS (CONTINUED)

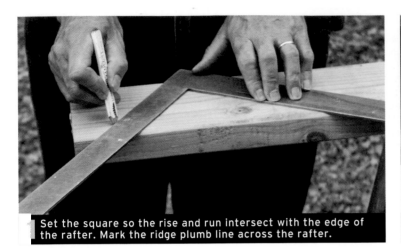

1 Set the square so the rise and run intersect with the edge of the rafter. Mark the ridge plumb line across the rafter.

Measure rafter length from ridge plumb line and mark here.

2 Mark the rafter length as shown. Then reset the square on the mark and pencil an extended bird's mouth level cut.

Combined thickness of wall plate and sheathing

3 Set the square on the level line in from the bottom of the rafter by the thickness of plate and sheathing. Mark the heel cut.

Heel cut

Level cut

4 With the rise and run on the edge of the rafter and the heel cut, mark the bottom plumb cut at the length of the overhang.

Finally, you need to figure the rafter length. You can step off rafters with a framing square (see "Stepping off Rafter Length," facing page), but that method is error prone. Better yet, use the table on the square's body (or blade). Here's how:

Framing-square math

1. Determine the run of the rafter. Let's say it's 12 ft. from the ridge centerline to the outer edge of the wall.

2. Find the row, "Length Common Rafters per Foot Run" on the square and follow it along until you reach the number above it that defines the pitch of the roof—let's say, 8.

3. Look in the row under the 8—you'll see 14.42. This is the length in inches an 8-pitch common rafter travels for each foot of its run. Multiply this by 12 (the run in our example): (14.42 × 12 = 173.04 in.).

You'll get the same results with the "Multipliers" table (see facing page). There you'll see a multiplier of 1.202 for an 8-pitch roof. Doing the math with a run of 12 ft. (12 × 1.202 = 14.424 ft.) and changing the decimal to inches results in 5 (0.424 × 12 = 5.088) or 14 ft. 5 in.

These computations produce the theoretical length of the rafter. In actual practice, you'll adjust how you measure the run, but the mathematics will be the same.

There are also books and websites with tables showing rafter lengths for various pitches. I usually figure the length using the Pythagorean theorem and a Construction Master calculator. The Construction Master delivers in feet and inches—much easier.

➔ See the "The Construction Master Calculator," p. 9.

Applying theory in the field

Real-life geometry allows you practical adaptations. Rather than defining the run from the outside edge of the top plate to the ridge centerline, define it from the point where the level cut of the bird's mouth meets the inside corner of the top plate.

➔ See "Rafter Cuts," p. 97.

This adjusted run allows you to lay a rafter out on its bottom edge, where you'll actually be cutting it. Here's the practical math:

STEPPING OFF RAFTER LENGTH

The hypotenuse between the rise and run marks on a square equals the rafter length per foot of run. Step off the rafter length by moving the square incrementally along the rafter, once for each foot of run.

When the rafter's actual run isn't an even increment of 1 ft., move the square beyond the last whole foot mark as if you were going to add another foot. But instead, mark the remaining distance in inches. Say the run is 6 ft. 9 in. You'd move the square 7 times. On the seventh move, mark the 9-in. point.

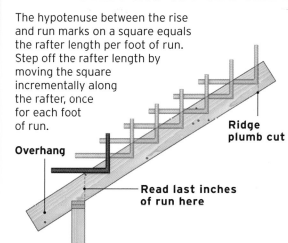

Ridge plumb cut

Overhang

Read last inches of run here

When you've finished the rafter layout, your lines should look like this, with the bottom edge of the rafter facing you.

TOOLS FOR CALCULATING RAFTER LENGTH

A framing square includes tables to compute the lengths of various rafter types. Follow the common-rafter lengths table until you reach the pitch of your roof. The number under it will tell you the rafter length per foot of its run. Use either the theoretical run or adjusted run, whichever one you prefer. Or you can multiply the run of your rafter by the multiplier listed for your roof pitch in the table at right.

MULTIPLIERS FOR COMPUTING COMMON-RAFTER LENGTH	
Roof Pitch	**Common-Rafter Multiplier**
3-in-12	1.031
4-in-12	1.054
5-in-12	1.083
6-in-12	1.118
7-in-12	1.158
8-in-12	1.202
9-in-12	1.25
10-in-12	1.302
11-in-12	1.357
12-in-12	1.313

1. Measure between the inside edges of the top plates. In our example, this would be 23 ft. 1 in. (24 ft. less the width of the top plates = 24 ft. – 11 in. = 23 ft. 1 in.).

2. Deduct the thickness of the ledger or ridge. (23 ft. 1 in. – 1½ in. = 22 ft. 11½ in.) That's all you need to do for a shed roof. For a gable roof, divide the result by 2: (22 ft. 11½ in./2 = 11 ft. 5¾ in.). This is the adjusted run to the inside edge of the top plate. Using this run to compute the rafter length with the framing square table results in a rafter length of 13 ft. 9⁹⁄₁₆ in.: (11 ft. 5¾ in = 11.48 ft. × 14.42 = 165.54 in. or 13.79 ft. or 13 ft. 9⁹⁄₁₆ in.).

Then pick a straight rafter–this one will provide a pattern for the rest. Mark the plumb cut at the ridge first. ❶ Measure the rafter length from the bottom of the plumb cut to the front edge of the bird's mouth level cut and mark that point. Then set the square on the mark with the rise and run intersecting the bottom edge of the rafter and draw the bird's mouth level line across the rafter. ❷

Hold the square on the level line of the bird's mouth and move the square back along this line until the width of the wall (plate width + sheathing thickness) aligns with the edge of the rafter, then mark the heel (or plumb) cut. ❸ Lay out and mark the tail plumb cut as you did the ridge. ❹ You may need a level cut on the tail, as well, depending on the width of the fascia, the thickness of the soffit material, and how far the fascia will hang below the soffit.

➜ See "Creating a Soffit," p. 120.

CUTTING RAFTERS

Once you've laid out the pattern rafter, cut it carefully. To minimize splintering on the rafter ends (and consequently in your hands), make plumb cuts from the short side to the long side. ❶ Cut the bird's mouth cuts just up to the corner. ❷ Finish the cuts with a handsaw. ❸ A lot of carpenters avoid having to pick up a handsaw by overcutting the bird's mouth with the circular saw, but that weakens the rafter. Don't be lazy.

Once you've cut out the pattern rafter, nail a temporary overhanging block to both ends. That will give you a fence to align the edges of the other rafters flush with the pattern rafter when you lay them out. ❹

Hold the production rafters against the block (crowns against the blocks) and trace the pattern. ❺

Cut the first two production rafters, then check their fit. They should sit absolutely flat on the wall top plates and fully bear on the ridge. If you haven't set the ridge yet, just hold a piece of ridge stock between the tops of the rafters. ❻ This is one operation where it helps to have help—preferably at least one person for the bottom of each rafter and yourself at the ridge.

Make any needed adjustments to the pattern rafter and/or its mate, then lay out and cut all the rafters. Stack them against the side of the building so they're ready to go. Then install the ceiling joists.

TRADE SECRET
When cutting stock marked from a pattern, remember that the entire pencil mark is outside the cut. The saw kerf should just remove the entire pencil mark.

1 Cut the ridge plumb line first. Minimize splinters by cutting from the short side of the angle to the long side.

3 Finish the bird's mouth with a couple of strokes of a handsaw held perpendicular to the rafter.

5 Lay an uncut rafter on a firm support and set the pattern rafter on it, pulling the alignment blocks against its side. Mark and cut.

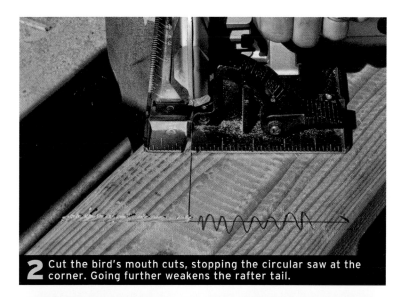

2 Cut the bird's mouth cuts, stopping the circular saw at the corner. Going further weakens the rafter tail.

4 Cut the tail plumb line. Then nail a block to the top edge of the pattern rafter at each end to align the other rafters flush.

6 Check the fit of the first two rafters by holding them on the wall plates. Fit scrap ridge stock between their upper ends.

Ordering material

- **Rafters:** Figure the number of rafters you'll need the same way you do floor joists (see "Estimating Floor-Framing Stock," p. 40). Then add four extras for fly rafters (rafters that extend beyond the wall and create overhangs on the gable ends). Calculate the length of the rafter stock and increase the length by the amount of overhang you plan. Then add the width of the rafter to this length to account for the angled end cuts.

- **Ridge stock:** The entire length of a rafter ridge cut must bear fully on the ridge board. Because a plumb-cut rafter end will be wider than the rafter stock itself, you'll need to order ridge stock that's wide enough to accommodate the additional length of the cut end. In roofs up to an 8 pitch, going up one nominal size is enough (for example, ordering 2×8 ridge stock for 2×6 rafters). For steeper pitches, go up two nominal sizes. In some cases, you may need to use LVL for the ridge. It's readily available in widths up to 16 in. It's common that a ridge will be sufficiently long to require multiple sections. Don't forget to increase the size of the ridge by the length of any overhang beyond the walls.

- **Roof sheathing:** Compute your roof-sheathing order by dividing the total square footage of the roof by 32. I don't use OSB for roof sheathing because it's heavier than plywood and not as stiff. In most cases, I use ⁵/₈-in. CDX plywood, even if ¹/₂ in. is specified. The thinner plywood can sag at the seams with time. One carpenter I know uses ³/₄-in. T&G OSB subfloor because it's less expensive than ⁵/₈-in. plywood. I like everything about that but carrying that heavy a panel 20 ft. up a ladder onto the roof.

INSTALLING CEILING JOISTS

The first step in setting rafters is actually setting the ceiling joists. They're critical to the structure. Without them, rafters produce enough outward thrust to bow out the walls.

Setting ceiling joists is not much different than setting floor joists. The main difference is that ceiling joists don't need a rim joist.

➔ See "Installing Joists," p. 58.

I often set ceiling joists back from the outside edge of the wall a little, so I don't have to clip their top corners to keep them from getting in the way of the rafters. Snap a line along the top plate about an inch from the edge to keep the joist ends lined up across the length of the plate. On shallow roof pitches, however, it's likely you'll have to angle-cut the top corners of the joists anyway so they don't stick above the rafters. ❶

Cut the ceiling joists long enough so they will lap the rafters by at least 3 in.–enough to accept three 10d commons without splitting. ❷ Ceiling joists supported on a beam must also lap at least 3 in., and will also take three 10ds. ❸ Toenail the joists to the beam and/or wall plates with three 8ds per joint.

Ceiling joists will often receive an L-shaped strongback tied to a stud and top plate at both ends, running down the middle of the joists. ❹ Strongbacks keep the joists on layout for the drywaller, and they help stiffen the entire ceiling assembly. Nail the two parts of the strongback together with 16d commons every foot or so, and drive two 16ds into every joist.

When you get to the task of setting rafters, most of the work will happen at the outside walls and at the ridge. That means you'll need to stand on the ceiling joists. Be careful here–ceiling joists aren't meant to take the loads floor joists are. Throw some sheets of sheathing on top of the joists to make a walking platform in the center. ❺ Tack the edges down so they don't slide off of their supporting joists.

1 Set the joists in about an inch so the corners don't interfere with the rafters.

2 Set ceiling joists to lap the rafters by 3 in., leaving room for three 10d nails.

4 An L-shaped strongback tied to both rake walls aligns and stiffens ceiling joists. Nail the strongback to each joist.

LAPPED JOISTS
OFFSET THE RAFTER LAYOUT

If the span of your building requires you to lap ceiling joists on an interior wall, you'll have to offset each pair of rafters by the thickness of the rafter stock, as illustrated at right.

Forward rafters fasten to the front side of one joist, rearward rafters to the rear of the other joist. Duplicate the offset at the ridge, of course. Mark the locations of joists and rafters on the ridge and top plates before installing.

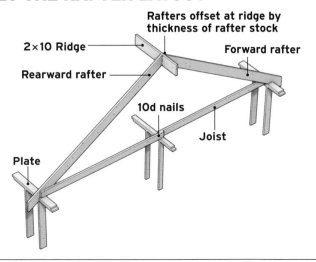

Rafters offset at ridge by thickness of rafter stock

2×10 Ridge

Forward rafter

Rearward rafter

10d nails

Joist

Plate

3 Ceiling joists that lap on top of a wall must do so by at least 3 in., and they must be fastened with at least three 10d commons.

5 Create a safe working surface below the ridge by tacking down sheathing on the ceiling joists.

OTHER WAYS TO KEEP RAFTERS FROM SPREADING WALLS

STRUCTURAL BEAM

If ceiling joists keep walls from spreading, why don't cathedral ceilings, which have no ceiling joists, collapse? Usually, it's because there's a honking big beam supporting the ridge. Rafters can't push the walls out without the center of the roof sagging, and a heavy beam prevents that from happening.

CEILING JOIST OR COLLAR TIE?

Not all ceiling joists rest on the outside wall plates. Sometimes, they're higher in the ceiling, as in Cape Cod–style houses. To keep the rafters from spreading the walls, joists generally have to be fastened within the lower third of the rafter span. Sometimes they can be higher, but that's for a design professional to figure out. Nearer the peak, there may be other horizontal members called collar ties.

Collar ties aren't always installed at every rafter pair, and they do nothing to keep the walls together. Nonetheless, they're quite important. In high wind areas, their purpose is to tie the tops of the rafters together to help them resist wind loads. Ceiling joists go up before setting the rafters. However, collar ties go on after you've set the rafters.

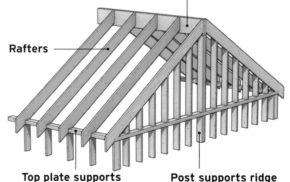

Structural ridge beam supports ½ the roof load.

Rafters

Top plate supports ¼ of the roof load.

Post supports ridge beam and creates load path to foundation.

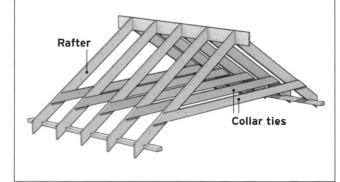

Rafter

Collar ties

SETTING THE RIDGE AND RAFTERS

1 Support the ridge with 2x posts offset from center by the ridge thickness. A cleat supports the ridge at the correct height.

2 Check and center the ridge by setting a pair of rafters on each end.

The ridge is the backbone of the roof, and your choice of material is therefore of critical importance. Choose ridge stock carefully. A slight crown is okay, but select material that's dead straight side-to-side and without cups or twists. And be sure to order stock long enough to support fly rafters if they're in your plans.

Your first step will be to set and brace 2× posts (here, 2×8s) that you can either incorporate into the rake wall when you build it or remove. Temporary support blocks, or cleats, attached to these posts will put the ridge at its correct height. The trick is to set the top edge of the support block so the bottom of the ridge will rest on it at the correct height.

To find the height of the support block, first find the height of the bottom of the rafters using this formula:

$$\frac{\text{pitch} \times \text{adjusted common rafter run (in inches)}}{12}$$

To that number, add the length of the plumb cut on the end of the rafter, and from that deduct the depth of the ridge. In this formula, pitch is the top number of the pitch definition, for example, 8 in an 8/12 pitch. Adjusted run is the result of the calculation you did when computing the rafter length (see p. 98). In our example, the math works out this way:

(8 × 11 ft. 5¾ in = 8 × 137.75 in./12= 91.83 in.)

Accounting for the plumb-cut length (7 in.) and ridge width (7.25 in.) gives us a support-block height of 7 ft. 8⅜ in.

(91.83 + 7 - 7.25 = 91.58 in. or 7.63 ft = 7 ft. 7½ in.)

This formula accounts for all ridges, including those wider than the rafter plumb cut.

Offset the posts from center by the thickness of the ridge and tack a cleat to the posts on the center side with its top edge at the height called for by your calculations. **1**

Most buildings will be too long to be spanned by a single-piece ridge board. In that case, position the joint to fall between two rafters and reinforce it with a scabbed-on piece of lumber. Make sure the scab doesn't interfere with placing rafters or sheathing. The scab is only temporarily a structural addition—it holds the ridge together until the roof sheathing is applied.

Once the posts are set, crown the ridge and mark the rafter locations on it and the wall top plates, including the location of any skylights or dormers. Then set the ridge on the cleats, secure it to the posts, and test-fit two rafters. **2**

➡ **See Photo "6," p. 101.**

If the fit of the rafters is exact, setting them is a straightforward process of placing them on their layout marks and nailing them to the ridge, plates, and ceiling joists. Install the rafters across the roof span, securing them to the ridge with either three 16d face nails or four 16d toenails. **3** It may seem that installing all the rafters on one side of the ridge and then the other would be easier, but doing so can easily push the ridge out of line. Instead, set 2 or 3 rafters on one side, then set those opposite them. **4**   >> >> >>

3 Set remaining pairs of rafters by end-nailing one through the ridge, driving nails into the opposite rafter at a slight angle.

4 To help keep the ridge straight, don't set more than a few rafters on one side before installing their opposites.

Scabbed cleat supports joint in multi-section ridge.

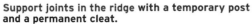

Support joints in the ridge with a temporary post and a permanent cleat.

TOP-PLATE LAYOUT

Include rough openings for skylights and other special features when you lay out your rafter locations on the top plate of the walls.

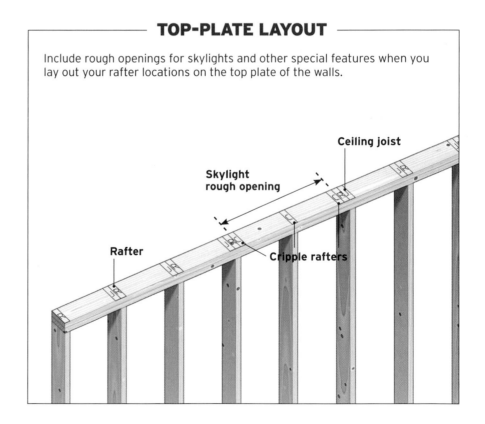

Ceiling joist

Skylight rough opening

Rafter

Cripple rafters

SETTING THE RIDGE AND RAFTERS (CONTINUED)

5 Nail the ceiling joists to the rafters to help keep the rafters from pushing the walls out.

6 Install any hurricane or seismic ties before sheathing the roof. A palm nailer makes the job fly.

Use two 16d toenails to fasten the rafters to the plates and three 10d commons to join the rafters to the ceiling joists. **5** Also, install any special hold-down hardware spec'd on the plans. **6**

If there's a skylight, box it out as you go, making the dimensions conform to the rough opening for the skylight specified by the plans. Double the rafters at either side if called for. **7**

➤ See "Installing Skylights," p. 118.

If there is a gable overhang, I usually frame it with fly rafters. These are identical to common rafters but with no bird's mouth cut. The rough framing lumber is usually covered with finish material such as pine, PVC, or aluminum coil stock.

The fly-rafter top plumb cut bears flat on the ridge, exactly as the roof rafters do. If the ridge is deeper than the rafters, you may need to rip the overhanging section so it will be flush with the bottom of the fly rafters so it won't interfere with the soffit.

The lower section of the fly rafter is supported by 2× purlins that fit in notches cut in the top of the first two rafters.

➤ See "Anatomy of a Gable Roof," p. 96.

Gang-cut the purlin notches by lining up the rafters and making a series of saw cuts 1½ in. deep. **8** Rough out the recess with a hammer claw and clean up the notches with a chisel. **9** Nail the purlins into the notched rafters. **10** Then face-nail the fly rafters to the ends of the purlins and the ridge. **11** Once you have all the rafters installed, you can sheathe the roof to stabilize it while building your gable walls. Make sure to nail the sheathing to the fly rafters.

➤ See "Erecting Rake Walls," p. 90.

If you're building a shed roof, deduct the full thickness of the ledger from your computations instead of half and nail the ledger to the wall.

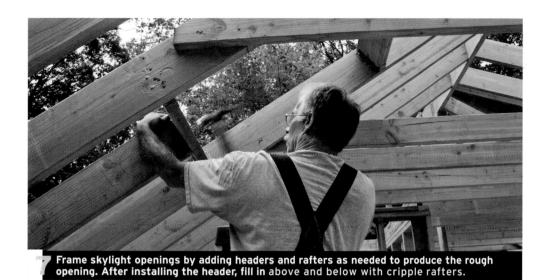

TRADE SECRET
The cheapest gable-rafter detail provides the least overhang, and therefore the least protection for the wall below. That's simply a fly rafter nailed over the wall sheathing. Typically, it's spaced out from the wall by 3/4 in. to 1 1/4 in. so the siding can terminate behind it.

7 Frame skylight openings by adding headers and rafters as needed to produce the rough opening. After installing the header, fill in above and below with cripple rafters.

8 Notch rafters for the purlins supporting fly rafters by lining them up and making a series of parallel cuts to the depth of the purlins.

9 Start removing waste with your hammer claw and then chisel out what waste you can't knock out with the claw.

10 Fit the purlins into the notches you cut and face-nail the purlins to the rafters.

11 Face-nail the fly rafters to the end of the purlins and the end of the ridge.

HIP ROOF FRAMING

Most hip roofs consist of a standard gable section whose ridge is centered between the end walls and is installed before the hipped sections. On each end of the gable ridge, a king common rafter–a common rafter not shortened by the ridge thickness–runs diagonally down to the center of the end wall. A pair of hip rafters runs at 45 degrees from the end of the ridge to the corners of the wall.

Shed roofs can also be framed as hips. When returning a shed roof with a hip, the rafter that runs between the end of the ledger and the wall plate that butts the house is likewise a common rafter.

Computing hip-rafter length

Except for the hip rafters, the pitch of all rafters in a hip is the same as the main roof (other than for so-called bastard hips, which are beyond the scope of this book).

The hip-rafter pitch is less than the pitch of the common rafters because the hip rafter travels further to its corner. The relationship is this: for every 12 in. of run of common rafters, a hip rafter travels 17 in. Thus, when laying out hip rafters, you'll use a run of 17 instead of 12 (see the sidebar on the facing page).

You can compute the length of hip rafters with the hip/valley function on a construction calculator. You can also figure it out mathematically or use the table on a framing square. To find it mathematically, first determine the hip rafter run. That formula is:

$$\frac{16.97 \times \text{adjusted common rafter run (ft.)}}{12}$$

In our example, the hip run would be 16.23 ft. (16.97 x 11.48/12 = 16.23 ft.).

Next, find the overall hip rise:

$$\frac{\text{Hip run} \times \text{roof pitch}}{17}$$

Here, roof pitch is the top number of the pitch or the theoretical rise, for example, 8 in an 8/12 pitch.

Plugging the numbers into the formula results in a hip rise of 7.64 ft.:

$$(16.23 \times 8/17 = 7.64 \text{ ft.})$$

Now, use the Pythagorean theorem and a square-root calculator to find the hip-rafter length:

$$(\text{Hip length})^2 = (\text{Hip run})^2 + (\text{Hip rise})^2$$
$$(\text{Hip length})^2 = 16.23^2 + 7.64^2$$
$$321.78 = 263.41 + 58.37$$

Finding the square root of 321.78 gives you 17.94 ft., the length of the hip rafter.

HIP ROOF ANATOMY

A standard hip roof runs at the same pitch as the main roof, but at 90 degrees to it. The hip rafters form the intersection of the two roofs. One common rafter, called a king, runs from the main ridge down the center of the hip roof to the wall plate. The short rafters that land on the hip rafter are called jacks.

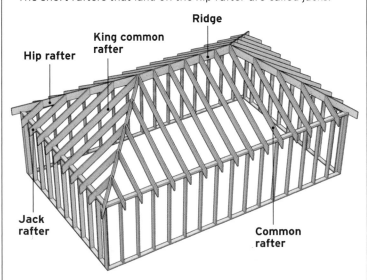

Ridge

King common rafter

Hip rafter

Jack rafter

Common rafter

Not all hip roofs are free-standing main roofs. Hips are also common on shed roof overhangs, or on porches, where a gable might appear overbearing.

MULTIPLIERS FOR COMPUTING HIP-RAFTER LENGTH	
Roof Pitch	Hip-Rafter Multiplier
3-in-12	1.016
4-in-12	1.027
5-in-12	1.043
6-in-12	1.061
7-in-12	1.082
8-in-12	1.106
9-in-12	1.131
10-in-12	1.161
11-in-12	1.192
12-in-12	1.225

Find the hip or valley rafter length by using these multipliers with the adjusted runs of hip or valley rafters.

To use a framing square, find the row, "Length Hip or Valley per Foot Run" on the square and follow it along until you reach the rise on the edge of the square (8 in our example). Look at the number in the row under the 8—you'll see 18.76 inches. This is the length of the hip rafter for each foot of the common-rafter run. Multiplying this number by the length of the adjusted common-rafter run (11.48 in our example) tells us that our hip-rafter length from the ridge to the inside edge of the wall plate or bird's mouth plumb cut is 17.94 ft.

$$(18.76 \times 11.48 = 215.36 \text{ or } 17.94 \text{ ft.})$$

You can also use the "Multipliers" table (above) as you did for figuring common-rafter lengths, but this time, multiply the number in the table appropriate to your pitch by the adjusted hip run (16.23 ft. in our example). Given the possibility of error with this much computation, you can see why a construction calculator is a good investment.

Jack rafters

The shortened rafters that intersect the hip rafter are called jack rafters. Their lower ends lay out and are cut like any common rafter. Their upper ends meet the hip rafter with a 45-degree compound miter. (More about how to figure jack-rafter lengths and cut them later.)

Ceiling joists in a hip roof

Ceiling joists in a hip roof run parallel to the main common rafters (and perpendicular to the hipped section of the roof) until they approach the end wall. As the ceiling joists reach the end wall plate, they will come into contact with the bottom edge of the hip-roof rafters. The solution is to change the direction of the ceiling joists, running those near the end wall parallel with the hip roof rafters.

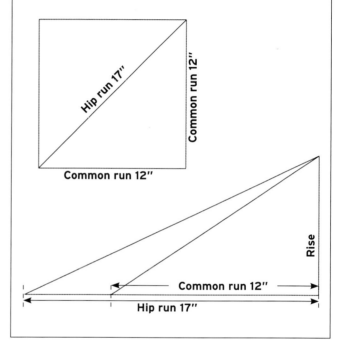

WHY HIP RAFTERS USE A RUN OF 17

Since we use 12 in. as the run for rafter calculations, we can imagine a hip rafter as bisecting a 12 in. square diagonally. Using the Pythagorean theorem, the hypotenuse of a right triangle with 12-in. sides works out to 16.97 in., which gets rounded up to 17 in. So, for every 12 in. of run the common rafters have, a hip rafter covers 17 in.

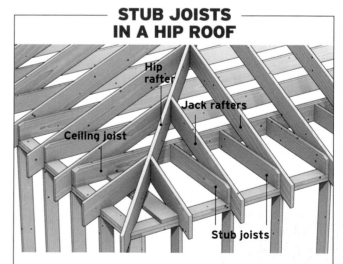

STUB JOISTS IN A HIP ROOF

Ceiling joists that run parallel to the common rafters run out of room as they approach the hip rafters. On a steep roof, the last joist might have enough room, but often not. In that case, you might have to double the second to last joist, and use it as a beam to support a bunch of stub joists that run parallel with the hip roof.

LAYING OUT HIP AND JACK RAFTERS

Mark a full plumb line across the hip rafter at the location of the bird's mouth heel cut (use a run of 17).

2 Using a common rafter already cut to specifications, measure the distance from the inside corner of the bird's mouth to the top edge.

Corner-to-edge distance on common rafter

6 Pencil two miter lines intersecting at 45 degrees on the rafter-length mark.

Rafter-length mark

7 Mark the ridge plumb lines on both sides of the rafter where the miter lines intersect the top edge of the rafter.

Once you've computed the actual length of your hip rafters—from the inside corner of the wall to the ridge—you'll use procedures modified slightly from the common-rafter layout to lay out the hip rafters.

➡ **See "Computing hip-rafter length," p. 108.**

Hip-rafter layout

Mark the approximate location of the ridge plumb cut about 3 in. from the top of the rafter (you'll make it exact later). Then measure down from that mark by the rafter length, add about 4 in., and mark the location of the bird's mouth heel cut. Set your framing square with the rise and run on the bottom edge of the rafter (using a run of 17) and mark the heel-cut line (a plumb cut), extending the line across the face of the rafter. **1**

To keep the top edge of the hip rafter in the same plane as the rest of the roof, you'll need to modify the method for laying out its

bird's mouth. First, take a common rafter and measure the amount of stock from the corner of the bird's mouth to the top of the rafter. This is the corner-to-edge distance. **2**

On your hip rafter, mark that corner-to-edge distance on the heel-cut line. That point represents the end of the level cut. **3** Set your framing square on the mark with the rise and run aligned correctly. Pencil the level cut from that point to the bottom edge of the rafter. **4** Then carry the bird's mouth plumb-cut line across and perpendicular to the top edge of the rafter. **5**

From the line you just marked, measure up the rafter and mark the rafter length in the center of the top edge. Strike a pair of 45-degree lines through this point. **6** Set your framing square with the rise and run on the bottom edge of the rafter and mark the upper plumb cuts where the 45-degree lines intersect the rafter edge. **7**

This double angle will allow the hip rafter to fit between the nearest common rafter of the main roof and the king common rafter of

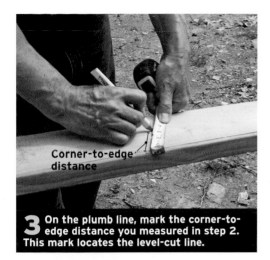

3 On the plumb line, mark the corner-to-edge distance you measured in step 2. This mark locates the level-cut line.

Corner-to-edge distance

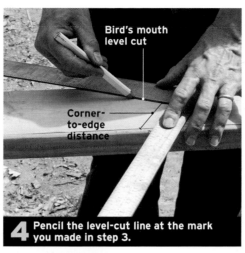

Bird's mouth level cut

Corner-to-edge distance

4 Pencil the level-cut line at the mark you made in step 3.

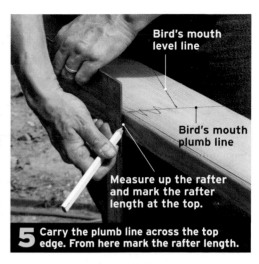

Bird's mouth level line

Bird's mouth plumb line

Measure up the rafter and mark the rafter length at the top.

5 Carry the plumb line across the top edge. From here mark the rafter length.

Double-bevel cut at base of overhang accommodates corner fascia.

8 Measure and mark the length of the overhang and mark the bottom plumb cut as you did the top—including the miter lines.

9 Cut the bird's mouth and make a pair of identical compound miters at both the top and bottom of the hip rafter.

the hip roof. (If the hip is for a shed roof, you'll need to cut only one bevel, and the bevel on the hip rafter at the other end of the shed roof will be on the other side of the rafter.)

Then figure the length of the hip-rafter overhang mathematically, with this ratio:

$$\frac{\text{Common-rafter overhang in inches}}{12} = \frac{\text{Hip overhang in inches}}{17}$$

Now measure from the square line on the top of the rafter and mark the overhang length on the center of the top edge of the rafter, just as you did when marking the length of the hip rafter. Pencil two 45-degree lines from that point to the edge of the rafter. From the intersection of these lines with the edges of the rafter, mark plumb lines on the sides of the rafter. **8**

Use a circular saw to cut the rafter at the appropriate marks, making 45-degree bevel cuts at the ridge line and bottom of the overhang. **9**   >> >> >>

HIP-RAFTER MITERS

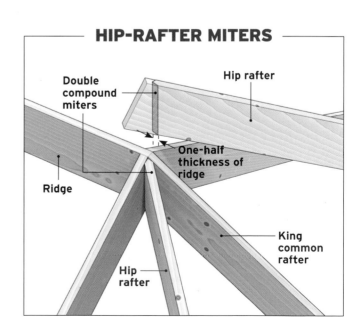

Double compound miters

Hip rafter

One-half thickness of ridge

Ridge

King common rafter

Hip rafter

LAYING OUT HIP AND JACK RAFTERS (CONTINUED)

Laying out jack rafters

Jack rafters (or just "jacks") are the progressively shorter rafters running from the top plate to the hip rafter. They oppose each other at the same points along the hip rafter, and because they travel up a diagonal, each pair is a different length.

Find the length of the first one by measuring over from the king common rafter 14½ in. (or whatever your internal gable-rafter spacing is). Mark this point on the bottom edge of the hip rafter.

Measure between that point and the inside edge of the layout mark on the top plate to find the length of the longest jack. (See "Taking Direct Measurements," facing page.)

This is the length of your jack rafter from the long side of the bevel cut to the inside edge of the top plate (front edge of bird's mouth). If you use a spacing of 16 in., your measurement will be from the short edge of the bevel to the top plate. You can also measure the distance from the layout mark and the intersection of the hip with the top plate and compute the jack-rafter length with a construction calculator.

Lay out the top plumb cuts at the same angle as your common rafters. Then cut the plumb-cut line with a 45-degree bevel. ❶ Cut out the bird's mouth, then the tail plumb cut (no bevel). Use the first rafter to mark the second, but be sure to reverse the direction of the top bevel cut. The mating rafter on the other side of the hip should be the same length but beveled the opposite way. ❷ Toenail jacks to the hip rafter and the wall plates with at least three 10d commons.

Figure the length of the remaining jacks by subtracting the common difference for each successive pair. The third scale on the framing square—or a construction calculator—will tell you how much this difference is (19¼ in. for an 8-pitch roof).

1 Mark top and bottom plumb cuts, and bevel the top cut at 45 degrees.

2 Use one jack to mark its opposite. Change the bevel direction at the top.

CUTTING JACK RAFTERS

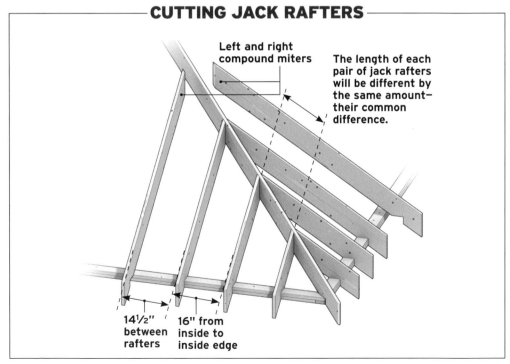

Left and right compound miters

The length of each pair of jack rafters will be different by the same amount—their common difference.

14½" between rafters

16" from inside to inside edge

TAKING DIRECT MEASUREMENTS

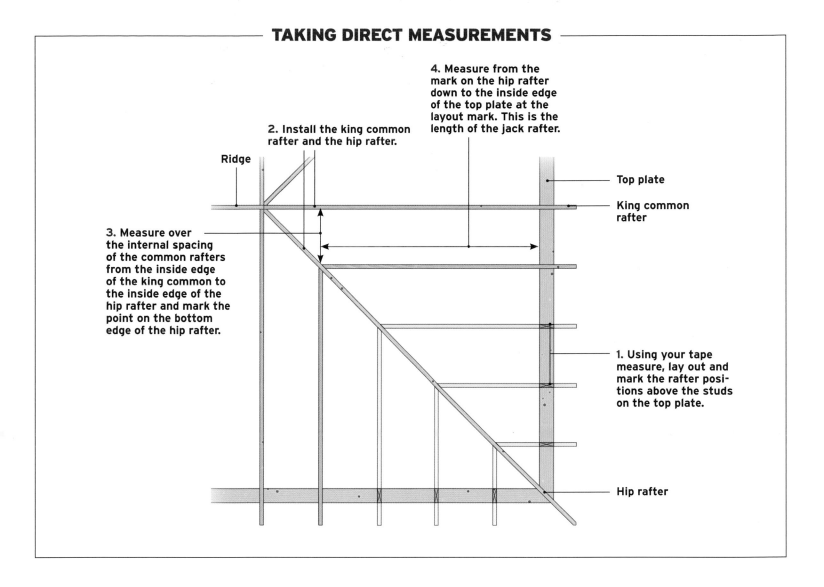

4. Measure from the mark on the hip rafter down to the inside edge of the top plate at the layout mark. This is the length of the jack rafter.

2. Install the king common rafter and the hip rafter.

Ridge

Top plate

King common rafter

3. Measure over the internal spacing of the common rafters from the inside edge of the king common to the inside edge of the hip rafter and mark the point on the bottom edge of the hip rafter.

1. Using your tape measure, lay out and mark the rafter positions above the studs on the top plate.

Hip rafter

Dropping the hip If you've read other carpentry books or talked to other carpenters, you may have heard the term "dropping the hip."

Traditional hip layout leaves the top edges of the hip rafter higher than the other roof planes. This puts a hump in the sheathing. You can bevel the top of the hip rafter to match the plane of the other rafters. I don't do this. No carpenter I know does this. Most simply "drop the hip" by cutting the bird's mouth deeper, lowering the hip rafter till its top edge falls in the same plane as the common rafters.

You can call on Pythagoras to cipher the exact drop. No one does this either. Most just cut the bird's mouth $3/8$ in. to $1/2$ in. deeper. It doesn't matter if the hip rafter sits a little low, as long as the jack rafters plane in with the common rafters.

Simply measuring the common rafters' height above the plate at the heel cut and laying out the hip rafter to be the same takes care of all this without guesswork or complicated math—and it keeps the hip rafter exactly in the same plane as the rest of the roof.

VALLEYS

Valley framing creates a variety of architectural effects, like this dormer. (Photo by Roe A. Osborn)

Traditional valley framing uses a valley rafter, concentrating the weight on a single board. (Photo by Brian Pontolilo)

Valleys also occur in doghouse dormers. Here, the cornice ties to the main roof.

A hip turns an outside corner, but its opposite—a valley—turns an inside corner. Valleys are found on T-shaped houses, doghouse dormers, and L-shaped houses.

Valley rafters are less common today than in previous generations of carpentry. That's because the jack rafters terminate on the valley rafter, not on the top plate of the walls. That concentrates a lot of weight on one structural member. About the only time a carpenter will install valley rafters now is when the plans call for a cathedral ceiling in a roof with a valley. That's a pretty rare occurrence and beyond the scope of this book.

In addition, most carpenters don't install valley rafters because there's a much easier approach, one that distributes weight more efficiently. It's called a California or blind valley.

In a California valley, the intersecting roof is framed on top of the main roof. The intersecting roof's jack rafters terminate on the main roof sheathing or, with increased loads, on a valley plate. The rafters of the main roof carry the load from the area above the valley down to the wall plates, which distribute the load more widely than a valley rafter does.

Beyond the valley, the intersecting roof is framed like a conventional gable roof.

CALIFORNIA VALLEY FRAMING

In a California valley, the jack rafters of the intersecting roof bear on the main roof sheathing or a valley plate, spreading the load more widely than a valley rafter.

Valley plate (optional depending on load)

Ridge

Jack rafters

$14\frac{1}{2}$"

Fly rafter

Common rafter of intersecting roof

Purlins

VALLEY-FRAMING BASICS

1 Start a dormer ridge like any gable ridge—supported by a pair of end rafters.

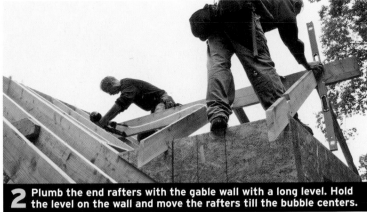

2 Plumb the end rafters with the gable wall with a long level. Hold the level on the wall and move the rafters till the bubble centers.

or

3 Support the end of a dormer ridge on blocking nailed between two roof rafters.

4 Nail a dormer ridge directly to a rafter, if you're lucky enough to land on one.

5 Sheathe the main roof around the dormer ridge.

Framing a valley—for example, when building an intersecting roof such as a dormer—starts out by figuring the ridge length.

First, add the length of the gable overhang to the length of the dormer wall plates. Then add the ridge extension from the wall-plate/main roof juncture using this two-step calculation:

1. Figure the intersecting ridge height. Unlike former calculations, don't deduct the measurement of the plumb cut—that's for when you want to find rafter length. Here, we're finding the top of the ridge.

$$\frac{\text{Pitch} \times (\frac{1}{2} \text{ the width between dormer plates})}{12}$$

2. Figure the ridge extension using the above result and the following formula:

$$\text{Extension} = \frac{12 \text{ in.} \times \text{Intersecting ridge height}}{\text{Main roof pitch}}$$

You can cut the back end of the ridge to the main roof pitch and toenail it to the sheathing. Add blocking between the rafters if there are no rafters under the sheathing at this juncture. However, I prefer to run the ridge long and tie it to the main roof rafter framing. I leave that area unsheathed until the ridge goes up.

Cut the ridge from straight stock, and install it as you would any gable ridge, capturing it between two pairs of rafters. **1** Make sure the end rafters are plumb with their gable wall. **2** Sight the ridge to be sure it's straight, and check it for level. Where the ridge runs into the framing, nail it to blocking between rafters **3** or if your layout works out, directly to a rafter. **4** Now, finish sheathing the main roof around the ridge. **5**

LAYING OUT VALLEY JACKS

1 Run a straightedge from the top of the rafter tails to the main roof and mark where the level meets the sheathing.

2 Snap a line starting at the ridge and running through the mark on the sheathing.

3 Measure square from the last common rafter to the chalkline; mark the end of the first valley jack.

4 On layout marks, measure between the ridge and chalkline to find jack lengths.

Jack rafters continue the common-rafter layout along the ridge. Lay a straightedge across the last few rafters extending it to the main roof. Mark the point where the bottom corner of the level contacts the sheathing. **1** Snap a chalkline through your mark starting at the top edge of the ridge. The ends of your jack rafters will fall along this line. **2**

Lay out the jack-rafter spacing on the ridge—at 16 in. (or the spacing you're using in the main roof). Set a framing square flush with the front edge of the last common rafter. Move the square to contact your chalkline and mark this point—it will be 16 in. from the front edge of the common rafter. This is the location of the first jack rafter. **3** Continue with the succeeding layout marks—32 in., 48 in., and so on—until you reach the ridge. These should correspond with layout marks on the ridge. At each layout mark, measure between the ridge and the chalkline to find the long point of the jack rafters. **4** Repeat these steps on the other side of the roof.

JACK-RAFTER NAILERS

On wider roofs where each jack rafter carries a larger load, designers often specify a 2× nailer be affixed to the main roof sheathing to spread the load where the jacks' level cuts meet the roof.

Especially with lower roof pitches, the width of the nailer is likely to be greater than the width of commonly available lumber—you may need to combine several planks.

I'm sure there's a way to figure the required width mathematically, but I've never bothered. To find the width of the nailer, measure the length of a level cut on the jack rafter. Find the length of the nailer by measuring from where the top of the ridge meets the main roof to where the outside edges of the wall plate meet the main roof.

Larger roofs bring larger loads, which sometimes require a wide nailer (or valley plate) to disperse the load from the jacks. (Photo by Justin Fink)

CUTTING VALLEY JACKS

Perhaps the most important point about cutting jack rafters–and sometimes the easiest to forget–is that you need both left and right jacks, and they aren't interchangeable.

On the bottom is a bevel cut that matches the pitch of the roof and the cut angles one way for the left-handed jacks and the other way for those on the right. On top is a standard plumb cut at the same angle as the common rafters. ❶

Measure from the plumb cut along the top of the rafter and mark its length on the top edge that will face the common rafters. ❷ From this point, mark a level cut at the roof pitch. ❸

Using the "Cutting-Angle Conversion" table below, find your roof pitch. The number corresponding to the pitch is the bevel angle of the level cut. Set a circular saw at this bevel and make the level cut. ❹ Nail the jacks in place, being sure to hit any rafters under the sheathing. ❺

CUTTING-ANGLE CONVERSION	
Roof Pitch	**Cutting Angle**
1/12	$4\frac{1}{2}°$
2/12	$9\frac{1}{2}°$
3/12	$14°$
4/12	$18\frac{1}{2}°$
5/12	$22\frac{1}{2}°$
6/12	$26\frac{1}{2}°$
7/12	$30\frac{1}{4}°$
8/12	$33\frac{1}{2}°$
9/12	$36\frac{1}{2}°$
10/12	$39\frac{1}{2}°$
11/12	$42\frac{1}{2}°$
11/12	$45°$

1 Lay out the top plumb cut of valley jacks at the pitch of the commons.

2 Measure along the top of the jack to its longest point.

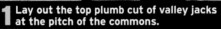

3 Mark the level cut using the common rafter pitch.

4 Set a circular saw to the pitch of the main roof and make the bevel cut.

5 At the chalkline, the jack should fit flat on the roof and on the ridge. Nail the jack to the main roof rafters and the ridge with 16d commons.

INSTALLING SKYLIGHTS

1 Use joist hangers to attach skylight headers to the side rafters. The joist hangers add stability to the installation.

2 Using the layout marks you made previously on the ridge, fill in above and below the opening with short rafters.

4 Most skylights come with hardware that fastens to the sheathing. Be sure to center the unit over the opening before affixing it.

5 Frame the corners of the light-well, joining the joists and rafters with stud material.

Y ou may have heard the old carpenter's axiom that there are only two kinds of skylights: those that leak, and those that haven't leaked yet. Well, that's old school. Buy a good-quality skylight (I've had great success with Velux® and Andersen®), and follow the installation instructions. I'll cover flashing later in Chapter 5.

> **See "Flashing a Skylight," p. 170.**

Frame the rough opening to the size speci-fied by the manufacturer. Use double rafters if required by the designer. The opening for this particular skylight was small enough that double rafters weren't required. Cut the stock for the headers to the width of the rough opening and install them with joist hangers. **❶**

If the skylight location comes close to at least one rafter that is part of the overall layout, I try to use it as a side of the open-ing. There will probably be intermediate rafters that terminate on the headers. Nail these to the header in the positions called for in the layout and finish the attachment with joist hangers. **❷**

Sheath the roof, and mark the skylight loca-tion by driving nails at its corners up through the plywood. Working from the outside, snap chalklines between the nails and cut out the opening in the sheathing along the lines. Be careful whenever you're cutting anything on the roof. The sawdust is very slippery. **❸**

3 At the corners of the frame, drive nails through the plywood from below, snap chalklines, and cut the opening with a circular saw.

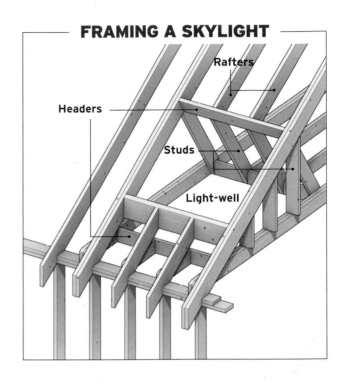

FRAMING A SKYLIGHT

Rafters

Headers

Studs

Light-well

6 Fill in between the corners with studs on a standard layout, making the well easy to insulate.

WHAT CAN GO WRONG

Because warm air rises into places like skylight wells, this is a crucial spot to insulate well. It's also a spot where it can be difficult for the insulator to work, and which probably won't be looked at very closely by any inspector. Consequently, it's common to see poor insulation jobs around skylights. Don't provide any excuse for sloppy work—use the same stud thickness and spacing as everywhere else to make it as easy as possible for the insulator to do a good job.

➡ See "Sheathing a Roof," p. 124.

Then, install the skylight. How this is done will vary from manufacturer to manufacturer, but most will have some sort of bracket that's screwed or nailed to the roof. Be sure the skylight sits square in the opening and that all four sides are equidistant to the sides of the opening. **4**

If you're installing a skylight in a cathedral ceiling, you're done. But if there's a flat ceiling under the roof, you need to frame a sky-

light well that extends through the ceiling joists. Skylight wells usually flare at the top and bottom to distribute the daylight more evenly. The angle of the flare is the designer's call. Check the plans for this information.

Frame the well opening in the ceiling joists, following the design. Establish the corners of the light-well by installing studs that run between the corners of the skylight opening and the corners of the ceiling

opening. **5** Fill in between the corners with additional studs on the standard layout. **6** Add additional studs, as you would in a wall. These studs provide nailing for drywall, and a place to contain insulation.

INSTALLING SOFFITS AND FASCIA ON EAVES

Traditional soffit and fascia techniques enclose the ends of the rafters in a box that includes some sort of screened ventilation openings. How the ventilation is handled varies with the soffit choice. Here, I'll show a traditional wood soffit.

The underlying framing would be the same for the other common soffit, made of perforated vinyl or aluminum, with the difference being only that instead of applying a 1× pine fascia, I would substitute a rough 2× soffit that would be wrapped in aluminum coil stock.

In most cases, I install preformed aluminum soffit vent. It's sold in 10-ft. lengths and cuts with tin snips. The vent has flanges on both sides that slip between the soffit boards and the framing. I use 1× or ³⁄₈-in. AC plywood soffit boards to hold the vent in place. Other soffit materials come with F-channels and instructions for mounting the board.

Usually, you'll want the vent centered, and if the plan specs won't accomplish that with standard-width boards, you may have to rip at least one of the soffit boards so it ends up just a gnat's hair past the ends of the rafter tails.

No matter the finish material, you need solid framing under it. Hold a 2-ft. level against the bottom edge of the rafter tail with its end against the wall. Using the top surface of the level, mark the wall at a point level with the bottom of the rafter tail. Level at another rafter tail and drive a nail at your marks.

Then set a 2×4 ledger on the nails with its leading edge even with the front of the fly rafter. Nail the ledger to the wall. ❶ Cut and nail 2×4 blocks between the rafter tails and the 2×4 ledger on the wall. ❷ This is all the framing you need to support the soffit vent along the eaves.

Fasten the first soffit board next to the wall, nailing only the inside edge—6d stainless-steel or hot-dipped galvanized siding nails. ❸ Slip the flange of the aluminum

vent into the gap at the un-nailed edge of the soffit board (make sure the vents angle away from the house). ❹ Then rip the second soffit board if necessary. Catch the other vent flange with this second soffit board and, holding it against the rafter tails, nail it to the framing. ❺ Go back and nail the un-nailed edge of the first board, too. No nails are needed in the vent itself.

The fascia comes next. Some carpenters bevel its top to match the roof pitch, but I

find that a waste of time. Instead, rip the fascia board so it will hang below the soffit enough to mask any irregularities, say, ¹⁄₂ in. to ³⁄₄ in., and just enough below the tops of the rafters that the roof sheathing can run over it. The fascia should end up flush, or just a little past the face of the fly rafter and even with the end of the soffit board. ❻

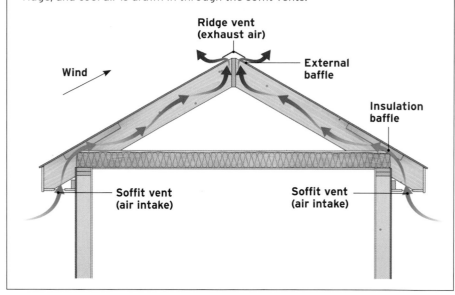

VENTING A ROOF

Code requires that roofs be vented, and that's usually done with intake vents in the soffits and exhaust vents at the ridge. The idea is that hot air exits the ridge, and cool air is drawn in through the soffit vents.

Ridge vent (exhaust air)

Wind

External baffle

Insulation baffle

Soffit vent (air intake)

Soffit vent (air intake)

CREATING A SOFFIT

A rafter overhang creates the cornice form. Lay out the tail plumb cut to create the overhang. Fascia width will dictate if a level cut is needed at the rafter tail.

Rafter

Blocking

Fascia

Soffit

1 Nail a 2× ledger on the wall, level with the bottom of the rafter tails. This ledger provides a nailing surface for the soffit.

2 Attach blocking between the ledger and the rafter tails to provide soffit nailers.

Blocking between ledger and each rafter tail

3 Nail only the inside edge of the first soffit board. This will leave a thin gap on the other side of the soffit board.

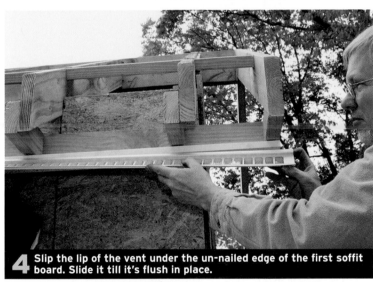

4 Slip the lip of the vent under the un-nailed edge of the first soffit board. Slide it till it's flush in place.

5 Trap the free lip of the vent with the inside edge of the other soffit board. Hold it against the rafter tails and nail it home.

6 Nail the un-nailed edge of the first soffit board. Then run the fascia flush with the fly rafter and with the ends of the soffit boards.

INSTALLING GABLE SOFFITS AND FASCIA

Gable soffits are simple—there's no venting. You'll want to close off the cornice to create a finished look, and one way to accomplish this is with a design detail unceremoniously called a pork chop, a simplified version of the old-style cornice return.

To start, rip the soffit board—which can be 1× or AC plywood—to the measurement from the front face of the fly rafter to the face of the wall.

Level over to the wall at the top and bottom of the fly rafter, mark the level points, and install a 2× nailer, as you would at the eaves.

See "Installing Soffits and Fascia on Eaves," p. 120.

Cut the top of the soffit board to meet its mate at the peak in a miter by setting your circular saw to the angle that matches the roof pitch.

See "Cutting-Angle Conversion," p. 117.

The bottom end can run long over the eave nailer and into the eave. ❶ Fasten this soffit board to the gable, then repeat the installation on the other side.

The next piece is the cornice return, and it finishes off the eaves nailer. Level over from the bottom edge of the eaves fascia to mark a line representing the bottom of the cornice return. Then measure from this line up to the soffit board. This will put the bottom edge of the cornice return level with the eaves fascia. ❷ Rip a piece of fascia stock to this height, beveling its upper edge at the angle of the roof. Cut it and nail it up. ❸

Rip the gable fascia to hang below the gable soffit the same amount as the eaves fascia does. Plumb-cut its ridge end to meet its counterpart in a miter, and let the lower end run long. ❹ Fasten the fascia to the gable sheathing, then cut it flush to the eaves fascia with a sharp handsaw. ❺

Finally, you'll need a small triangular piece of fascia to cap off the end of the eaves. Its angle will be that of a level cut on your rafters, which you can compute by subtracting the level-cut angle from 90 degrees. So, for example, the plumb cut of an 8-pitch roof is 33.5 degrees. Subtracting this from 90 degrees leaves you with an angle of 56.5 degrees. Cut this piece so it's flush with the bottom of the cornice return. ❻

SIMPLE GABLE FASCIA

If you don't have a gable overhang, you can just nail the gable fascia, or rake board, to the wall. It's simple and it's common to bring the fly rafter out from the wall with utility-grade 5/4 stock and tuck the siding under the fly rafter.

Nail the spacer to the wall along the edge of the roof. When you install the fascia, the spacer creates a recess behind it. Install the siding without worrying too much about accurate end cuts. The fascia will cover them. Fill in the remaining space at the bottom of the fascia with a triangular-shaped piece of fascia material, called a "pork chop."

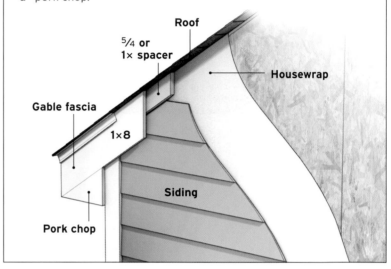

INSTALLING A GABLE SOFFIT

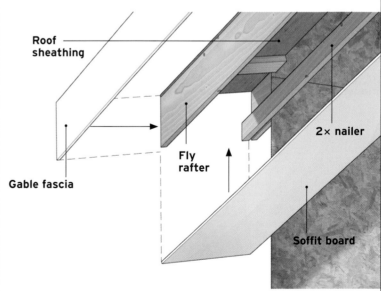

Gable-soffit installation is uncomplicated. Make sure the bottom of the 2× nailer is level with the bottom of the fly rafter. Then attach the soffit board tight to the wall and flush with the outside edge of the fly rafter. The fascia should cover the fly rafter and the exposed edge of the soffit board.

1 Miter the top end of the soffit and nail it to the bottom edge of the fly rafter and the eave nailer. Let the bottom end run into the eaves.

2 Use a level to extend the plane of the bottom edge of the eaves fascia and to locate the bottom of the cornice return.

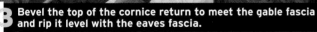

3 Bevel the top of the cornice return to meet the gable fascia and rip it level with the eaves fascia.

4 Plumb-cut the top of the gable fascia and let its bottom end run a little past the eaves fascia.

5 With a sharp handsaw, trim the gable fascia flush with the eaves fascia.

6 Nail the triangular cap to the gable fascia first to keep the pieces flush.

TRADE SECRET

People object to wood trim because paint peels from it. That's often because moisture gets in the wood. Sealing end grain at installation is more than half the battle in keeping paint on. Use oil-based primer—it soaks in better than latex primers. Prime all six sides of every board before installation. It's okay to prime a fresh cut and nail it up wet.

SHEATHING A ROOF

Unlike walls, you can't sheathe a roof on the ground then raise it into place. Roof sheathing strikes me as one of the most dangerous carpentry operations—you're up on a slanted surface, often with intermittent foot support, handling heavy, awkward sheets of plywood. Do not attempt this on very windy days. On any day, you should spend considerable energy, thought, and time on safety.

When working on a roof, fall-protection is an absolute necessity. One approach is to wear a harness and rope. However, I'm not wearing a harness for several reasons. First, I find the rope gets in the way, particularly when handling sheathing. It's also a low roof, and I've set up roof scaffolds near the eaves, and there's scaffolding with guard rails below. Either one would probably stop a fall, and the scaffolds provide a surface for standing—2×10 or 2×12 planks resting in steel brackets temporarily nailed through the sheathing into the rafters. I also nail 2×4 cleats on the sheathing every 4 ft., after a section of sheathing is down and nailed. There is no substitute for good judgment, both about the conditions and your abilities. Ultimately, you're the person responsible for your safety.

I like to stage hauling the sheathing to the roof on the floor directly below the roof, employing a helper to hand it up through the rafters after cutting it on the ground or the floor below. That puts a small break in the lifting, distributes the workload, and keeps sawdust—which acts like a lubricant under foot—off the roof.

Measure and cut the first piece so its edge lands in the center of a rafter. Snap a chalkline 4 ft. up from the leading edge of the fascia or subfascia, align the sheathing with the line, and nail it. **1** Strike chalklines on the layout along the rafters to guide the nails, and use the same nailing intervals as for any sheathing—every 6 in. along the edge and 12 in. in the field. **2** In addition, as with floor or wall sheathing, stagger the sheets so that no four corners meet.

➡ See "Laying Subfloor," p. 66.

When laying successive sheets of sheathing, set their lower edge on the rafters just above the installed sheathing to keep them from sliding, then lower the sheet into place. **3** Watch your footing especially here—leaning forward shifts your center of gravity, and can cause your feet to slip. Avoid excessive leaning by holding the end of the sheet, or extending your grip by hooking the claws of your hammer around the upper edge of the sheet.

When there are hips and valleys, the sheathing has to be cut at an angle. **4** Snap a line up 4 ft. from the previous row of sheathing to represent the top of the piece you'll cut and install next. Measure for the top of the sheathing along this line. Transfer the top and bottom measurements to a fresh piece of sheathing, and snap the angled line between them. **5** It's not a bad idea to cut such pieces ¼ in. short, to avoid having to hand them down to be re-cut.

At the top of the roof, hold the sheathing back from the ridge by the amount recommended by the manufacturer of the ridge vent you intend to use. **6** This is usually 1 in. to 2 in.

Steel brackets and 2×10 planks provide a staging and walking area as well as extra safety against falls.

In addition to roof scaffolds, 2×4 cleats nailed on the sheathing every 4 ft. provide improved footing.

When possible, cut roof sheathing off the roof. You can work on sawhorses and keep slippery sawdust off the roof.

1 To lay out the first course of sheathing, snap a chalkline 4 ft. up from the lower edge of the fascia.

2 Nail the sheathing with 8d common or deformed-shank nails at least every 6 in. on panel edges and 12 in. in the field.

3 To lay successive panels, support the bottom edge on the previously installed sheathing and lower the new sheet into place.

4 To cut sheets for hips and valleys at angles, use lines snapped on the rafters at 4-ft. intervals as benchmarks for measurements.

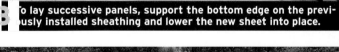

5 With the sheet on sawhorses, snap a line at the measurements taken on the roof to mark the cuts for angled sheathing.

6 Ridge vents require an opening. Cut the top sheet short by the amount specified by the ridge-vent manufacturer.

INSTALLING TRUSSES

In much of the country, roofs are commonly built with trusses. They can be faster to install and don't require the knowledge of roof geometry that rafters do. Trusses are engineered and made in factories, typically from 2×4s, although some specialized or larger trusses use heavier members.

There is much more to be said about trusses than we have space for here–larger trusses require more expertise and equipment, hip trusses require a few extra details, windy days require you to find some other way to fill your time, and so on.

Every truss order should come with both a plan and installation guidelines. Follow them religiously. When in doubt, check with the manufacturer, or with the Truss Plate Institute® (www.tpinst.org).

Material delivery

Trusses save time because they provide both the roof and the ceiling framing in one piece. Most are light enough that they can be muscled to the top of the walls, but it's pretty easy to damage them in this way. Suppliers can often deliver trusses to the top of the walls with a boom truck. If not, it may be worthwhile to hire a crane for an hour or two. If you do that, have the crane place the roof sheathing on the uppermost floor before it sets the trusses. Don't overload the floor with the sheathing, spread it in a couple of stacks, and make sure these stacks are set above bearing points.

Some crews use the crane to set each truss, and if it's still around at the end of the day, they'll have it set the bundles of roof sheathing on the trusses.

Be very careful–a large, concentrated load can damage the trusses or topple the whole roof. Break the sheathing into smaller bundles and distribute them evenly. Never place big loads near the ridge, but always low, and support them at least in part with struts to the plates. When in doubt, err on the side of caution.

If you aren't going to have the supplier deliver them to the tops of the walls, then have a flat area prepared for storage. Use framing lumber to level this surface.

Working efficiently

Trusses cost more than the lumber used in a site-framed roof, so any savings come in labor. To realize those savings, plan to work efficiently. Before delivery, be familiar with the truss plan and aware of any special situations such as trusses that need to be supported in particular spots.

Although many trusses seem identical, they might not be. Take the time to be certain before installing them. Have the top plates, including those of any center bearing wall, laid out for the trusses as you would for rafters.

Most trusses are designed for 2-ft. centers. To line up all the truss tails and ensure your fascia will be straight, snap a line down one of the wall plates 1 in. from the outside edge. ❶ Measure in the correct distance from the tails, and mark the lower chord of each truss to align with this chalkline. Install the truss with the mark aligned on the chalkline. ❷

TRUSSES ARE MADE FOR ALMOST ANY ROOF FORM

Almost any stick-framed roof shape can be done with trusses, including ones that incorporate a room within the roof. Nomenclature for the structural members is the same for all styles–top (or rafter) chord, bottom chord, and web.

The simplest truss is a king-post truss, which can span about 25 ft.

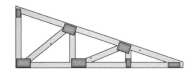

A mono-pitch truss for shed-roof buildings spans about 25 ft.

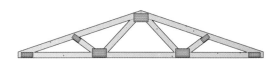

Fink trusses span over 40 ft.

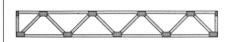

Parallel-chord trusses are for flat roofs. Standard spans are available up to 30 ft.

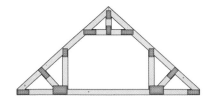

Attic trusses provide usable space within the truss, with spans to over 30 ft.

The sloping bottom chords of scissors trusses can increase interior volume, providing space for a cathedral ceiling. Spans up to 40 ft. are possible.

1 To be sure of straight fascia, snap a line on one wall plate 1 in. from the outside edge. (Photos by Donald Blum)

2 Mark the trusses at the distance of the overhang plus half the wall thickness and align this mark on the chalkline.

3 Lay the trusses near their layout marks to ease placement as they're raised.

A temporary catwalk framed down the center of a building makes a safer working area for dragging and setting trusses.

Arranging your material

When setting trusses, you'll be doing a fair amount of work in the center of the building. To cut your "travel" time, set up a temporary catwalk that extends from end to end and is just below the plate height. Start at one end with a gable end truss. Have four or five other trusses ready.

Set these trusses near the far end of the house, and drag the end truss close to but not hanging over the end wall. Stack the other trusses on the end truss like fallen dominoes, so that within four or five trusses, the bottom chord of one falls on its layout. Bring the rest of the trusses up, and continue stacking them with their bottom chords close to their layout marks. **3** >> >> >>

> ### ⚠ WARNING
> Each member of a truss serves a specific purpose, and cutting or damaging one can destroy the truss's structural integrity. Never modify a truss without the designer's approval.

> ### ⓘ WHAT CAN GO WRONG
> Lots can go wrong, and it's usually because of inadequate bracing or overloading the building with other materials. First and foremost, follow the manufacturer's instructions to the letter.

INSTALLING TRUSSES (CONTINUED)

BRACING THE FIRST TRUSS

2×6

To catch and temporarily hold the first gable truss, firmly affix 2×6 or larger stock to the gable wall near the center of the truss.

Nail or screw to solid framing.

4 Nail cleating to the top chords to keep the trusses consistently spaced and braced. (Photos by Donald Blum)

6 Before bracing, plumb the first gable wall using the longest level you have.

7 Diagonal bracing is crucial, and must be installed at least every 25 ft., unless the truss maker says to install it more often.

Bracing the trusses

The final truss should be another gable truss. For initial braces, nail together at least a pair of 2×6s in an L-shape, then nail them to the end wall next to this truss, about ⅔ of the way to the center of the building from each outside wall.

The 2×6s should reach to the top chord of the truss in that spot, and an equal distance down the wall. Be sure to nail to solid framing, not just sheathing. Wider trusses may call for more braces.

Stand up the end truss against the 2×6 braces and align the trusses with the chalkline on the plate. Nail the truss temporarily to the braces and permanently to the end wall plate. Don't depend on this brace for more than the first few trusses—they need diagonal bracing before they're safely set.

This is the most precarious time in raising a truss roof. The only bracing in place is the L-shaped 2×6s. The next goal is to raise about five more trusses, and install permanent diagonal bracing to create

a block of trusses that can anchor the next few trusses. So, raise the next truss in from the gable and nail it to the plate.

Near the top of the truss on each side, nail cleating to space the truss correctly (usually 22½ in.) from the end truss. **4** You can use manufactured truss spacers that fold out like an old-fashioned carpenter's rule, but remember, they're a spacing tool, not a brace.

Repeat this procedure until there are four or five trusses up, installing hurricane ties or blocking between the truss heels as you go, if called for. **5** Use a long level to plumb the end truss and brace it in the center to an interior wall with a long 2×4 running through the other trusses you've raised. **6**

Although you have a brace installed, don't relax yet. Install sway braces by cutting 45s on the ends of two long 2×4s. Thread them through the trusses you've raised, and nail them between the top of the top chord of the end truss and the bottom of the top chord of the innermost truss, near the wall plate. **7** Use 2 16d commons in each

5 As with rafters, it's a lot easier to install hold-down hardware before sheathing the roof. (Photos by Donald Blum)

8 Bottom-chord braces stiffen the ceiling, keep trusses from rotating, and space the chords for drywall installation.

truss where the brace contacts the top chord. This bracing is usually repeated every 25 ft., although sometimes more closely depending on the design. These braces are critical—don't ignore them.

You'll also need to brace the bottom chords. **8** Here, nail 16-ft. 2×4s to the tops of the chords as specified by the design. Mark the truss layout on the edge of these 2×4s to aid in spacing the bottom chords.

Continue adding permanent bracing as you raise the trusses—don't wait until they're all up. If it turns windy, you want the trusses braced. Some truss roofs require additional bracing. Long webs, typically near the highest part of the truss, sometimes get lateral bracing, which is usually a series of long 2×4s nailed perpendicular to the webs. The purpose of these braces is to prevent these longer webs from buckling under load.

LATERAL TRUSS BRACING

Not all roof trusses require lateral bracing, but don't skip it if it's called for. Particularly on trusses with tall webs, loads from above can cause the web to buckle and the truss to fail. Lateral bracing ties the webs together so they act in unison to resist loading.

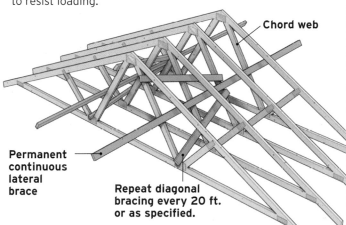

Chord web

Permanent continuous lateral brace

Repeat diagonal bracing every 20 ft. or as specified.

TRUSS UPLIFT

Truss uplift occurs in heated homes when the bottom chord bows upward in the center of a house. The chord's top surface is in the relatively damp attic, while its bottom surface is being dried by heat escaping through the ceiling. The differing moisture content can bow the chord up by

an inch or more, and you can't prevent it by restraining the truss—it's likely the truss will break.

The solution is to attach the truss to the top plates with special clips that allow movement, and not to attach the drywall to the trusses within about 2 ft. of any center wall. That allows the truss to move independently without cracking the drywall corner.

Installing sheathing

Only after all the bracing is in should you begin to sheathe the roof. That's no different than on a site-cut roof, except that because of the 2-ft. spacing, you may be required to use panel clips between the trusses. Because trusses are always part of an engineered design, it bears reiterating that following the design completely is crucial to the strength of the roof. Any change you make can affect the structural integrity of the design. Unless you're an engineer, don't mess with a truss plan.

EXTERIOR WINDOWS AND DOORS

MOST EXTERIOR WINDOWS AND doors install fairly easily. Making sure they set plumb and level in their openings will be one of your primary concerns, but installation requirements don't end there. Stopping leaks is critical, and most leaks in the sidewalls occur around windows and doors. No longer can you get by with simple flashing on top of a window or door frame. In this chapter, you'll find techniques for sealing windows and doors that will meet IRC weatherproofing requirements.

FLASHING

Flashing the Sills,
p. 132

Detailing the Corners,
p. 134

INSTALLING WINDOWS

Installing Vinyl Flanged Windows, p. 136
Sealing and Shimming Windows, p. 138

INSTALLING DOORS

Installing a Prehung Exterior Door, p. 140

New Windows and Doors in an Old House, p. 146

FLASHING THE SILLS

1 Make a 6-in. cut in the building paper at the sill level on both sides of the opening.

2 Cut both upper corners of the building paper about 6 in. diagonally.

3 Fold back the flaps of the tar paper and temporarily staple them out of the way.

6 Remove the lower half of the backing, smoothing the membrane as you go.

7 Cut the membrane along each side, down to the sill. Don't let it stick to anything.

All siding leaks, particularly where it meets windows or doors. This is why flashing is essential—particularly in rainy climates. It moves water away from window or door framing and out onto the face of the siding, where gravity can bring it to the ground.

Flashing goes on in two stages—the first before you install the window or door, the second after the unit is in place. Although the steps shown here illustrate procedures for a window, the same techniques apply when flashing a door opening.

➤ See "Installing a Prehung Exterior Door," p. 140.

Begin by cutting the tar paper or house-wrap so you can pull it back on the sides and top of the opening. Start at the edge of the opening and, using a utility knife, make a horizontal cut about 6 in. to either side at the sill level. **1** Make the same cut diagonally at each upper corner. **2** Then temporarily staple back the side and top flaps to get them out of your way. **3**

Rough sills should be sloped, and there are a couple of ways of doing this. The first uses clapboard, the second, commercially manufactured materials.

➤ See "Manufactured Alternatives," p. 135.

For clapboard, cut a piece of cedar siding to fit on top of the rough sill. Nail it with its thin edge facing out. **4** Then cut a piece of 12-in. membrane, about 1 ft. longer than the opening is wide. Peel the backing on the upper part of the membrane and adhere it to the wall across the opening, with about 6 in. of exposed adhesive above the sill (4 in. for a 2×4 wall). **5** Remove the lower backing and adhere the bottom section of the membrane. **6**

Cut the membrane along the studs on both sides, folding it out to keep it from adhering where you don't want it. **7** Then fold and stick the membrane smoothly to the sill. **8**

4 Slope the sill for drainage by nailing a piece of tapered clapboard to it.

5 Remove the backing from the top half of the membrane and adhere it to the walls.

8 Apply tension and fold the membrane smoothly back over the rough sill.

TRADE SECRET

Remember these two things about flashing (they apply also to building paper, housewrap, siding, and roofing): Upper layers lap lower layers, and side joints—such as a joint in tar paper or housewrap or where siding overlaps flashing along a door or window—need to lap by at least 4 in. (more is better).

FLASHING MEMBRANES

Several manufacturers produce adhesive flashing membranes in a variety of widths. I generally use 12-in. and 6-in. widths. All have a non-sticky face and a sticky face covered with a backing, or release membrane—a slit in the middle makes peeling and installation easier.

One of the differences between membranes is their adhesive, which may be asphalt, butyl, or acrylic. One is advertised as a "co-polymer adhesive." I don't know what that means, but I do know that membrane sticks like white on rice. Before you use a membrane, check with the window and membrane manufacturers—some vinyl flanges are incompatible with asphalt and butyl adhesives.

How sticky the membrane is will vary with temperature (they're stickier in the heat) and the surface you're adhering to. What doesn't vary is that membrane adhesives stick very well to themselves—I've thrown away more than one piece whose sticky side accidentally touched itself.

Membranes stick well to housewrap, smooth surfaces, such as powder-coated aluminum coil stock, and other metal flashings that have been cleaned of manufacturing oils. However, they stick with varying tenacity to wood. OSB, especially, can be a problem because it's manufactured with wax sealant. And if the OSB is wet, forget it. Let it dry.

If you're having adhesion problems on a substrate, try priming it with a proprietary primer or regular spray adhesive. Let the primer dry to the touch before applying the membrane. The solvent in the primer or spray adhesive will dissolve membrane adhesives, so it won't stick to wet spray primer. Pressure helps membranes adhere. Burnish them down with your hand or a laminate roller.

Peel away the backing to expose the adhesive, but only an amount you can work with.

DETAILING THE CORNERS

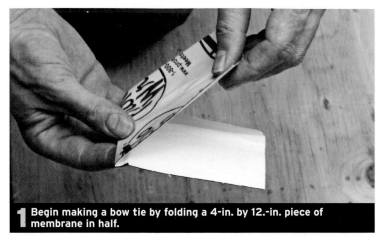

1 Begin making a bow tie by folding a 4-in. by 12.-in. piece of membrane in half.

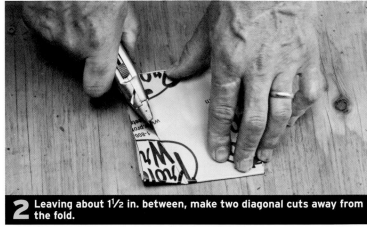

2 Leaving about 1½ in. between, make two diagonal cuts away from the fold.

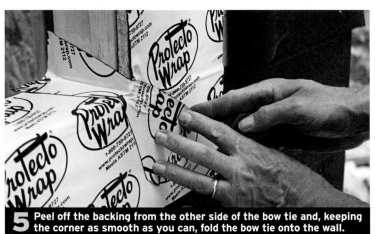

5 Peel off the backing from the other side of the bow tie and, keeping the corner as smooth as you can, fold the bow tie onto the wall.

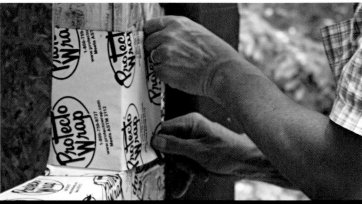

6 Lap the bow tie with another piece of adhesive membrane. Repeat the process on the other corner.

Detailing the lower corners is the trickiest part of flashing the sills. You need to get some sort of waterproof material to conform to three planes at once: the jack stud, the rough sill, and the sheathing. This can be done with standard adhesive membrane or with commercial materials made for this purpose (see "Manufactured Alternatives," facing page).

To use adhesive membrane, cut a piece about 4 in. by 12 in., and fold it in half. **1** Make two diagonal cuts, each starting about 1 in. from either side of center and extending toward the corners, leaving about 1½ in. of material in the center. **2** When opened up, you'll have a bow-tie shape. **3**

Remove the release paper from one half of the bow tie, and adhere it to the rough sill and the face of the jack stud, with the narrow part of the bow tie at the corner. **4** Rub the adhered portion of the bow tie so it's well secured.

Remove the remaining release paper and adhere the rest of the bow tie to the face of the wall, keeping tension on it as you go, so it lies relatively smooth. **5** It will crinkle up some, but don't worry about that.

Bow ties don't extend very far up the jack stud, so I lap them with a 6-in.-wide piece of membrane. **6** In high-wind areas, such as along the coast, I'd extend this piece the entire height of the jack stud.

TRADE SECRET
Flashing the corners with membrane is much easier on a warm day. If it's cold, warm the bow ties before application. And on sheathing, if it's cold or damp outside, you'll get much better adhesion if you spray the sheathing with primer or spray adhesive before installing the membrane.

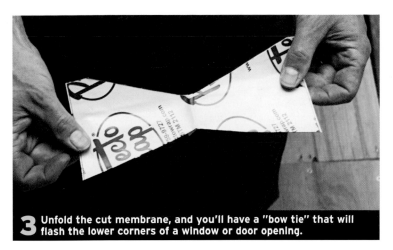

3 Unfold the cut membrane, and you'll have a "bow tie" that will flash the lower corners of a window or door opening.

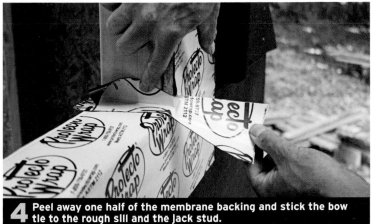

4 Peel away one half of the membrane backing and stick the bow tie to the rough sill and the jack stud.

MANUFACTURED ALTERNATIVES

SILLS AND CORNER FLASHING

Sloping the rough sill with a clapboard works pretty well, but there are manufactured alternatives that can make the job easier.

One fairly inexpensive product that I use is Protecto Wrap®'s PSDS, which combines a sloping closed-cell foam surface with a wicking membrane that wraps to the outside. In addition to the sloped surface, this product provides a low back dam. Other sill-drainage options include multi-piece rigid plastics that glue together or DIY sheet-metal pans like I make for doors.

I don't use bow ties much since I learned of an unreinforced membrane by Protecto Wrap, which they simply call Detail Tape. It has a release film on both sides, and when that's removed, the stuff stretches like Silly Putty®. Several companies make rigid plastic corners.

Sold in rolls, this closed-cell foam drainage system is cut to fit and incorporates a back dam.

This unreinforced membrane for corners is stretchy enough to conform to the jack stud, rough sill, and face of the wall.

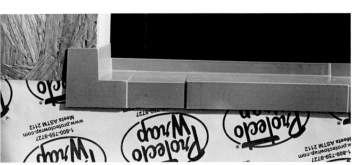

Manufactured drainage pans come in several pieces and are glued together to fit the individual opening.

Premade plastic corners are another product that make detailing openings quick, easy, and waterproof.

INSTALLING VINYL FLANGED WINDOWS

Plastic flanges are the main attachment device for most modern windows. Roofing nails or galvanized screws fasten them to the framing.

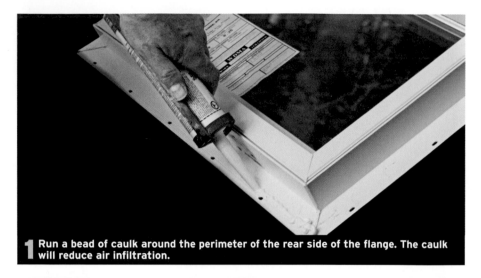

1 Run a bead of caulk around the perimeter of the rear side of the flange. The caulk will reduce air infiltration.

4 Check for plumb and level, shift the window as needed, and tightly nail the flange to the framing.

With the sill flashing addressed, it's time to install the window. Most windows sold today are secured to the house with plastic nailing flanges that integrate into the flashing system and ultimately are hidden by the siding or trim.

Here, I'm showing the installation of a sliding window, but the process is pretty much the same with any other type. One word of caution—read the manufacturer's directions. If they differ from what's said here, follow them. Not all windows are the same, and to benefit from the manufacturer's warranty, you have to follow their instructions. In addition, enlist the help of a friend—window installation is far easier with a helper than alone.

Securing the frame

Apply a bead of caulk around the perimeter of the rear of the flanges. **1** Don't use cheap caulk—this seal has to last the life of the window. I prefer urethane or butyl caulk (check with the window manufacturer—butyl isn't compatible with all plastics used for flanges). Lock the sash(es) shut till you've nailed the window securely. They'll help hold the window square, making leveling easier.

Set the window into the opening, bottom first. **2** Tack it loosely with a couple of 2-in.

galvanized roofing nails. **3** Check it for plumb and level and move it as needed. **4** Then drive the nails home, always adhering to the manufacturer's nailing schedule. There are a lot of holes for nails in most window flanges, and it's often unnecessary to fill them all.

Sealing the unit

With the window secured, cut a length of membrane long enough to start 4 in. above the window and extend below to cover the membrane at the sill. Run this piece over the side flanges, starting about 4 in. above the top of the window. To do this without adhering the membrane where you don't want it,

peel back about 6 in. of the backing and stick the top of the membrane where you want it. Then continue peeling the release paper from behind, aligning the membrane with the edge of the window as you go. **5**

Run a piece of membrane across the top of the window, lapping the upper flange and the two vertical pieces of membrane you just installed along the sides of the window. **6** Fold the tar paper on the sides and top over the membrane and staple the paper. Membranes are self-healing and won't leak around the staples. **7** Then seal the cuts in the building paper at the top and bottom of the window with additional membrane. **8**

2 Lock the window shut so it holds its shape and set it in the opening, bottom first.

3 Hold the window in place with one or two loosely driven 2-in. galvanized roofing nails.

5 Cut membrane for the sides. Peel and stick 6 in. at the top of the window, then peel and align the membrane down along the flange.

6 Lap the window's upper flange and the two side pieces of membrane with membrane across the top.

7 Fold the tar paper back over the membrane and secure it with staples.

8 Seal diagonal cuts in the tar paper with membrane. If using housewrap, apply the manufacturer's tape.

TRADE SECRET
In high-wind areas, you can take the additional step of taping the building paper to the window flange. Cut the building paper so its edge is about 1 in. away from the edge of the window and lapping the flange. Use adhesive membrane or housewrap tape.

SEALING AND SHIMMING WINDOWS

FOAM GUNS

Foam guns are awesome for sealing around windows and doors. They use essentially the same foam as you've seen in home centers, the cans with the screw-on cap and straw dispenser. The trouble with the cans is twofold. First, once you start using a can of foam, you have to finish it, or the remaining foam will harden inside the can within days. Second, it's impossible to stop the flow of foam exactly when you want to.

Foam guns take care of both issues, but always leave a can of foam on the gun. It won't harden for a month or longer. If you take the can off without replacing it, the foam within the gun will harden and the gun will be ruined. The flow of foam can be started and stopped with precision, and the amount of flow can be easily metered. Foam guns use special cans of foam, which are available from a variety of online sources and from well-stocked lumberyards. Foam guns come in a range of prices. The cheaper ones are well worth it, even if you're only sealing the windows and doors in a single addition.

1 With vinyl windows, fill large cavities with closed-cell foam backer rod.

2 Caulk over the backer rod to complete the window seal.

Once you've finished outside, go inside to finish your window installation. For vinyl flanged windows, this means sealing the cavity around the window (with foam or caulk), and for wood units, it means shimming and sealing.

Shimming is important. If the jambs bow out, the window won't seal well. If the jambs bow in, it will be difficult to operate. Sealing prevents air flow, which can cause significant heat loss, as well as allow interior moisture to condense in the cavity in the winter. That's why you want to use foam or caulk, not fiberglass insulation. Fiberglass may be good insulation, but it's lousy at stopping air flow. Sealing a window also creates a dead air space on the exterior that tends to stay at the same air pressure as outside. That helps prevent air-pressure differentials during storms from sucking rain water in behind the window. Don't use silicone caulk. No paint will stick to it.

Finishing vinyl windows

To seal the interior of a vinyl window, you can use disposable cans of foam that come with their own applicator straw, but they're harder to control than a foam gun.

Be certain to use minimal-expansion foam. High-expansion foam can put enough pressure on the jambs to make the windows inoperable. Some manufacturers (mostly of inexpensive vinyl windows) void their warranty if any foam is used. When the window manufacturer forbids foam, use caulk. So you don't have to fill the entire opening with caulk, first insert closed-cell foam backer rod, then caulk on top of it. **1**, **2**

Finishing windows with extension jambs

Windows, such as the ones in the photos on the facing page, can be ordered with factory-installed extension jambs. The ones shown here are made from fiberglass on the outside, but the extension jambs are wood. Manufacturers also offer wood windows clad with vinyl or aluminum that have wood extension jambs. They install just like the fiberglass units shown here.

Hold a level against the side jamb, and add shims as needed to make the jamb straight. **1** Depending on the height of the window, shims will usually be needed in one or two spots on each jamb. Fasten the inside of the window by nailing through the extension jamb with 8d finish nails. **2**

→ See "Installing Extension Jambs and Stools," p. 220.

Score the shims with a knife, then snap them off flush with the studs. **3**, **4** Finally, seal the cavity around the window with foam. **5**

1 For wood windows, set a 4-ft. level against the jamb and insert shims to keep the jambs straight.

2 Nail through the jambs and shims into the framing.

3 Use the jamb as a guide to cut partway through the top shims with a sharp knife.

4 Pull the top shim toward the inside of the window to snap it along the cut. Cut and snap the remaining shims.

5 Air-seal the jamb to the framing with low-expansion foam.

BIG WINDOWS

Not all windows are single units easily handled by one or two people. Mulled (joined together) units can run several hundred pounds. Installing them can be tough on the ground floor, never mind higher up. The trick is to have help and to remove the sashes, which account for most of the weight. Place the frame in the opening, reinstall the sashes, and finish the installation.

Sometimes even a small window can be awkward to get up a ladder. In that case, and with a high window, work with one or two helpers inside. Have them maneuver the unit sideways through its opening, then straighten and place it while you attend to the fastening.

Remove the sashes to lighten big windows for installation.

INSTALLING A PREHUNG EXTERIOR DOOR

Doors get more attention than windows. This is because, as I learned from my carpentry mentor, "All doors leak." I've never regretted acting on that assumption.

Doors leak because on the latch side, they are only secured in the center, at the latch. Wind pressure can move the top or bottom of the latch side, admitting rain. In addition, the proximity of the bottom of the door to the ground makes it subject to backsplashes and drifting snow. Unless a door will be well sheltered by a roof, I always make a sill pan with an integral dam to go between the framing and the door sill.

Making a sill pan

To make a sill pan, cut a piece of 12-in. metal flashing–aluminum coil stock, copper, or galvanized–1 ft. wider than the door opening. ❶ Measure how far the door sill extends inside the exterior trim, add 1 in., and mark this dimension from the rear edge on each end of the flashing. ❷ At the same time, make a mark at 1 in. from the rear edge. Align the 1-in. marks with the face of a sheet-metal brake and make a 90-degree bend. This flap will extend up just inside the door sill as a dam. ❸

> **See "Siding Brakes," p. 197.**

Release the bent flashing from the brake, flip it over, and make a 90-degree bend in the opposite direction at the sill-depth marks you made. ❹ This flap will hang down over the building paper below the sill.

Mark the two flaps at 6 in. from each end, and cut the flaps at these points with snips. ❺ Bend the ends of the pan up. ❻

Cut the tar paper at the top and sides of the opening as you would for a window, fold the tar paper back out of your way, and staple the flaps. Flash the door sill with adhesive membrane, just as you would a window, treating the corners with a bow tie, an unreinforced membrane, or a pre-made corner. ❼

> **See "Flashing the Sills," p. 132.**

Insert the pan in the sill opening atop the membrane and nail it in place with roofing nails. ❽ Using urethane or butyl caulk, seal the holes in the back corners created by the fold. ❾ >> >> >>

1 Use snips to cut sheet metal for a sill pan about a foot longer than the width of the door opening.

4 Flip the sheet in the brake and align the sill-depth marks for the bend. This flap will lap the tar paper or flashing below the opening.

7 Cut and move the tar paper flaps out of your way. Cover the rough sill with membrane and detail the corners as you would a window.

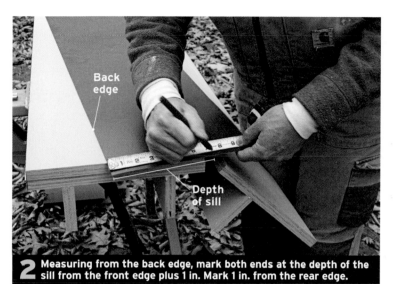

2 Measuring from the back edge, mark both ends at the depth of the sill from the front edge plus 1 in. Mark 1 in. from the rear edge.

3 Insert the sheet in the brake and align the 1-in. marks for the bend. Bend the sheet, creating a back dam.

5 Snip both flaps at 6 in. from the ends. The distance between the cuts should be equal to or slightly smaller than the rough opening.

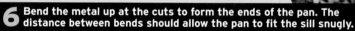

6 Bend the metal up at the cuts to form the ends of the pan. The distance between bends should allow the pan to fit the sill snugly.

8 Use roofing nails to secure the pan in the opening. The self-healing membrane will prevent leaks around the nails.

9 There's always a small hole at the folded back corner of a sill pan. Seal it with urethane or butyl caulk, not silicone.

INSTALLING A PREHUNG EXTERIOR DOOR (CONTINUED)

Sealing doors (and cased windows)

Except for patio doors, which generally have flanges, exterior doors come trimmed with brick molding or some sort of 5/4 flat exterior casing. Older-style windows or custom units can also come with this sort of casing. Using the techniques shown here, seal and flash these window units just like a door.

First, check the top of the sill pan for level. If need be, add shims to create a level base. ❶ If you don't get the sill level, there's no way you'll get the door plumb and square. Caulk below the shim before setting it permanently, then nail it in place so it doesn't move when you set the door.

Because there are no flanges to seal with adhesive membrane, cased doors and windows require a different approach. Some carpenters bed the casing in caulk, and I'll do this on a well-sheltered unit. When there's any chance of wind-blown rain, though, I take a different approach.

Cut a piece of adhesive membrane about 4 in. longer than the opening is tall. Slit the release paper along its length about 2 in. from one edge, being careful not to cut into the membrane itself. This takes a delicate touch and a sharp blade. ❷

Leaving the 2-in. backing strip in place and allowing it to overhang into the door opening, remove about 4 in. of backing from the wider side and adhere the membrane at the top of the opening. Then adhere the wider section down the opening, peeling away the backing as you go. ❸

Once the membrane is adhered to the wall, fold the 2-in. section back over the membrane and staple it through the release paper. ❹ Then remove the 2-in. backing, exposing the sticky side. ❺ Do this on both sides of the opening, and along the top. The back of the unit's casing will adhere to this, making a good seal. >> >> >>

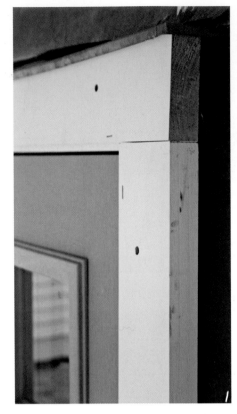

Doors and windows with flat casing (left) or brick molding (right) require different installation techniques than flanged units.

Patio doors Sliders and patio doors usually have flanges, like windows. Installing them is a hybrid operation. Install a sill pan as you would for a door, but otherwise flash them like flanged windows.

Because of the great weight of the door panels, these units aren't installed as one piece. Install the frame first, carefully keeping it plumb and level. Then lift the sliding pane into the frame according to the manufacturer's instructions.

1 Place shims atop the sill pan to level the framing. If the sill is not level, setting the door plumb and square will prove impossible.

2 Slit the backing down its length about 2 in. from the edge. Use a sharp blade and don't cut through the membrane itself.

3 With the 2-in. backing in place, stick the membrane so the slit in the paper more or less aligns with the edge of the opening.

4 Fold the 2-in. flap of membrane back and staple it to the wall through the release paper.

5 Remove the 2-in. strip of release paper shortly before installing the unit.

TRADE SECRET

Very often, a sagging door can be fixed by removing the screws from the top hinge farthest from the hinge pins and replacing them with longer ones that penetrate the framing.

INSTALLING A PREHUNG EXTERIOR DOOR (CONTINUED)

Installing the door and frame

With the sill pan and the flashing membranes in place, the final task in sealing a door is to run a thick bead of urethane or butyl caulk along the back of the pan to seal the sill. ❶ Although the pan does a good job keeping water from the framing, the caulk is needed to stop air infiltration. Remove all the packing material from the unit except for the clip at the latch hole.

Set the door in the opening, sill first. To keep from smearing the caulk, tilt the unit and move it into the door frame tilted until the inside bottom edge of the casing hits the pan. Then push the unit in the opening until the casing contacts the walls. ❷

Drive one 16d galvanized finish nail most of the way through the casing into the framing near the upper hinge. ❸ Then check the unit for plumb. ❹ Adjust it as needed by moving the bottom of the unit to one side or the other, then finish nailing off the casing. If the manufacturer doesn't have a specific nailing schedule, I use about one 16d finish nail every 16 in.

Remove the latch clip. From the inside, shim the cavity behind the upper hinge, and drive two long screws through its inner holes. ❺ Usually, doors are shipped with these screws missing and the holes predrilled. Predrill these holes if they don't come that way, to avoid splitting the jamb. These screws are usually supplied, but if they aren't, use #10 by 2½-in. or 3-in. screws. For very heavy doors, I've used 4-in. or 4½-in. screws. This is a crucial step, as most of the weight of the door hangs from this hinge. If it's not secured to the framing, the door will certainly sag with time. Add shims just below the other hinges as well, securing them with 8d or 10d finish nails through the jamb. ❻ Some doors call for long screws through these other hinges as well.

Shim behind the latch and dead-bolt plates, using the supplied screws. ❼ The latch holes in the jamb weaken the jamb. Some doors come with a reinforcing plate here. Whether or not there is reinforcement, long screws that penetrate the framing here will reduce the chance of the door falling prey to a well-placed boot.

Close the door, and check to see that the gap along the hinge side is even. If it's not, add shims where needed. Finish the installation by installing a drip cap. This is a simple, Z-shaped piece of sheet metal you can bend on site to fit the thickness of the door casing. It's also readily available in most lumberyards, although typically in aluminum, not copper, as shown here.

Cut the drip cap a couple of inches longer than the head casing. Carefully snip along the creases to allow the front of the cap to fold in and the middle of the cap to fold down at the ends. ❽, ❾ Measure carefully, and the cap should fit snugly around the head casing. Trim the building paper to fit closely to the casing on the sides and fold it over the drip cap above. ❿ Seal the corner and bottom cuts in the building paper with pieces of membrane. ⓫

1 Air-seal the door sill by laying down a thick bead of caulk along the pan.

2 To avoid smearing the caulk, tilt the unit as you place it. When the back of the casing contacts the framing, push it home.

3 Tack the unit in place with one nail through the casing or brick molding near the upper hinge.

4 Check for plumb, adjusting the bottom of the unit side-to-side as needed.

5 Shim behind the top hinge and secure the unit to the framing with long screws.

6 Shim just below each hinge and nail into the framing through the jamb and shims.

7 Shim the latch jamb straight and behind the latch and dead-bolt holes.

8 Cut the drip cap long and snip the corners as on a sill pan.

9 Fold the drip cap down to create ends at the frame and set the drip cap in place.

10 Fold the building paper over the top flange of the drip cap and tight against the wall. Secure with roofing nails.

11 Use pieces of adhesive membrane to seal the diagonal cuts in the building paper.

NEW WINDOWS AND DOORS IN AN OLD HOUSE

When changing out an old door or window, my goal is usually to replace the old unit without having to cut the existing siding (which is often brittle and covered with lead paint), while at the same time installing a modern flashing system that extends behind it.

Removing the old unit

If the existing paint is in good condition (unlike the peeling paint in the photos), cut the caulk and the paint in the joint between the siding and the trim with a utility knife. That way, pulling out the old unit won't chip the siding. Take the sashes out of the old unit first. Often, this is accomplished from the inside by removing the stops that hold the sashes in place. Be brutal—you aren't saving the unit.

Once the sashes are out, remove the interior trim. (If you want to save it for re-use, carefully drive the nails through with a $\frac{1}{32}$-in. nailset.) Remove the exterior casing with a pry bar. In many cases, once the casing is removed, the old jambs will simply push out. If not, cut a side jamb in half with a reciprocating saw, then pull the jamb out one piece at a time. Take appropriate precautions if you suspect lead paint is present.

Once the old unit is out, slide a fine-toothed metal-cutting blade in a reciprocating saw between the siding and the sheathing and cut any siding nails within 6 in. of the opening. ❶ This will allow aluminum coil stock to slip behind the siding as the base for the new flashing.

If the reciprocating saw damages the siding, cut the nails with a hacksaw blade held in your hand. That's a lot slower, but it's way faster than trying to match or patch 200-year-old clapboards.

To flash the sill, start with a piece of membrane that covers the sill and extends to the edge of the siding. Extend this membrane onto the siding below, but don't go any lower than the trim will cover. Treat the corners as you would a new window. ❷ Cut two legs of coil stock wide enough to extend from the edge of the window or door opening under the siding at least 4 in. Make them long enough to cover the sill membrane and extend 4 in. above the opening. Slip them under the siding, making sure they cover the sheathing edge. ❸ Once the legs are done, slide as wide a piece of coil stock as will fit behind the siding above the opening, lapping the two legs. ❹ It's often easiest to do this with two pieces long enough for a generous center overlap.

➔ See "Detailing the Corners," p. 134.

Installing the new unit

Install the window without its exterior trim, as centered in the opening as possible, and secure it with nails through the jambs. Keep the jambs flush with the face of the coil stock, even if that kicks the unit out of plumb. In old houses, plumb and level isn't as important as how they fit to the existing structure.

1 With the old unit removed, cut the nails behind the siding with a reciprocating saw and a fine-toothed metal-cutting blade.

2 Flash the sill as on a new unit, bringing it onto the siding below, but high enough that trim or the next siding course will cover it.

Cut membrane legs to the length of the coil stock, but with one edge of each leg about 2 in. from the slit in the backing. With the 2-in. backing toward the siding, apply the legs to the face of the coil stock. Peel and adhere about 6 in. at the top and line up the membrane edge with the inside edge of the coil stock, pulling off the wide part of the baking as you go.

➔ See "Sealing Doors (and Cased Windows)," p. 142.

Then fold the 2-in. side of the membrane over so the sticky side will face out and peel away the backing. ❺ Repeat these steps on the other side and across the top. ❻

End-prime the exposed siding. Then rip the casing to fit from the edge of the window frame to the siding and nail it in place with galvanized or stainless-steel finish nails. ❼ Old siding can be brittle, so predrilling holes to prevent nails from splitting the siding is a good idea. Finally, install a drip cap that slips as far as you can manage behind the siding above the unit. ❽

3 Slide metal flashing under the old siding, covering the edge of the sheathing.

4 Slide metal flashing under the siding above so it covers the flashing legs.

5 Apply membrane to the flashings, folding its outer edge, sticky side out.

6 Keep the exposed sticky side close to where the top of the casing will be.

7 End-prime the siding, rip the trim to fit against the siding, and nail it in place.

8 Slip a drip cap well under the siding above the unit.

Lead paint For centuries, painters have known that lead makes paint better. Lead paint was commonly used on houses until it was banned in 1978. According to the fellow who taught the EPA lead-safety class I took, it wouldn't be unusual for a Victorian-era house to have half a ton of lead in its exterior paint.

Lead paint can cling more or less harmlessly on a wall for decades—even a century—but start working on that wall, and you may generate a cloud of toxic dust. Lead dust can cause neurological problems and reduced intelligence, particularly in children. Children living in homes undergoing remodeling have been poisoned by construction dust. Children of remodeling carpenters have been poisoned by lead dust from their fathers' work clothes. Replacing doors or windows in older houses requires some knowledge of lead safety.

In April 2010, the EPA began requiring certification for contractors working on houses built before 1978. Contractors working on such homes must follow safe practices, including testing for lead, sealing off work areas, and cleaning up with a HEPA vacuum and damp wipes.

The same rules don't apply to DIYers, but smart ones will follow lead-safe work practices anyway. Lead dust from DIY remodeling is no less toxic than lead dust from professional remodeling. The certification class is 8 hours long, so the particulars are beyond the scope of this book. However, most of the details can be found at www.epa.gov/lead.

ROOFING

T HE RANGE OF ROOFING MATERIALS is staggering. It includes asphalt shingles, clay tile, concrete tile, metal, slate, fake slate, and wood shingles, as well as various rubber, hot-mopped asphalt, and fiberglass systems used on low-slope or flat roofs. All of them, properly installed, keep out water and stay on the roof through severe winds. However, the vast majority (about 80 percent of American houses according to my quick and unsubstantiated research) are topped with asphalt shingles, and they'll be the primary focus of this chapter.

Roofing goes on in layers, and although it's easier to understand the installation of each material by discussing it separately, you'll install the materials in sequenced courses. Once you've completed a sequence, you'll move your safety supports up the roof and begin another. Read the entire chapter before proceeding with a roofing job.

ROOFING MATERIALS

Three-tab shingles resemble roofing slates and have to be lined up precisely.

Architectural shingles look more like wood shingles and install in an easy, random pattern.

Asphalt patches adhere to overlying shingles to provide wind resistance.

Step flashing consists of sheet metal pieces intended to shed water where the roof meets a vertical surface like a wall or chimney.

Drip edge extends beyond the trim to support the shingles and carry rainwater past the front of the rake or fascia.

There are two main types of asphalt shingles—three-tab and architectural. Three-tab shingles emulate roofing slates, but architectural shingles create a random wood-shake look. They also tend to be thicker, heavier, and more costly (which buys a longer warranty), but they're easier to install and waste less. Small patches of asphalt adhesive across the middle of each shingle adhere succeeding courses to those already installed. The adhesive goes to work once the sun warms it up, sealing the shingles together to resist wind.

If your roof intersects with a vertical surface, like a wall, dormer, or chimney, you'll need flashing—sheet metal used to direct runoff down the wall and across the top of each course of shingles where they meet the wall.

In addition, there is drip edge and underlayment. Drip edge is pre-bent sheet metal that supports the ends of the shingles an inch or so beyond the roof. It folds down onto the fascia, then kicks out slightly at the bottom so that runoff will drip into space, rather than down the fascia. It's available in powder-coated aluminum (probably used on 90 percent of the roofs in America), galvanized steel, copper, and a hybrid of copper laminated to an aluminum backing made by York® Manufacturing.

The most common underlayment is tar paper, although in cold climates the building code requires an adhesive ice barrier membrane, which most carpenters refer to as "ice and water," after the Ice & Water Shield® manufactured by Grace Construction Products®. Grace had the first popular version of this material, but there are many similar products available.

The original purpose of ice barrier was to prevent water backed up by an ice dam from leaking into the house, but it's now used as a backup anywhere prone to leaks. Ice barrier is thicker and far tougher than tar paper. The bottom is coated with an adhesive, which is covered with a plastic release film. The top is available uncoated or coated with a sandy mineral compound. I prefer the uncoated membrane. The minerals always loosen and can be slippery underfoot.

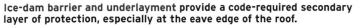

Ice-dam barrier and underlayment provide a code-required secondary layer of protection, especially at the eave edge of the roof.

Apply ice barrier by rolling it into position, then removing the release membrane from below to expose the adhesive.

STORING AND LIFTING SHINGLES

If you store shingles in too hot a place, the asphalt adhesive beads will stick the shingles together. During the warm months, store shingles in the shade and carry them to the roof when needed. In the winter, cold shingles become stiff, so I store them in a sunny spot.

The hardest part of roofing is getting the shingles from the ground to the roof. Production roofers, who'll blast out a roof in a day, often have them boomed up to the ridge by the delivery truck. I'm slower than that, and only want what I can install that day on the roof. Consequently, I often end up carrying them up the ladder. A bundle of shingles weighs at least 70 lb., so with some of the heavier architectural shingles, I carry only half a bundle at a time. Alternatively, I hire a younger laborer whose back is less creaky than mine, or I rent a power ladder.

Ordering shingles Shingles are sold in bundles, each typically containing one-third of a square. One square equals 100 sq. ft. So, a conversation with the lumberyard might sound like this: "Send 24 and a third squares of 40-year (that's the warranty period) black architecturals."

Measure for starters, caps, drip edge, and flashing—if the shingle abuts a wall, you need one piece of step flashing for every 5 in. of wall length measured along the roof.

Always order extra. The color of extras you get next week might not match. Five percent extra is plenty for a straight gable roof and more than enough for architectural shingles. A roof with a lot of hips, valleys, and dormers might take 20 percent more. If you're not sure, ask the supplier to send a salesman. That puts the ball in their court if you end up short or with a big overage.

DRIP EDGE, ICE BARRIER, AND UNDERLAYMENT

The first stuff to go on a roof is the drip edge on the eaves. Drip edge comes in 10-ft. lengths, so most roofs require several pieces. The joint is a simple overlap, but there is a consideration. Any time you overlap building materials, be it drip edge, a long drip cap, aluminum fascia cover, or vinyl siding, think about the direction from which it will be viewed most often. If the piece closest to the viewer laps the one farther away, the joint will be nearly invisible. Lap it the other way, and it's a sore thumb.

Installing drip edge on the eaves

Working on scaffolding, start the drip edge at the end of the roof farthest from the usual view point, extending the end past the roof sheathing on the rake edge by about 1 in. ❶ This extension will become one side of the joined corner with the drip edge on the rake.

➡ See "Joining Drip Edge," p. 156.

Begin fastening drip edge with roofing nails. You only need two or three nails at this point—you'll use a lot more when you lay the starter course of shingles. Lap the second piece over the first, extending it past the roof edge here as well. Continue nailing to the end. ❷ Trim the drip edge to an extension of about 1 in. ❸

Installing the ice barrier

Next is the ice barrier. You can roll out the entire edge of the roof at once, but I find it easier to work in roughly 10-ft. lengths.

Leaving the backing in place, roll out the first piece, lined up with the leading edge of the drip edge. ❹ On steep roofs, you might need to keep the membrane in place with a couple of staples. In any case, remove the backing and smooth the barrier as you go. ❺ Then repeat this step with the second piece, lapping it over the first by about 6 in.–more if the manufacturer says to.

In cold climates, the IRC requires ice barrier to extend at least 2 ft. past the inside of the wall. Ice barrier comes in a 3-ft. width, so with wider overhangs, you'll need two courses to extend that far up the roof. In high-wind areas it's also a good idea to install ice barrier at roof/wall intersections, extending it up the wall. >> >> >>

Viewed one way (left), a lap in the drip edge is hard to see. Viewed the other way (right), the lap is obvious.

SEQUENCE MATTERS

Underlayment

Drip edge goes over underlayment on the rake.

Shingles

Ice barrier

Starter shingles

Drip edge goes beneath underlayment on the eaves.

TRADE SECRET

If you're involved in a major rehab job that includes new vents, run them through the roof before roofing. That way they'll be ready for you to install the vent boots.

Approx. 1" to edge of roof sheathing

1 Nail the first section of drip edge on the eaves, running the end past the roof edge to allow for the corner joint.

2 Nail the subsequent sections of drip edge every couple of feet and allow the end of the last piece to run long.

3 At the roof edge, trim the drip edge to length, leaving an overhang of about 1 in.

4 Roll out the ice barrier, leaving its release membrane in place.

TRADE SECRET

I prefer the kind of ice barrier material without a mineral surface. I find it provides better traction. This may seem counterintuitive, until you realize the mineral grains aren't that well adhered. Stepping on mineral-surfaced ice barrier isn't as slippery as loose sand, but the comparison isn't wholly inaccurate.

5 Position the edge of the ice barrier along the drip edge and pull the release membrane from behind the ice barrier.

At a wall, run ice barrier up the wall for additional protection.

DRIP EDGE, ICE BARRIER, AND UNDERLAYMENT (CONTINUED)

6 Staple the first course of tar paper even with the drip edge. Lap succeeding layers and install 3 courses in one sequence.

7 Fashion the drip-edge corners and nail the first piece of rake drip edge over the tar paper.

8 Overlap the first section of drip edge with the second and nail it in place.

At a wall, run the tar paper up 3 in. or more. It backs up the flashing and will be lapped by the tar paper and siding you'll install on the wall.

Installing underlayment

Underlayment has two purposes. First, it provides a layer of insurance against leaks. Second, it allows you to cover the roof quickly with something that will keep out the rain—simply staple it down. It used to be that all roofing underlayment was simply tar paper. That's not so anymore, although most of the time, tar paper is what's used. It's cheap and usually does the job.

On low-slope roofs, 2 to 4 pitch, depending on the shingle manufacturer, you may have to install a double layer under the shingles. I usually forego that and cover the whole roof with ice barrier instead. (Roofs shallower than a 2 pitch aren't common and require specialized roofing that's beyond the scope of this book.)

Tar paper can become troublesome on steep roofs or if you need to leave it in place for a long time before shingling. It tears around the staples and can blow off in a good wind. Worse, on steep roofs, when you step on the tar paper, it can come loose. That's an excitement you don't need. I've had that happen on roofs as shallow as a 6 pitch. The solution is to use a reinforced underlayment. There are several on the market, and they're far less likely to tear.

Whether using tar paper or reinforced underlayment, roll out the first course of material, square and trim it flush to the roof sheathing at the rake edges, lap it over the ice barrier by at least 3 in., and staple it down. **6** Staple the edges every 6 in. to 12 in., and every 18 in. or so in the field. If

it's windy, use more staples and always be cautious when you step. Then install subsequent layers.

I usually run three courses of tar paper at a time. That way, I'm not too far above my roof scaffolds, and a 10-ft. piece of drip edge, which on the rake goes over the tar paper, neatly covers up that amount. At adjacent walls, run the tar paper up by 3 in. or more.

Installing drip edge on the rakes

As mentioned above, the drip edge on the rake goes on after you tar paper the roof. The best reason I've heard for this is so the drip edge can secure the end of the tar paper against wind. If you're using drip edge with guttering, make sure the rear panel of the gutter goes behind the drip edge.

MOVING UP

When installing roofing, work as far up from your roof scaffolds as you can comfortably reach—three underlayment courses is an average amount. Then install rake drip edge and as many shingle courses as fall within your reach.

When you feel you're stretching too far, install another set of roof scaffolds and repeat the installation sequence from there. Continue this process to the peak.

Running no more than three courses of tar paper at a time keeps them reachable from one roof scaffold.

WHAT CAN GO WRONG

Cold weather requires some caution. It's impossible to stand on any sort of pitched roof that has frost on it. Don't even try. Wait until the sun melts the frost. And it should be self-evident, but if there's snow or ice on the roof, well, I recommend the Caribbean until the frozen stuff melts.

Watch the weather If it's a hot day on the ground, it'll be a lot hotter on the roof. Asphalt shingles soften in the heat, and up to a point, that makes them easier to work. But the sun can make them so soft that standing on them causes damage. Soft-soled shoes help, but you need to get off the roof if your shoes begin to damage the shingles.

On hot days, start as early as the neighbors will let you. I've been on roofs as soon as it was light enough to work and off those roofs by 10 A.M. When the sun moves to the far side of the house, you may be able to get up there in the afternoon, but the residual heat of the day can keep shingles too soft to walk on for hours.

Before you install the rake drip edge, however, you need to fashion the drip edge corners with the following steps:
• Cut and fold the eaves drip edge.
• Cut and fold the bottom of the rake drip edge.
• Push the corners together.

→ **See "Joining Drip Edge," p. 156.**

Once you've made the corner, install the first section of drip edge on the rakes. ❼ Then install additional tar paper courses and succeeding pieces of drip edge. Nail these sections, overlapping the preceding ones. ❽ Form the joints at the ridge.

DRIP EDGE WITH GUTTERING

With guttering, make sure the rear panel of the gutter goes behind the drip edge so runoff drains in the gutter and stays off the fascia.

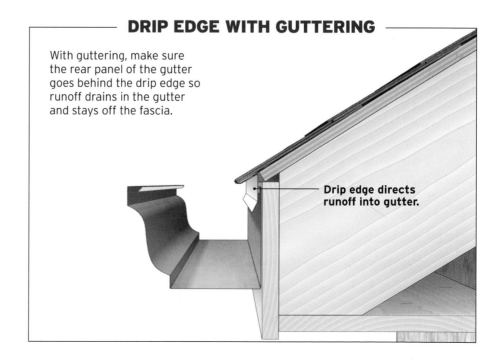

Drip edge directs runoff into gutter.

JOINING DRIP EDGE

To put the finishing touches on drip edge, you'll have to make two joints—where the rake meets the eaves and at the peak. The eaves joint is trickier. The good news is that these joints don't need to look perfect. Frankly, they're usually 20 ft. or 30 ft. in the air. Perfection at that height isn't visible from the ground. What's important to remember is to fashion the eaves joint before you install the first piece of drip edge on the rake.

Place the drip edge on the rake with its bottom edge touching the eaves drip edge. On the eaves drip edge, mark the intersection of the two pieces. ❶ Remove the rake drip edge and on the eaves drip edge, use snips to cut the front fold back to your mark. ❷ Fold the rectangular face back against the rake board, and pinch the angled

section to close it up. ❸ Repeat those cuts and folds on the rake drip edge. ❹ Merge the folds of the rake drip edge in the eaves drip edge. ❺ Then push the metal tight together. ❻ Nail the rake drip edge in place.

The peak is much easier. Simply run the first piece of drip edge past the peak, slit the face, and fold the other side down. And when your roof features a valley, extend the drip edge and ice barrier into and across the valley.

➤ **See "Roofing Valleys," p. 172.**

DRIP EDGE AT THE PEAKS AND VALLEYS

To join drip edge at the peak of a roof, eyeball the joint at the peak of the fascia and cut a slit in the front of the drip edge along that line.

Then simply fold the drip edge over the peak. Don't make the notch very big—leave enough material so that when you make the fold, some of one side of the drip-edge face slips behind the other.

At valleys, extend the drip edge into and across the valley then install the ice barrier across the valley also.

Cut a slight notch in the drip edge at the peak.

Fold the unfastened leg of the drip edge down on the roof surface.

When a dormer meets a main roof, extend the drip edge into the valley.

Run the ice barrier membrane over the drip edge and into the valley.

1 On the back face of the eaves drip edge, mark the point where it intersects with the rake drip edge.

2 Using sharp tin snips, cut the eaves drip edge up to the mark you made.

3 Fold the rectangular face of the eaves drip edge back against the rake and the triangular section up against the top.

4 Set the first section of rake drip edge in place and cut and fold the rake drip edge the same as the eaves corner.

5 Insert the cut tabs of the rake drip edge into those of the eaves drip edge.

6 Push the corner sections together for a tight joint and nail the rake drip edge over the tar paper.

LAYING OUT SHINGLES

1 Strike a chalkline along the eaves to align the first course.

2 Snap a line up the center of the roof to line up the correct offset for three-tabs.

3 Adjusted guidelines keep three-tabs aligned and end tab from being too small.

Top to bottom, three-tab and architectural shingles lay out the same way. Side-to-side, their layout is different. With architectural shingles the pattern is random, so the starting and stopping points are irrelevant, as long as the shingles at the edges are at least 6 in. long. With architecturals, apart from paying attention to the last shingle length, the primary layout concern is keeping the courses straight and spaced evenly on horizontal lines.

Three-tabs, however, have a regular pattern. First, the notches, or keys, of the odd-numbered courses should line up with each other up the roof, and the keys of even-numbered courses should line up with each other also. Second, the keys of each course should fall at the halfway point of the tabs in the course below and above it. And finally, you might want to cut the tabs at the ends of the roof to the same size. This isn't strictly necessary, as few people pay that close attention to roofs, but it's a nice touch. And even if they aren't quite the same size, the shingle ends should never be less than 2 in. wide. So in addition to keeping three tabs straight on the horizontal, you must keep their offset consistent across the roof.

Laying out the horizontals

To keep the courses straight on the horizontal, you'll have to snap chalklines as controls across the roof, starting at the first course and at the top of every few courses thereafter. **❶** The lines will serve as checkpoints, and between the lines you'll use the course below to align succeeding courses.

The first chalkline acts as a guide for locating the top of the first course and needs to account for the ½-in. to ¾-in. overhang beyond the drip edge. I like the longer overhang, so I begin by snapping a chalkline 11¼ in. up from the drip edge. Most shingles are 12 in. deep from top to bottom, so aligning the tops of the first course with a chalkline that's 11¼ in. up provides that ¾-in. overhang. If your shingles are a different depth, subtract ¾ in. from that depth and mark both ends of the roof at that dimension. Then snap your first chalkline between the points. (In our illustration, starter shingles are not installed. If this is your first roof, install the starters after snapping the chalklines.)

Laying out the three-tab offsets

To get an even layout, mark the center of the roof at the top and bottom and snap a chalkline. **❷** Measure over from the center to within 1 ft. of the rake edge to see how the shingles would work if the layout began with the edge of the shingle on the center-line. Since each tab is 12 in., the whole-foot measurement nearest to the edge of the roof represents where the last key of a course of shingles centered on the roof would fall.

If the amount of roof left beyond the end of your measuring tape is 2 in. or more, mark that point—a course started at the center of the roof will be good. Measure over, again from the center, an additional 6 in. to check where the keys of the courses above and below will fall. Again, if your measurement indicates that the cut tabs at the rake will be longer than 2 in., it's good. Mark that point as well.

If either measurement indicates that your tabs will be shorter than 2 in., snap a line parallel to and 3 in. (a quarter a tab width) to either side of the center line. Check the layout from this new line as you did from the center line. It should now result in tabs at the rake wider than 2 in. Double-check this layout on the opposite edge of the roof.

Go back to the marks you made by the rake and from each snap lines parallel to the rake and 2 ft. toward the center of the roof from those marks. These are gauge lines to locate the edges of the first shingles in alternating courses. **❸**

As you shingle the roof, the edge of a shingle or the center of a key of every course should land on one of these lines in an alternating pattern.

LAYING OUT SHINGLES

For both architectural and three-tab shingles, keep the top-to-bottom spacing consistent between courses by striking horizontal lines every several courses. For three-tabs, keep the keys in line by snapping a pair of chalklines from eaves to ridge. The first line locates the end of the first shingle in the first and all the odd-numbered courses. The second line is 6 in. closer to the rake and locates the end of the first shingle in the second and all the even-numbered courses.

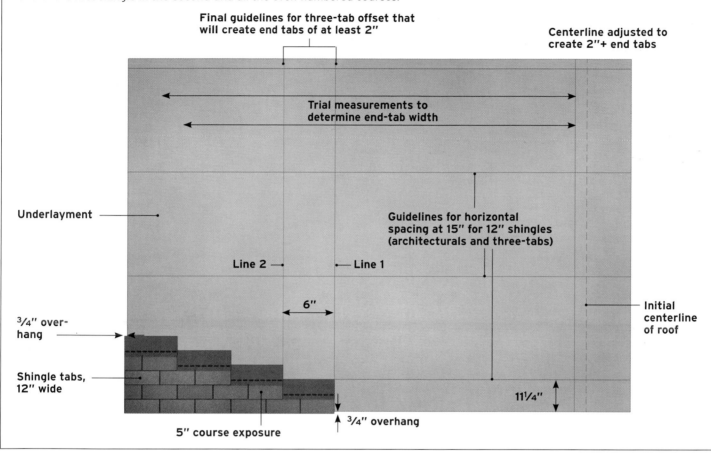

Final guidelines for three-tab offset that will create end tabs of at least 2"

Centerline adjusted to create 2"+ end tabs

Trial measurements to determine end-tab width

Underlayment

Guidelines for horizontal spacing at 15" for 12" shingles (architecturals and three-tabs)

Line 2 → ← Line 1

Initial centerline of roof

6"

¾" over-hang

Shingle tabs, 12" wide

¾" overhang

11¼"

5" course exposure

Starter shingles will go on first, and you can use your guidelines to make sure the joints in the starters don't fall under the joints in the shingles. In other words, don't lay a starter shingle with its edge on one of your guidelines.

→ See "Installing the Starter Course," p. 160.

After the starters, you'll install the shingles. Where I begin depends on the roof configuration. If it runs from rake to rake with no intervening dormers, then I overhang the rake drip edge by ¾ in. with the first shingle and go, just making sure that the joints in the first course of shingles are offset from those in the starter course. If there's a wall, I'll usually start there and work toward the rakes. Also, if there's a dormer, you have to lay out the shingle courses so that they meet in a straight line above it.

→ See "Running Field Shingles," p. 161 and "Shingling around Obstructions," p. 165.

Proper nailing is crucial. There is always a line on the shingles showing the top of the nailing area. Sometimes there's also one that shows the bottom. Lacking the lower line, just keep the nails below the upper line and high enough on the shingle so they'll be covered by the next course.

Nail the shingles as directed by the manufacturer, who usually provides nailing lines.

INSTALLING THE STARTER COURSE

Shingles always require a starter course—a strip of un-tabbed shingles—under the first exposed course. The purpose of starters is twofold. First, they provide a layer of waterproofing below the joints in the first course of exposed shingles. And second, they provide wind resistance at the bottom edge of the first exposed course.

The nails that hold shingles to the roof go through the center of the shingles. Without some help, the bottom edge of shingles would literally flap in the breeze, and a stiff wind could get enough purchase on the shingle to blow it off. The asphalt adhesive patches on the starter strips hold the first course down and prevent this.

Making your own starters

You can buy manufactured starter shingles, but I usually make them from three-tab shingles, even when I'm going to install architectural shingles. (The starter course has to lie flat, and the varying thickness of architectural shingles makes them unsuitable for conversion into starters.)

To make your starter strips, use a straightedge and a utility knife to cut off the tabs. ❶ Use a scrap of plywood for a cutting board and cut from the back, or you'll quickly dull the blade.

Installing the starters

If you're going to install three-tabbed shingles, use your layout guidelines to make sure the edges of the first exposed course are offset from the starter edges by at least 6 in. Adjust the starter shingle accordingly. With architecturals, you can be safe by just starting with a full-length starter strip.

Align the starters, homemade or store-bought, over-hanging the front edge of the drip cap and nail them just above the asphalt strip with 4 roofing nails. ❷ Generally, the first nails should be within 1 in. to 2 in. of the shingle edge, and the center nails about 1 ft. from each edge. Do the same thing along the rake. ❸

1 Cut the tabs from three-tab shingles to make starter strips. Discard the tabs and install the uncut strip.

2 Drive nails close above the asphalt adhesive in locations where they won't be exposed by cutouts in the overlying shingles.

3 Set starter strips on the rake with the adhesive strip toward the edge and nail them up the rake as you did on the eaves.

RUNNING FIELD SHINGLES

Most of the rest of what you need to know about shingling is how to stagger the courses. My normal approach with both architecturals and three-tabs is to run several courses at once, working from a roof scaffold to the limits of my reach.

Offsetting three-tabs

I start the first course of three-tabs with two whole shingles. Start the second course with one half and one whole shingle, the third course with one whole shingle, and the fourth with one half shingle. This staggers the joints nicely, and I can nail on four courses of shingles from one spot. With three-tab shingles, this layout will continue all the way up the roof.

Staggering architecturals

With architectural shingles, it changes a little. Because of their randomness, you don't have to slavishly adhere to a layout when using architectural shingles. You can use the scrap from the end cuts to start the next courses, making sure that the width of your cut first shingle will stagger the joints between the remaining shingles adequately. You do have to pay attention to this. The joints between architectural shingles are easy to miss.

Unless you're adjusting the exposure (the amount of the shingle showing from the bottom edge up to the bottom edge of the next course) to hit the peak perfectly, shingles have a built-in mechanism to govern the exposure between your control lines. (In fact, a lot of tract-house roofers never snap control lines.) With three-tab shingles, you align the bottom of the shingle with the tops of the tabs below. With architecturals, set the bottom edge of the upper shingle along the top edge of the laminations in the shingle below.

You can leave the ends uncut until you've done the entire roof and run a chalkline to guide your cutoff with a hook-blade knife. Or you can mark the cutline on each shingle and cut it before nailing it.

Staggering the courses of shingles in a stair-step pattern allows you to move across the roof nailing several courses at a time.

Joints in architectural shingles are easy to miss. Pay attention to avoid placing the joints in one course too close to those in another.

ALIGNING SHINGLES

With three-tab shingles, align the bottom of the upper course at the top of the keys in the lower course.

With architectural shingles, set the bottom edge of the upper shingle along the top edge of the laminations in the shingle below.

SETTING SCAFFOLDS

Roof scaffolds are planks that rest in metal brackets nailed through the sheathing into the rafters. I set my first roof scaffolds as soon as working from a ground scaffold becomes too big a stretch.

Place the bracket on top of the current top row of shingles, with the plank support arm below the shingle exposure line. Nail through the elongated holes in the brackets with whatever size nail (typically 10d to 16d) the bracket manufacturer says to use. Set these nails pretty tight—they get shingled over and are permanent.

When using adjustable brackets, I set them just beyond level, so they pitch toward the roof. Place clear scaffolding planks on the brackets. Ensure they don't come off the brackets by nailing them in place. To remove the brackets, drive them upward with a hammer until the nail heads reach the wide part of the elongated slot, and lift the brackets off the nails.

Nail roof brackets through the sheathing and into the rafters below.

Use dedicated scaffold planks or clear framing lumber secured to brackets with nails.

PLUMBING VENTS

Vent boots consist of a neoprene dome laminated to a metal or plastic flange. The neoprene has a number of concentric circles stamped in it and can be torn or cut at these to fit various diameter pipes.

Shingle up to the pipe, notching the shingle around it. Open up the dome to the correct diameter and slip the boot over the pipe and the shingle below. Continue roofing over the boot's flange, cutting the shingles to fit and sealing the edges to the flange with roofing cement.

The rubber gasket on the vent boot should fit the pipe snugly.

Use a hook blade to cut the overlying shingle to fit the boot.

RIDGE CAPS

1 Align the cap shingles on a chalkline snapped 6 in. down from the center.

2 Install the ridge vent per the manufacturer's instructions.

3 Use the longer nails supplied with the ridge vent to secure the cap shingles.

4 Apply a bed of roof cement to seal the last cap shingle.

5 Cut the bottom 5 in. from a cap shingle for the final shingle.

6 Seal the nails through the final cap shingle with roofing cement.

Almost all roofs today get ridge vents. Like skylights, ridge vents are proprietary systems, but most have similarities. And most are capped with what are cleverly called "cap shingles," which lap the ridge, half on each side. Cap shingles can be bought as such, particularly for architectural shingle roofs. You can also make cap shingles for both architecturals and three-tabs by cutting three-tabs in thirds.

Snap a line along one side of the roof, 6 in. from the center of the ridge. This line is to keep the cap shingles straight. At each end of the roof, nail two cap shingles on, over-hanging the drip edge even with the shingles, using the nail lines as you did for whole shingles. Maintain the same 5-in. exposure, as well. **1**

Install the ridge vent according to the manufacturer's instructions. **2** Continue running the cap shingles over it using the longer nails supplied with the ridge vent. **3** Bring the caps in from both ends toward the middle, lapping the joint one full cap shingle. Trim about half of the upper section from another cap shingle. Nail it on and run two beads of roofing cement across it. **4**

Trim one more cap shingle to just the 5 in. that would normally be exposed, and nail it on. **5** Cover the exposed nail heads with roofing cement. **6** Hips get capped in the same way, except that hips never get vents, and you have to trim the top and bottom shingles at 45 degrees.

TRADE SECRET
For chalklines that might show, such as the cap shingle line, use blue chalk. It washes away. Red chalk does not. There is a red chalkline visible on the roof of my mother's house, which I re-shingled 25 years ago.

STEP FLASHING

Step flashing keeps water out of the joint between the roof and the wall.

Counter flashing covers lower layers such as step flashing when wooden siding is planned for a wall.

Because sheet-metal flashing material can be bent to a variety of shapes, it can serve a wide range of purposes, including the detailing of corners and edges. Step flashing is probably the most common application, and it's used where a wall rises above a roof. Step flashing comes pre-bent, or in packs of 50 flat pieces that are 5 in. by 7 in. I bend them, using a homemade bending jig.

➡ **See "Installing Kick-Out Flashing," p. 168.**

When the house is getting wood siding, the siding must be at least 2 in. above the roof. I use step flashing that runs 3½ in. up the wall, or I extend a piece of counter flashing (an upper flashing that covers the top of a lower flashing) down over the step flashing. That's because wood siding should be kept at least 2 in. off of a roof to prevent it from soaking water into its end grain. That 2-in. gap below the siding leaves smaller types of step flashing exposed. Use powder-coated aluminum coil stock for the counter flashing—it will hide the shiny finish of the step flashing. Additionally, powder-coated coil stock takes paint very well, so you can finish it to match the house color.

Add a piece of step flashing at every shingle. Lay the step flashing atop the shingle with the flashing's bottom edge aligned at the top of the shingle exposure. There are arguments about the right place to nail step flashing—some for nailing it to the roof, some for nailing it to the wall. What everyone agrees on is that step flashing shouldn't be nailed to both the roof and the wall. The reason for this is that the rafters will shrink more than the wall studs. Flashing nailed to both can be torn.

I nail it to the wall for additional reasons. First, it's one less nail hole in the roof. Second, you can count on siding nails going through the step flashing, and that eliminates any need to nail it to the roof. In any event, use one nail placed high up on the step flashing. Place the next shingle over that piece of step flashing.

To make sure the wall/roof intersection is waterproof, cover every shingle with a piece of step flashing.

Once a shingle is covered with step flashing, then each shingle also overlies that piece of step flashing.

SHINGLING AROUND OBSTRUCTIONS

When shingling a dormer, you have to lay out the courses so they meet in a straight line above it. That will maintain an even layout around dormers (and chimneys). To establish that line, measure up from the eaves (1) and strike a line across the roof. Measure down from this line (2) to locate the course lines.

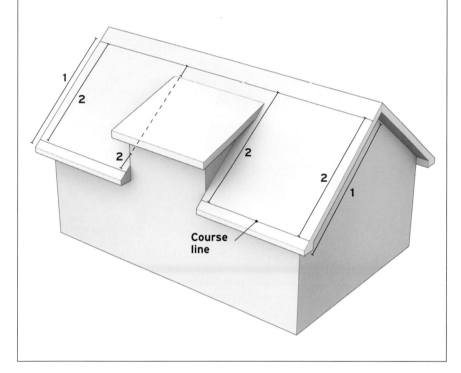

Course line

PERFECT EXPOSURE

Unless your roof happens to be an exact multiple of the shingle exposure, using a typical, consistent 5-in. exposure means the top course of shingles will be narrower than all the rest. That doesn't bother me, or most other carpenters. It's so far up on the roof that it's usually not noticeable. However, if you really want to show your roofing chops, you can adjust the exposure of the shingles so that last course is spaced the same as the rest.

First, measure from drip edge to the horizontal center of the roof. Add 1 in. for the overhang at the eaves, and subtract 5 in. for the cap shingles. (The cap shingles actually measure a bit less than 12 in., with half extending onto each side of the roof, but the bend where they cross the peak eats up some of their width.) Divide the resulting number by 5 (the standard course width), and round up. That's the number of courses of shingles. Now, divide the adjusted roof height by the number of courses. Rounding up ensures that the exposure is no more than 5 in., which is usually the maximum allowed.

You'll probably get some number like $4\frac{7}{8}$ in., and you'll need to lay out each course at that exposure. Making a short story pole is a good idea, say one that goes up five courses. In our example, the marks would be at $4\frac{7}{8}$, $9\frac{3}{4}$, $14\frac{5}{8}$, $19\frac{1}{2}$, and $24\frac{3}{8}$. Assuming five courses between control lines, you would snap chalklines every $24\frac{3}{8}$ in. up the roof, and use the story pole to govern exposure between the controls.

Use a story pole to govern custom shingle layout between horizontal control lines.

FLASHING DORMER CORNERS

Corners are always the tricky part of dormer roofing. Getting flashing to conform to three planes is a challenge, and worse than windows, dormer corners have to be done in two pieces.

Most roofers overlap two pieces of flashing metal, which leaves a pinhole at the corner. Because of how the side flashing is installed, most of the water is directed past this pinhole, and it isn't usually subject to meaningful leakage. Generations of roofs have lasted for decades with just a dab of asphalt cement sealing this hole. That makes me nervous though, and since I discovered flexible adhesive membrane, I've backed up this hole with a secondary layer that leaves me a lot more comfortable.

→ See "Flashing the Sills," p. 132.

Detailing the corners

To flash the corners, you can start by running some ice barrier on the roof at the corner and up the wall 6 in. or so, but even though it's excellent insurance, it's not strictly necessary.

With or without the barrier, install the shingles up to the face of the wall, notching the last row around the corner. Detail the corner with a piece of flexible membrane. Run this membrane onto both faces of the wall, and around the corner on the roof. Be careful not to take it farther than will be covered with shingles or flashing. ❶

Installing the flashing

The front piece of flashing will lie atop the shingles below. Start with a piece of flashing that's at least 6 in. by 8 in. To keep the visible edge from kinking, use hand benders to fold a hem along the bottom edge. ❷ Then about 3 in. from one end, cut halfway through the narrow dimension. ❸

→ See "Installing Kick-Out Flashing," p. 168.

At the end of the cut, bend the flashing to an angle slightly less than the roof/wall intersection. That creates a spring tension that helps hold it in place. ❹ Install it so it sits around the corner, nailing it to the wall near the top of the metal. ❺

The flashing that completes a dormer corner from the side is step flashing. Bend it in half lengthways and nail it to the wall so its bottom edge laps the first piece of corner flashing. Extend the step flashing bottom edge about 1 in. past the face of the dormer. ❻ Sharply fold the flashing from where its top passes the dormer edge to the fold, letting the corner conform to the face of the dormer. ❼ Nail this corner to the face of the dormer. ❽

Extending the step flashing beyond the corner directs most of the water beyond the dormer face and onto the top of the roof shingles. The counter flashing at the bottom of the wall will lap the side piece.

→ See "Shingling around Obstructions," p. 165.

1 Use flexible membrane to back up the flashing at corners, wrapping and adhering it to both sides of the corner and the shingles.

4 Bend the longer flap to slightly less than the angle between the roof and the wall.

7 Fold the exposed corner of the step flashing back to the wall. Snug it in place to remove as many wrinkles as possible.

2 Hem the bottom edge of the first piece of flashing to keep it flat, straight, and kink free.

3 Cut halfway across this first piece of flashing so the resulting flap matches the width of your step flashing.

5 Set the first piece on the corner and nail it to the front of the wall, over the last course of shingles.

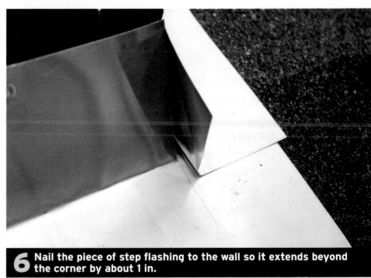

6 Nail the piece of step flashing to the wall so it extends beyond the corner by about 1 in.

8 Pinch the folded corner of the step flashing to a sharp crease, and nail the folded corner to the wall.

WHAT CAN GO WRONG

To avoid premature corrosion, use nails that are compatible with the flashing material. Use copper nails with copper flashing, galvanized nails with galvanized flashing, and galvanized or aluminum nails with aluminum flashing. Otherwise, the dissimilar metals will create a small electrical current that will corrode the metals, especially in the presence of moisture.

INSTALLING KICK-OUT FLASHING

When a roof ends on a wall face, it's important to detail the bottom of the step flashing correctly. An extremely common mistake is to simply extend the step flashing to the end of the roof, where it dumps its water onto or into the siding. This is one of the most common rot spots. To avoid this problem, it's necessary to use what's called a kick-out flashing. Kick-out flashing is bent to divert the water away from the wall and into a gutter. It's installed as the lowest piece of step flashing.

There are commercial versions available, but I bend my own. Start with a piece of flashing about 12 in. by 9 in. It can be bigger, but I wouldn't go smaller. Bend it in half longways. ❶ The next two bends won't stay in place until the end, but they set the stage. On the wall side of the bend, mark a line square to the crease and 4 in. from the bottom end. Keeping hand benders ¼ in. to ½ in. away from the initial crease (to avoid tearing the metal where the bends meet), grasp the wall side of the metal along this line and fold the metal 90 degrees. ❷

Once released, the metal will flatten out some, but that's okay. Now grasp the roof side of the flashing with the hand benders held at a 20- or 30-degree angle aimed at the point where the other two bends meet. ❸ Bend upward—it won't be pretty. ❹ Next, use your hands to begin folding the metal. It will fold in from the corner like you're wrapping the end of a Christmas present. ❺ When you've squeezed this bend as tight as you can with your fingers, place it on a flat surface and hammer the bend flat. ❻ I like to trim the open bottom corner round for looks.

1 Start the kick-out flashing by bending a piece of coil stock in half.

Kick-out flashing diverts roof water away from the wall and allows it to flow into a gutter.

2 Bend the wall side of the flashing to about 90 degrees, keeping the bender away from the first bend to avoid tearing it.

3 Grab the roof side with hand benders whose edge is aimed at the bend in the wall side.

4 Bend the corner you have grasped with the hand bender and turn it upward at a 20- to 30-degree angle.

5 Force the last two bends into place with hand pressure, creasing the flap like wrapping paper.

6 Keeping the metal on a flat, solid surface, lightly hammer the crease flat.

TRADE SECRET

When figuring out how to bend a particular piece of flashing, I experiment by folding paper. If you can fold it from paper, you can probably fold it, albeit with more difficulty, from sheet metal.

If the flashing is expensive stuff like copper, I go an extra step. When I'm happy with the paper model, I make another model out of cheap aluminum, just to find any differences between folding paper and folding metal before I turn to the good stuff.

FLASHING A SKYLIGHT

Most skylights come with manufactured flashing—a solid top and bottom, step flashing for the sides, and counter flashing to cover the rest.

To start, I like to detail the skylight with ice barrier for extra insurance. **①** Run the shingles up to the bottom of the skylight, notching them as needed, then install the bottom flashing. **②** If the skylight comes with fasteners, use them. They're designed so they won't protrude into the skylight's finished surfaces. Continue roofing, installing the step flashing as you would against a wall. **③** At the top, install the upper flashing, running the shingles around it as the manufacturer dictates. **④** Install the counter flashing, using the screws that are usually supplied. **⑤**

1 Minimize the chance of skylight leaks by detailing the installation with ice barrier before flashing.

2 After running the shingles up to the bottom of the skylight, notching them where necessary, install the bottom flashing.

3 Step-flash skylights like any roof-to-wall intersection, covering the shingles with flashing and the flashing with the next course.

4 Add the one-piece top flashing, lapping the shingles as directed by the skylight manufacturer.

5 Install the counter flashing—it waterproofs the bottom, step, and top flashings.

FLASHING A ROOF BELOW A WALL

1 Use a sheet-metal brake to bend the apron flashing to an angle slightly less than the roof's intersection with the wall.

2 Hem the bottom of the counter flashing on the brake to keep the edge straight and flat.

Whenever a roof intersects the front face of a wall, as on a dormer, an L-shaped (or apron) flashing is used for the transition. I run it from one corner of the dormer or wall to the other, lapping multiple pieces by 6 in. or so when needed.

Run the shingles far enough up on the roof so the flashing will cover them. Then bend a long piece of 12-in.-wide flashing on a brake to slightly less than the angle between the roof and the wall. **1** I usually bend the metal so 4 in. goes on the roof and 8 in. goes up the wall. Bending about half an inch of metal back under the main flashing at the bottom creates a hem that makes it more rigid and helps it to lie flat on the shingles. **2** This L-shaped flashing is simply nailed to the wall, with the nails kept at least 3 in. above the shingles. **3** It covers most of the top row of shingles, as well as the corner flashing assembly described previously.

➔ See "Flashing Dormer Corners," p. 166.

3 Nail the flashing to the wall. Using a helper when transporting long pieces of flashing minimizes the chances of unwanted kinks.

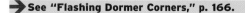

ROOFING VALLEYS

Snap reference line on roof sheathing 18" from center of the valley.

1 Always cover valleys with ice barrier that laps the underlayment along the bottom of the roof.

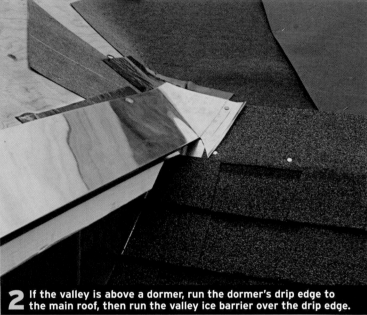

2 If the valley is above a dormer, run the dormer's drip edge to the main roof, then run the valley ice barrier over the drip edge.

There are several ways to detail valleys. The shingles can terminate on a sheet-metal pan, which is great in snow country. You can do a woven valley, where both roofs are shingled at the same time, and the shingles overlay the valley alternately. My favorite way is the cut valley. It's fast, simple, and reliable.

Installing the ice barrier

In all cases, first cover the valley with a layer of ice barrier. Snap a reference line 18 in. from the center on one side of the valley to keep the ice barrier straight. This sheet of ice barrier should lap the ice barrier at the eaves and, in a dormer valley, should extend onto the tops of the shingles below the valley. **1**

Installing the shingles

On a dormer valley, install the drip edge first, running it into the valley where the ice barrier will lap it. **2** Snap a line down the center of the valley. **3** Roof one side first, running the shingles at least 1 ft. onto the other roof and keeping any nails at least 6 in. from the valley center. **4** Clip the top corners of these shingles to direct water down. **5**

Roof the second side, letting the shingles run entirely past the valley center line. Use an old pair of tin snips to cut the shingles along this line. **6** Finally, lift the edges of the overlapping shingles and adhere them to the lower layer with a bead of roofing cement. **7**

3 Snap a line down the valley center using soluble chalk (blue or white).

4 Lap the shingles from one side through the valley, keeping all nails at least 6 in. up from the centerline.

5 Snip the top corners of the side's shingles to direct water down.

6 Run the second roof's shingles over the first roof's. Trim them to the chalkline with snips.

7 Seal the lapping shingles to those below with roofing cement.

TRADE SECRET
Use an old pair of tin snips for trimming shingles—you don't want to dull your new snips on the mineral surface.

CHIMNEY CRICKETS

When there's a chimney (or in the odd circumstance, a wall) at the bottom of a roof, water is diverted around it by a "cricket." A cricket is much like the back section of a doghouse dormer, just a section of roof that goes back to the main roof, creating a valley on either side that bypasses the chimney.

• Detail the valley with ice barrier.

• Cut and wrap the step flashing on the side of the chimney around the upper corner.

• Using coil stock as an oversized piece of step flashing, install it at the bottom where the cricket meets the chimney out onto the main roof to divert water away from the chimney.

• At the top, run one piece of step flashing past the other to cover the point where the ridge of the cricket meets both slopes.

• Shingle the cricket like a doghouse dormer.

With dark shingles, bend the flashing so the dark side of the coil stock shows from below. With white shingles, make the white side show.

Most chimneys today are framed, so the siding serves as counter flashing. Masonry chimneys are harder. With new stone chimneys, I coordinate with the mason so he can set counter flashing into his mortar joints. That's the best approach with brick chimneys too. On a re-roof when there's no mason on the job, I'll use a diamond blade in an angle grinder to cut a reglet, which is a fancy word for a groove, about 1/2 in. deep, in the masonry above the step flashing. Bend up a piece of counter flashing to cover the step flashing. Hem the bottom to keep it straight. Bend the top of the counter flashing to make a 1/2-in. lip and set the lip in the reglet. Fill the reglet with polyurethane or butyl caulk.

TRADE SECRET
Don't set aluminum flashing in mortar—it will corrode. Use a longer-lasting material such as copper, lead, stainless steel, or PVC.

Use ice barrier in the valleys of a cricket, taking care to keep any folds smooth as you apply it.

The last piece of step flashing on the side of the cricket should fold around the corner.

Make a long piece of step flashing from coil stock to move water well past the corner of the cricket.

Two pieces of step flashing are slit and folded over the peak, and they bypass each other on the wall.

Crickets create a pair of valleys that divert water to the sides of a chimney or wall.

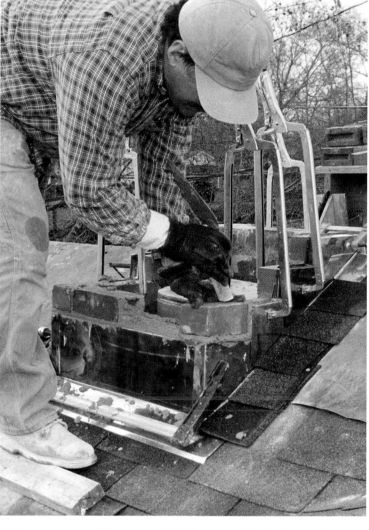

With new masonry chimneys, work with a mason to set the counter flashing in the mortar joints. (Photo by Tom O'Brien)

FLASHING AN EXISTING CHIMNEY

On existing chimneys, use an angle grinder to cut reglets in the mortar.

Bend a lip in the counter flashing and set it in the reglet.

Seal the counter flashing with polyurethane or butyl caulk. (Photos by Daniel S. Morrison)

SIDING

PEOPLE TEND TO SEE SIDING mainly as one of the chief stylistic elements of a house. And supporting that perception is the fact that the variety of siding materials available today is greater than at any point in history.

If you really think about it, however, good looks are secondary. No matter the material, siding's primary purpose is the same—to protect the walls of the house from most water intrusion. By itself, siding will keep out a large portion of the rain, but all siding leaks, particularly when the rain is wind driven. It's the combination of the siding and the drainage plane behind it—the tar paper or housewrap, along with the window and door flashing—that keeps water out of the walls. Together, these materials keep water from penetrating to the framing and rotting the house. In fact, after the roof, siding is the most important element in any house's longevity.

PREPARATION
Siding Materials, p. 178

Running Exterior Trim, p. 180

WOOD SIDING
Installing Clapboard Siding, p. 182

Installing Cedar Shingles, p. 186

ENGINEERED SIDING
Installing Fiber-Cement Siding, p. 192

VINYL SIDING
Installing Vinyl Siding, p. 194

SIDING MATERIALS

Cedar siding

The most common wood siding is cedar–clapboards and shingles. Lightweight and easy to work with, cedar is naturally rot-resistant and long-lasting. It's gotten a bad rap in recent decades for peeling paint, but that has little to do with the material and lots to do with poor installation. Properly backprimed and installed, cedar siding should hold paint for 20 years or longer. It can be painted or stained, or installed raw and left to weather. Cedar clapboards come with one side smooth and one side rough; which side faces out is a purely aesthetic choice.

Engineered wood

The other wood sidings on the market today are so-called engineered wood sidings. There are several brands, with a core of either hardboard or OSB. Less expensive than the cedar they're meant to mimic, all must be painted. Earlier generations experienced failures from moisture, and it's still debated whether that's because of inherent defects or poor installation. Manufacturers claim new products address these concerns, and some offer extraordinary warranties. I won't cover installation here, except to say it's much like installing cedar, but that you should always follow the manufacturer's instructions.

Fiber cement

The other popular engineered siding is fiber cement. It's heavy, made from a blend of wood fiber and Portland cement. It's essentially fireproof, a boon in areas subject to wildfire, and it holds paint extremely well. It requires a few special techniques, can break if handled incorrectly, and can't be hand-nailed.

Vinyl siding

Finally, there's vinyl. It's probably the most popular siding in America because it promises low up-front cost and low maintenance. Vinyl, for the most part, installs using the same tools as wood siding, but the techniques differ considerably.

Cedar clapboard is an iconic siding. Long-lasting, it's what most other siding imitates.

Common on traditional homes, particularly in the Northeast, cedar shingles are the most labor-intensive siding choice.

Often made from recycled or plantation-grown wood, engineered siding comes with great factory warranties.

Rot-proof and highly fire-resistant, fiber cement has a reputation for holding paint for decades, as on this clapboard and shingle siding.

TRADE SECRET

Don't cheap out on nails, particularly for siding installed with exposed fasteners. Most manufacturers allow hot-dipped galvanized nails, but they're only corrosion resistant until the galvanization is used up in an ongoing chemical reaction. This can take a century in the desert, or a year on the coast. Use stainless-steel nails. Yes, they cost a lot more, but compared to the total cost of a siding job, that extra money is small potatoes.

Aluminum and steel siding

Two other siding materials are aluminum and steel. Popular choices in the past, I haven't seen them installed in the 30-plus years I've been in the trade. The large amount of energy required for aluminum-siding production, along with increased costs of raw materials, pushed aluminum siding out of the broad marketplace in the 1970s. Due to the increased difficulty of cutting and installing heavier steel, along with its tendency to rust, steel siding suffered a similar fate. Their decreased use puts them beyond the scope of this book.

Vinyl is the most popular siding in America because of its low initial cost and its low maintenance.

Ordering siding

Like roofing, siding is usually sold by the square, or 100 sq. ft. You can sometimes buy individual pieces of some siding, such as cedar clapboards, fiber cement, and vinyl.

Measure a house for siding by measuring each wall and calculating its area. Subtract the area of the windows and doors. Five percent is usually enough to figure for waste, but figure more for complicated houses with lots of ins and outs. As illustrated below, you can easily figure the area of a gable if you know the house width and the roof pitch.

Measure individually for corners, window trim, water tables, vinyl-siding accessories, and the like. You will also need to order nails. Your supplier should be able to tell you how many based on the amount of siding. If you're siding with shingles, you'll need undercourse—a starter row across the bottom of the walls. Undercourse is inexpensive, knotty shingles.

CALCULATING THE AREA OF A GABLE

Sketch the gable and divide it into two triangles along the center line down from the peak. The base of the triangles is a line level with the top of the siding on the sidewalls. Mentally flip one of the triangles so it sits atop the other, forming a rectangle, one of whose sides equals the height of the peak. The other side of the rectangle is half the width of the gable. Multiply these two sides together.

For example, say the house is 28 ft. wide, and the roof is an 8 pitch. The height of the ridge will be 8 in. for every foot along the base: 14 × 8 in. = 112 in., or 9 ft. 4 in. Mentally flipping one of the triangles forms a rectangle 14 ft. by 9 ft. 4 in. Figuring the area becomes a simple multiplication problem—here, 9 ft. 4 in. × 14 ft. = 130.6, rounded to 131 sq. ft. Round up to the nearest square foot to avoid shorting your materials.

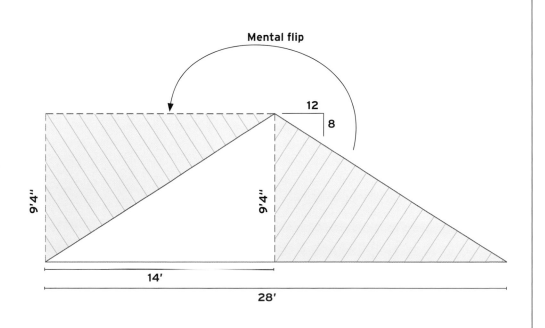

Mental flip

12

8

9'4"

9'4"

14'

28'

RUNNING EXTERIOR TRIM

The first step in any siding installation is always installing the trim pieces. Common trim details include corners, water tables, and in some cases such as with vinyl siding, window trim. It can also include trimming the soffit and fascia if it wasn't done during framing.

→ See "Installing Soffits and Fascia on Eaves," p. 120, and "Installing Gable Soffits and Fascia," p. 122.

In most cases, trim other than the soffit and fascia is nothing more than the outside and inside corners. The material used for corners varies widely. It can be raw cedar, if you're going to let the siding age naturally. If the house is to be painted or stained though, prime or stain any raw wood on all six sides before installation. That minimizes the entry of moisture from behind. Moisture from behind is one of the leading causes of paint peeling in the front.

A variety of products, such as the finger-jointed pine I use, come factory primed. The only painting you need to do is on cut ends. Another option is PVC trim. It's pricey, but it doesn't need back-priming. Fiber-cement trim usually comes primed, but it's advisable to prime cut ends. Don't use oil-based paints on fiber cement. The oils can react with the alkali in the cement and saponify, or make soap. Then the next layer of paint won't stick. When using engineered or synthetic trim, follow the manufacturer's instructions.

Installing outside corners

In most cases, 1× stock works fine for corners, but sometimes the siding laps will be thicker than that. Use stock thicker than the siding will be at the laps and cut it long enough to extend from the soffit to 1 in. past the bottom of the sheathing. Inside corners will go up a board at a time, but you can assemble outside corners as a unit. ❶ On tall corners, you'll probably need joints in the boards. Make scarf joints by cutting the ends of the boards on a miter saw at 45 degrees. Prime the cuts, and assemble them so the upper board laps the lower one. This allows moisture to drain. Be sure to offset the joints by at least 4 ft. ❷ Run adhesive membrane on the corner. This is a vulnerable area because of the large number of joints formed where the siding meets the trim. Extend the membrane about 6 in. in both directions. ❸

Set the boards in place and press them tight to the house. ❹ Nail the corners in place using corrosion-resistant (hot-dipped galvanized, or better still, stainless-steel) siding or finish nails long enough to penetrate the framing at least 1½ in. Nail each side about every 2 ft. ❺

Installing inside corners

Inside corners are easy. Like outside corners, they should be thicker than the siding, with scarfed joints. Prepare them with adhesive membrane and drive the nails at an angle. Alternate which side you nail from, and place a nail every 2 ft. or so. ❻

1 Preassemble outside corners. It's easier to get a flush joint working on sawhorses than on a ladder.

2 Assemble scarf joints so the upper half laps the lower to drain out water.

3 Add adhesive membrane to corners to seal around nails for extra protection in these vulnerable areas.

4 Set the outside corner assembly in place, snug against the wall.

5 Fasten the assembled corner to the house with corrosion-resistant nails.

6 On inside corners, angle the nails. It's easier to nail and pull the corner tight.

WATER TABLES

A traditional but optional siding trim detail is a horizontal board around the base of the building called a water table. The material for the water table can be cedar, cellular PVC, or primed pine. I tend to use the latter only when the water table will be well off the ground (1 ft. or more) and protected by a generous roof overhang.

If the wall is flush with the foundation or overhangs it, extend the water table onto the foundation by about 1 in. Miter the corners, prime or seal the end cuts, and fill the joint with sealant such as polyurethane caulk during assembly. Nail the water table to solid framing such as plates or studs, using corrosion-resistant nails long enough to penetrate 2 in.

Drip-cap molding is not the same as drip cap material used to flash windows and doors (which a lot of carpenters use, but I don't). It's available at any lumberyard. Fasten it to the top of the water table with the lip, or back dam, against the wall. This keeps water from getting behind the drip cap and kicks out the bottom of the lowest course of siding. The cornerboards will land atop the drip cap. (An alternative is to run the corners first and butt the water table to them.)

Cut the bottom of the corners at an angle that's a little greater than that of the drip cap's slope, and rabbet the back of the corners to fit around the drip cap's back dam. This angle keeps most of the corner from resting directly on the water table, where it can trap water.

Water tables are horizontal trim boards at the bottom of the siding.

Prime outside miters and seal the joints for longevity.

Drip-cap back dam keeps water out and angles the first course of siding.

With a drip cap, rabbet the cornerboard to fit over the back dam before assembling.

INSTALLING CLAPBOARD SIDING

When people think of siding, traditional cedar clapboards are probably what comes to mind. Most other horizontal siding is an emulation of this classic material.

Clapboards are installed so the uppers lap the lowers from 1 in. to 2 in. Lapping them at more than 1 in. enables some variation in the exposure. For example, clapboards intended for a 4-in. exposure measure 5¼ in. wide.

Take a look at a well-built older home with clapboard siding. Odds are that the siding courses line up with the window tops and bottoms all the way around the house. This was accomplished by varying the exposure (the amount of siding exposed from the bottom of one course to the bottom of another) of the siding courses slightly. For example, a ⅛-in. decrease in exposure isn't noticeable from one course to another, but over 16 courses, for example, it adds up to 2 in.

Calculating clapboard exposure

Clapboards can be installed with a uniform exposure, but it's worth the effort to align them with the windows. Odds are, there will be one or two windows where this won't work, but in most cases, the windows will be uniform in size, and the clapboards can be adjusted to fit.

Measure from the bottom of the sheathing to the bottoms and tops of the windows and add ½ in. to 1 in. for the amount the bottom course will extend over the foundation. ❶ Mark those dimensions on a story pole. Measure the walls in sections—from the bottom of the siding to the bottom of the first-floor windows, from the bottoms of those windows to their tops, from the tops of the first-floor windows to the bottom of the second-floor windows, and so forth. Divide the measurements by the nominal exposure, say 4 in., to find the approximate number of courses in those sections.

For example, suppose the distance up to the bottom of the first-floor windows is 37 in. Dividing 37 by 4 yields 9.25. Round that to 9 courses. Now, divide 37 by 9 to find the course spacing of about 4⅛ in. Using 5¼-in.-wide clapboards, that still provides the minimum 1 in. lap required, while aligning the ninth course with the bottom of the window.

Now, say the window measures 67 in. tall—67 divided by 4 is 16.75. Rounding up to 17 gives an exposure of $3^{15}/_{16}$ in. Rounding down to 16 courses gives an exposure of $4^{3}/_{16}$ in. Either exposure is fine, but I'd probably go with $4^{3}/_{16}$ in. because it's closer to the 4⅛-in. exposure of the clapboards below, and it saves a course of siding.

Marking a story pole

Cut a story pole the height of the wall. Calculate the exposures you'll use, and mark them on the pole in pencil. ❷ Unless it's an easy number to add in a series—say 4½ in.—then it's smart to do the math on a construction calculator. These marks represent the bottom of the clapboards. You want marks to locate the tops of the clapboards, though,

so that you can strike a series of chalklines along the wall to guide installation. To locate the marks for the tops of the claps, simply hold a scrap of clapboard on each existing line and strike a line along the top of the scrap with a pencil. ❸ (Screw a block to the story pole to hook the bottom of the clap.)

Cedar siding is supposed to be nailed to the studs, although a lot of carpenters ignore this rule. I don't, and I snap vertical chalklines on the wall where the studs are. ❹ The first piece of siding to go on the wall is a starter strip, ripped from the top inch of a clapboard. ❺ Nail this at the bottom of the wall, even with the bottom of the corners. ❻ All the other clapboards overlay the one below, and the purpose of the starter strip is to space the bottom of the first clapboard away from the wall by the same amount.   >> >> >>

This 19th-century Connecticut building's clapboards are spaced so their bottoms come even with the head and sill of the windows.

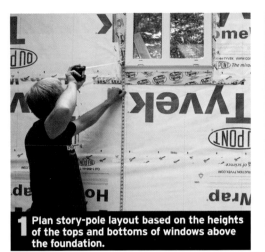

1 Plan story-pole layout based on the heights of the tops and bottoms of windows above the foundation.

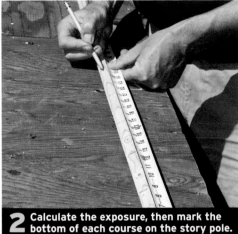

2 Calculate the exposure, then mark the bottom of each course on the story pole.

3 Hold siding scrap on the course-bottom marks, then mark the tops of the siding.

4 Snap vertical chalklines along the wall to identify stud locations.

5 Rip a 1-in.-wide strip from the top of a clapboard as a starter.

6 Nail the starter strip to the wall to kick out the bottom of the first course.

TRADE SECRET

When installing wood siding or trim on a wall intersecting a roof, maintain a minimum 2-in. gap between the wood and the roofing shingles. Otherwise, the wood will wick up moisture from the roof, fostering rot and peeling paint.

MAKING A STORY POLE FOR CLAPBOARDS

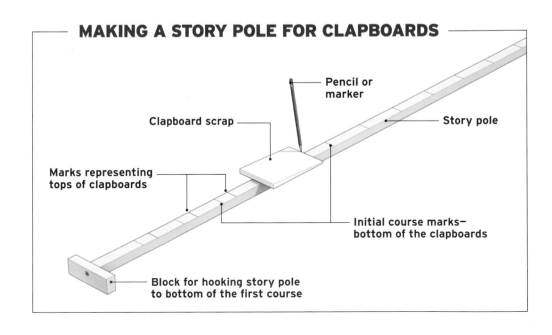

Pencil or marker

Clapboard scrap

Story pole

Marks representing tops of clapboards

Initial course marks— bottom of the clapboards

Block for hooking story pole to bottom of the first course

INSTALLING CLAPBOARD SIDING (CONTINUED)

7 Snap a line that locates the top of the first course of clapboards. Nail it in place with its bottom edge even with the cornerboards.

8 Cut the first board to length and prime or seal the end grain of this and all subsequent pieces before installation.

9 Once the first course is installed, hook the story pole to its bottom and lay out the remaining courses of siding.

10 Nail clapboards about 1¼ in. above the bottom of the previous board—enough that the nail completely misses the board below.

Hook the bottom of the story pole on the bottom of the first clapboard and mark the top of each course at both sides of the wall and on both sides of interruptions such as windows. **9** On runs longer than 8 ft., snap lines between the marks. On shorter walls, marking the ends will keep the courses well enough aligned.

After the first course, nail succeeding courses at every stud—a bit more than 1 in. up from the bottom of the clapboard. This should be just high enough to miss the underlying clapboard. That's important. Wood siding expands and contracts across the grain with seasonal changes in humidity. The tops of clapboards have to be free to move with these changes or the clap will crack. If the nail on the upper clap penetrates the lower board, that lower clapboard is restrained in two places and unable to move without cracking. If that crack spreads down to the exposed face of the clapboard, water can get in and cause the finish to fail. **10**

Installing the clapboard

Snap a chalkline to locate the top of the first clapboard, then measure the first board and cut it to length. **7** If a run is shorter than a clapboard, the most accurate way to measure is to hold it in place, fit tightly to the corner trim, and mark it in place. Then cut it on a miter saw and prime or stain the cut ends. **8** Nail the first course into the floor framing with its lower edge even with the cornerboards.

DETAILS FOR CEDAR SIDING

As with cornerboards, or any painted exterior wood, priming or staining the end cuts is very important. Either stain or a stain-blocking oil-base or acrylic primer is acceptable.

It's a pain in the neck to keep an open can of primer around. Instead, put the primer in a plastic container, such as one that take-out soup from a Chinese restaurant comes in. Clean containers such as this can be had at paint stores and home centers. Slit the lid to fit the brush handle, and you've got a ready-to-use system that keeps the paint and the brush from drying out.

Field joints in clapboards are inevitable, and they should be scarfed. Make the cuts on a miter saw. Prime the ends, and nail both boards. To avoid cracking the clapboards, predrill when nailing near the ends.

If you're working with a cased window, or a flanged window that gets a wider trim detail, be sure to add a metal drip cap.

Keep paint or stain in a plastic container. Slit the lid for the handle of a paint brush.

Scarf field joints in clapboards and install them over a stud.

Predrill when nailing close to the ends of clapboards.

Install metal drip cap before installing siding above windows or doors.

Cedar siding Cedar siding is produced by a number of mills in different configurations and sizes. Here, I'm installing primed, finger-jointed 5¼-in. clapboard—probably the most common and economical cedar siding.

Most of my installation tips apply to other clapboard configurations as well, but there are some differences. Verify the guidelines for the cedar siding you're using with the manufacturer or the Western Red Cedar Lumber Association (www.wrcla.org).

TRADE SECRET

Cedar siding doesn't have to be painted—it can be installed raw and last for a century. However, if it's going to be painted or stained, it has to be coated on all six sides. If you install raw cedar, consider that a permanent choice, as any coat of paint applied to its exterior without back priming a couple of years down the road will be doomed to early failure.

WHAT CAN GO WRONG

The same compounds that make cedar rot-resistant also give it its wonderful smell. But not everyone finds that smell wonderful. Some develop severe allergy symptoms, and worse is possible (all wood dust is considered a carcinogen). Wear dust protection when working with cedar.

INSTALLING CEDAR SHINGLES

Use a rack to hold shingles at the right height and to arrange them to offset joints from one course to another.

1 Cut a ½-in. by ½-in. rabbet in a 1×2 board for the bottom of the rack and fasten a piece of ¼-in. plywood.

Like clapboards, cedar shingles can be installed with varying exposures to align with windows or doors. They are often, but not always, installed with the same kind of trim details as clapboards, and they must be installed over properly flashed housewrap or building paper. As with clapboards, I add a layer of adhesive membrane to the corners. But that's where the similarities end.

At the very least, shingles or shakes are far more labor intensive than any other kind of siding. That's because shingles have to be installed so their joints are offset from course to course by at least 1½ in. In any three courses, no joints should align. It takes time and care to get this right. I build racks to hold the shingles in place while I'm nailing them up so I can fiddle with their placement (see "Calculating clapboard exposure," p. 182). Usually, I make an 8-ft. and a 4-ft. rack of ¼-in. plywood and a rabbeted 1×2.

Building a shingle rack

Cut a ½-in. × ½-in. rabbet in a piece of 1×2 and screw that to the ¼-in. plywood with the rabbet facing up and in. **1** The shingles will sit in this rabbet. Cut two or three strips of aluminum flashing (two for a 4-ft. rack, three for an 8-footer) about 1 in. wide and 2 ft. long, and fasten these to the back of the plywood with screws driven into the 1×2. **2** Use ¾-in. screws from behind for all the connections.

→ See "Calculating Clapboard Exposure," p. 182.

Marking the story pole

The length of shingles varies too much for you to lay them out along their tops, so a story pole for shingles has to work with the bottoms of the courses. To do this, shorten the story pole by the distance between the bottom of the rabbet and the bottom of the installation board. **3** Compute your exposure and lay out the story pole as you would for clapboards, except don't adjust the layout to work with the tops of the shingles. **4** >> >> >>

2 Use aluminum coil stock to cut strips for hanging the rack. Fasten them to the bottom of the rack with two screws.

3 Measure the un-rabbetted dimension and shorten the story pole by this measurement.

4 Lay out the story pole for the bottom of the shingles, extending the marks to the edge of the board with a combination square.

SHINGLE PANELS

To speed up the installation of cedar shingles, manufacturers also supply them attached to plywood panels that apply more like short, wide clapboards. The material cost is greater, but installation is a lot faster. However, panelized shingles cannot be installed with varying course widths, so odds are their bottoms won't align with the windows.

Manufactured shingle panels install much faster than using traditional methods. (Photo courtesy Michael R. Guertin)

Shakes? Shingles? Shakes are split from cedar logs and are thicker and rougher than shingles. Shingles are sawn and are thinner, more uniform, and tapered.

There are several grades of each, and the grades vary depending on whether the material is western red cedar or eastern white cedar. Additionally, shingles and shakes come in different lengths, and their permitted exposure depends on a combination of the grade, species, and length. Like cedar clapboards, cedar shakes and shingles can be installed painted, stained, sealed, or raw. Sound complicated? It's not, really. Just check with the manufacturer or the Cedar Shingle and Shake Bureau (www.cedar bureau.org).

Where I work, the most common shingle or shake sidewall product is R and R shingles. That stands for resawn and rebutted and means the shingles have parallel edges and square bottoms. What I'm installing here are 16-in.-long, raw, eastern white cedar R and Rs, with a 5-in. exposure.

INSTALLING CEDAR SHINGLES (CONTINUED)

Installing the undercourse

Seal each corner with a layer of adhesive membrane, extending the membrane about 6 in. in both directions. ❶ Then install any cornerboards and trim called for by your design.

➡ See "Running Exterior Trim," p. 180.

Fasten the shingle rack to the wall with screws through the tops of the aluminum straps, lapping the bottom of the rabbet over the foundation by 1 in. ❷ Start with a course of undercourse, arranging them in the rack. Space the undercourse, and all shingles, 1/8 in. to 1/4 in. at their sides to allow for expansion. Use stainless-steel shake nails long enough to penetrate the framing by at least 1 in. to fasten the undercourse (and all succeeding courses) about 1 in. up from the exposure line and 3/4 in. from each edge (but see "Special Nailing Procedures," facing page). ❸ Don't worry about hitting studs, and don't nail through the rack straps, or even right next to them. Skip those nails, and when you have finished the undercourse, go back and unscrew the shingle rack. Carefully pull down so the straps slip past the back of the shingles. Now, nail the shingles next to where the straps were.

Installing the shingles

You could reinstall the rack for the first course of shingles, which goes directly over the undercourse, but I find it easier to skip the rack for this course. Just flush the bottoms of the first course with the undercourse shingles, offsetting the joints between these shingles by at least 1 1/2 in. from the undercourse joints. ❹ Then align the story pole on the bottom of the first course and mark both sides of the wall at the story-pole marks, which you adjusted down to align with the bottom of the shingle rack.

➡ See "Installing Clapboard Siding," p. 182.

For the next course, fasten the rack with its bottom edge on the story-pole marks. Arrange the shingles in the rack so the joints will offset correctly. Nail this row of shingles then remove and reset the rack for the next course. Repeat this to the top of the wall.

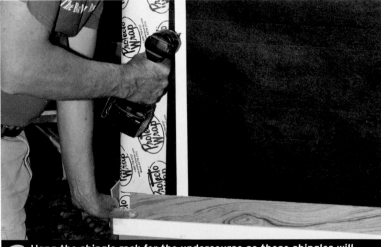

1 Back up corners in shingled walls with a layer of adhesive membrane at least 6 in. on both sides of the corner.

2 Hang the shingle rack for the undercourse so those shingles will lap the top of the foundation by about 1 in.

3 Nail the undercourse and all shingles 1 in. above where the bottom of the next course will fall.

4 Skip the shingle rack for the first visible course. Flush the bottoms with the undercourse, and stagger the edges by at least 1½ in.

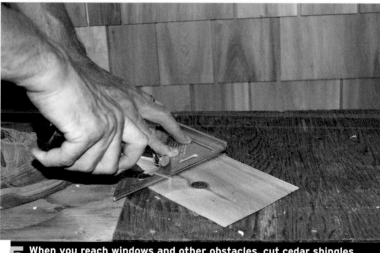

5 When you reach windows and other obstacles, cut cedar shingles with a sharp knife and a square.

When you get to windows or the top course, you'll need to cut the shingles to length. Cedar is so soft, these cuts can be made with a square and a sharp knife. **5** When trimming the thinner section near the top of a shingle, tin snips work well. In fact, there's no need for power tools to install cedar shingles. It's pretty cool to work with a material so timeless that a carpenter from a century ago would immediately recognize the tools being used today.   >> >> >>

SPECIAL NAILING PROCEDURES

On eastern white cedar shingles wider than 7 in. and western red cedar shingles wider than 8 in., nail the center of the shingle with two nails spaced 1 in. apart. Shingles of this size are likely to split, and the idea here is that this nail placement will make the split happen in the center of the shingle between the nails, and each remaining half will still be held fast by two nails.

GETTING THE SPACING RIGHT

Many shingles come with a nail line embossed in them (top). If yours don't, mark your hammer handle with the nail height and use that to gauge their placement from the bottom of the shingles (bottom).

INSTALLING CEDAR SHINGLES (CONTINUED)

Woven corners overlap each other in a way that eliminates the need for cornerboards.

1 Overlap the corner by enough to trim the edge of the end shingle properly.

3 Using a block plane, finish trimming the first shingle flush with the material on the other side of the corner.

5 Alternate the overlaps to stagger the joints from one course to the other.

Weaving corners

Woven corners are a traditional cedar-shingle detail. Instead of butting against cornerboards, the end shingles of alternating courses lap each other at the corner. To weave a corner, you need to shingle both adjoining walls at the same time. You don't need to do all of both walls at once, but you do need to shingle each course out 4 ft. or so on each wall, to give yourself enough area to work with. Of course, if one or both walls are short, then do the entire area at once. You can also leave the corners till last, installing and trimming the final shingle in each row after shingling the body of the wall.

When you get to an end shingle in a course, nail it in place so its edge overhangs the corner. **1** Use a sharp knife to trim that shingle to within about 1/8 in. of the face of the lower-course shingle on the other side of the corner. **2**

Finish flushing up the trimmed shingle with a plane. **3** You don't need a fancy plane here—just a small, basic standard-angle block plane. Move to the other side, and nail that end shingle in place so it laps the one you just installed. **4** Flush it up with a knife and a block plane as you did the first side. Change which wall you start on so that the corner laps alternate. **5**

2 Trim the first shingle to within about 1/8 in. of the profile of the shingle and wall on the opposite side of the corner.

4 When you get to the last shingle of the adjoining course, nail a shingle lapping the one you just trimmed.

TRADE SECRET

Weaving corners is not necessarily limited to outside corners, but it's easier. You can weave inside corners. It's more work, and it doesn't look a lot different than when an inside corner-board is used. In short, it's probably not worth the trouble to weave an inside corner.

GOING WITH THE GRAIN

Wood grain is rarely straight; most often it angles toward one edge or the other. Knife (or chisel) cuts will tend to split the wood along the grain. Cut in a direction so that if the shingle splits, the split will run to the scrap edge and not into the part you're keeping. Grain direction can change, so you may need to cut from each end of the shingle.

For example, on the shingle shown below, cutting up on the right side would not likely cause a visible split, but cutting down would. However, cutting on the left side is more complicated. Within about an inch of the edge, I'd cut up, but farther in from the edge, I'd cut down.

INSTALLING FIBER-CEMENT SIDING

I installed fiber-cement siding on my own house in 1999. It may have been the first house in Connecticut sided with that material. I had to buy it two states away. Now, it's ubiquitous. It has a lot of advantages, including fire resistance (very important in parts of the country prone to wildfire), price, and an excellent ability to hold paint. Fiber cement is available in a variety of styles—smooth lap siding, wood-grain lap siding, shingles, shingle panels, and in 4×8 and larger grooved panels, primed, finish painted, or raw. Additionally, there are several manufacturers. Installation methods vary, and you should follow the instructions from your manufacturer.

Fiber-cement layout

Fiber cement doesn't lend itself well to varying exposures the way cedar does, because the siding doesn't taper. You can vary the exposures, but you'll end up with gaps at the bottom of some of the panels. In most cases, it's best to maintain a consistent exposure. Instead of trying to hit the tops and bottoms of all the windows, I'll usually pick an exposure that puts the bottom of a course of siding at the top of the windows. I still use a story pole for layout, with the pole marked for the bottom of the courses. ❶ I also use a pair of hangers bent from tie-down strapping to hold the siding while I nail it. ❷

Align the bottoms of the hangers with the course mark made with the story pole. Don't nail right next to the hangers right away. Nail the rest of the course of siding, leaving it loose next to the hangers so they can be removed without scratching the courses below. You can also use commercially available siding gauges that hang on the previous course and support the next course at a set exposure.

Carrying and cutting

Carry fiber cement lap siding with an edge up or it will break. ❸ There are several methods of cutting it, and siding manufacturers provide blades that can be used in a circular

1 Use story poles to mark the bottom of the courses of fiber-cement siding.

4 Drill-powered shears are a low-dust way to cut fiber cement. Use them with a square for clean cuts.

saw. However, they produce a ton of dust that not only gets everywhere you don't want it but can also cause silicosis, a degenerative and incurable lung disease. If you use a saw, use a dedicated fiber-cement saw with dust collection.

I prefer fiber-cement shears that attach to a drill. ❹ They make little dust, are easy to take up on a scaffold, and don't cost an arm and a leg. Use them with a layout

square for right-angle cuts. Work on a bench (some framing lumber thrown on top of sawhorses is fine). Place the siding on a couple of pieces of 5/4 or 2× to support the stock while providing room for the shears to work. No matter what tool is used to cut fiber cement, it's important to support both sides of the cut, or the siding will break near the end of the cut and leave a ragged edge. Cut fiber cement to leave 1/8-in. joints and seal

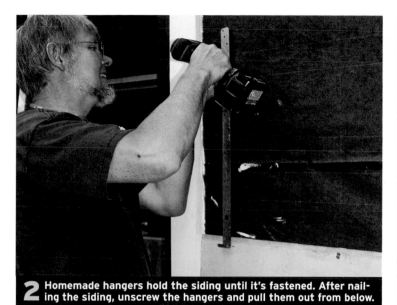

2 Homemade hangers hold the siding until it's fastened. After nailing the siding, unscrew the hangers and pull them out from below.

3 Fiber-cement siding can be brittle. Carry it with an edge upright or it can break.

5 Because of its hardness, fiber-cement siding must be installed with a pneumatic nailer.

6 Butt field joints, and back up the joint with a piece of flashing. Tack it to the wall above and lap it on the course below.

the joints with polyurethane or butyl caulk. Caulk every joint as you go up, so succeeding courses lap the caulked joints.

Nailing fiber cement

Blind-nail fiber-cement siding with a roofing gun and 1½-in. corrosion-resistant nails, or with a siding gun and 2-in. corrosion-resistant nails. **5** Because fiber cement is blind-nailed (the nails are hidden by the next course of siding above), I'm comfortable using galvanized fasteners. Pay attention to the manufacturer's nailing schedule (usually no closer than ³⁄₈ in. to the ends and within 1 in. of the top of lap siding). Hold the siding firmly against the wall while nailing or the impact of the gun can crack the siding. Nail into studs and keep the edges of fiber-cement siding 2 in. above roofs. Start lap siding with a 1¼-in.-wide starter strip, as is done with cedar lap siding. Back up the joint with a piece of metal or plastic flashing. **6**

INSTALLING VINYL SIDING

1 Cover corners behind vinyl siding with aluminum flashing, extending the flashing at least 1 ft. beyond the corner on each side.

2 Establish the end points of the soffit nailer by leveling over to the wall from the subfascia.

5 Cut the first soffit section (and all vinyl) with a miter saw. Cutting this material slowly will avoid cracking it.

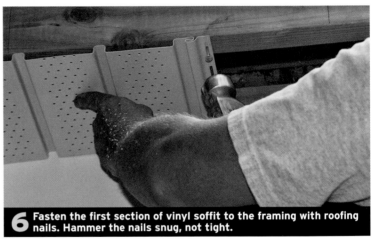

6 Fasten the first section of vinyl soffit to the framing with roofing nails. Hammer the nails snug, not tight.

Say "vinyl siding" and people think of vinyl lap siding—by far the most common type. But it's also available in a variety of other styles, including shakes. The primary reason for using vinyl siding is to create a low-maintenance exterior. That includes the soffits and fascia, as well, which are usually vinyl and aluminum, respectively.

Installing a vinyl soffit

Like all siding, tar paper or housewrap and flashings are critical to keeping water out. The Vinyl Siding Institute's (www.vinylsiding.org) installation manual recommends covering the corners and 1 ft. beyond with rigid flashing such as aluminum. I think adhesive membrane works just as well or better but hesitate to ignore such specific instruction.

Install the aluminum flashing first. **1** Then fasten a 2× nailer for the soffit panels to the wall. Level over from the subfascia at each end of the wall to find the elevation. **2** Snap a line on the wall. **3** Fasten the nailer on and just above this line with 10d commons or

longer. **4** Cut the vinyl soffit panels on a miter saw ¼ in. or so shorter than the distance between the wall and the subfascia. **5** The Vinyl Siding Institute says to cut vinyl with a plywood blade installed backward in the saw to avoid cracking the material. I'll do that in the cold, but I rarely bother in the summer, instead cutting more slowly.

Nail the first soffit section to the subfascia and the nailer using 1¼-in. or longer roofing nails through the centers of the slots in the panel. **6** Don't set the nails tight here, or in any piece of vinyl. Vinyl has to be allowed to move with changes in temperature. Tack the other side of the first piece of soffit with a nail through one of the vent holes. Don't worry much about supporting this end—the fascia will hold it up. Hook the buttlock (the edge of the piece of vinyl siding or soffit opposite the edge with the nail slots) of the second section into the flange of the first piece. **7** You'll feel it click in. Continue this procedure until the soffit is complete. Trim the last piece on a miter saw or with snips. **8**   >> >> >>

3 Snap a line between the end points to locate the bottom of the soffit nailer.

4 Fasten the nailer to the wall, aligning its bottom with the chalkline.

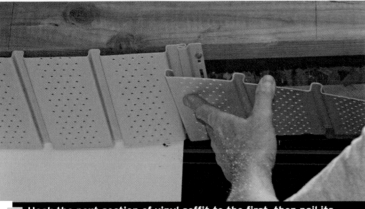

7 Hook the next section of vinyl soffit to the first, then nail its opposite end.

8 Trim the last soffit section on a miter saw or with snips (usually more convenient) and install it as the other sections.

Temperature tactics Unlike most other siding, vinyl doesn't change dimension with changes in humidity, but it does move—a lot—with changes in temperature, expanding in the heat and shrinking in the cold. You can hear it moving when the sun hits it on a cold morning. Consequently, you have to take thermal expansion into account during installation.

Never install vinyl siding so its ends fit tightly between two surfaces—it will buckle in the heat. Instead, cut it about $1/2$ in. short—about $5/8$ in. short if the heat is extreme and about $3/8$ in. short when installing in the cold. Vinyl trim always has a channel into which the siding slips, hiding gaps and cut ends.

INSTALLING VINYL SIDING (CONTINUED)

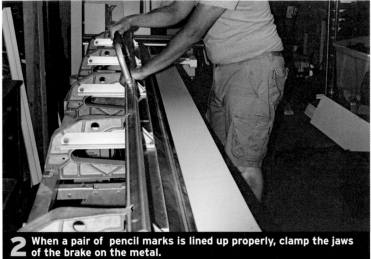

1 Mark the bends and cuts on both ends of the aluminum coil stock. For each bend or cut, line the marks up with the jaws of the brake.

2 When a pair of pencil marks is lined up properly, clamp the jaws of the brake on the metal.

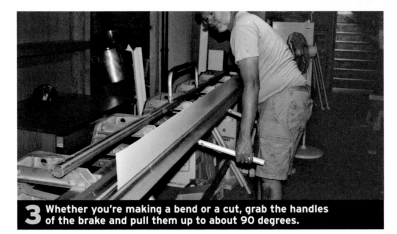

3 Whether you're making a bend or a cut, grab the handles of the brake and pull them up to about 90 degrees.

WARNING

Be careful when working with sheet metal. The edges can be sharp, particularly the cut edges. Gloves are strongly recommended.

Preparing the fascia

Start with the eaves fascia, cutting and bending as many sections of aluminum flashing as you need to cover it. In general, you'll cut the flashing first, hem it (bend an edge completely back on itself to stiffen it and to avoid a visible cut edge), and then bend it to conform to whatever structural element it's going to cover.

First, using snips, cut the flashing to a length that will fit the brake (see "Siding Brakes," facing page). Cut as many pieces as you'll need to cover the subfascia, and be sure the total length of the pieces will include any laps (about 2 in. each) and any extension over the ends of the fascia board.

Using a pencil, mark the widths between bends, the width of the hem, and the overall width of the piece on each end of the stock. **1** For example, in this case I wanted the flashing to hide the bottom edge of the fascia, covering the thickness of its 2× stock and extending an additional 1 in. over the soffit-panel edges. I also wanted a 3/4-in. hem on that extension, to stiffen the flashing and present a finished edge. This meant that I needed to cut a piece 9 1/4 in. wide to start with (6 in. for the face of the fascia plus 1 in. slipped behind the drip edge, 2 1/2 in. for the thickness of the fascia board plus the extension over the soffit, and 3/4 in. for the hem). So, I marked each of these dimensions on the aluminum stock.

To cut the aluminum flashing, slip the metal into the brake, align the pencil marks with the jaws, and clamp it shut. **2** Grab both sides of the bending handle and raise it until the metal is bent at about 90 degrees. **3** Slip the metal out a couple of inches and clamp it again. Score the inside of the bend with a sharp knife once or twice, then reclamp it on your marks and bend it back and forth until it breaks. Some brakes have slitters that negate the need for this step (see "Cutting Coil Stock," facing page).

If you're just putting a bend in the flashing, you can skip the scoring and rebending steps, of course.

To hem a flashing, bend the metal as far as the brake will go. That won't fully bend the metal back on itself, however, so here's what you do: release the clamp, take the metal out of the brake, and slip the hem bend under the jaws. Clamp the brake tightly to cinch the hem. With thicker metal, you may need to push the hem flatter with a hammer before clamping it in the brake.

SIDING BRAKES

Siding or aluminum brakes are essential tools for making crisp bends in finish aluminum. But they cost thousands of dollars, far more than makes sense for a DIYer. Fortunately, they can be rented.

Plan to bend all the metal for the job at one time so you can rent the tool for just a day. Bend up more than you need to allow for mistakes. Alternatively, you may be able to hire a contractor to handle this part of the job for you.

Coil stock Powder-coated aluminum coil stock is sold in rolls of varying lengths and widths. I usually buy 50 ft. by 2 ft., but it depends on what jobs are on the horizon. Don't be tempted to open the top of the box and pull out the roll. It's a lot easier to cut a slot along one of the box's long corners and feed the coil out through there. That keeps the rest of the coil in the box where it's safe. Alternatively, you can buy vinyl coil stock that bends much like the aluminum.

CUTTING COIL STOCK

To cut coil stock, bend it, then pull it out of the jaws an inch or so. Reclamp and score the metal.

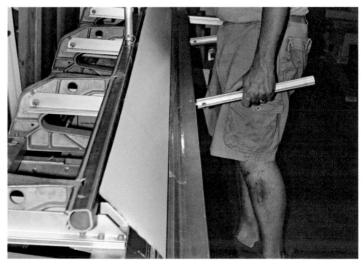

After scoring the metal, flexing it back and forth should break it along the score. The edges will be sharp.

INSTALLING VINYL SIDING (CONTINUED)

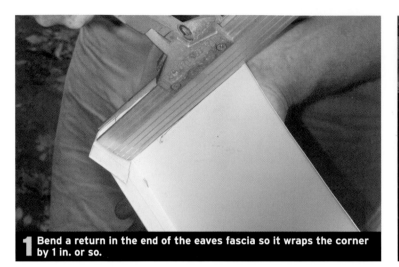

1 Bend a return in the end of the eaves fascia so it wraps the corner by 1 in. or so.

2 Slip the cut and formed piece of aluminum for the eaves fascia behind the drip edge.

3 Nail the returned end of the eaves fascia to the subfascia. Nail the fascia to the eave with painted aluminum nails.

4 Cut and bend a custom piece to fit the cornice return, lapping the returned end of the eaves fascia. Nail it in place.

Installing the fascia

Snip the bend in the fascia that will cover the bottom of the subfascia about 1 in. from the end and use a hand bender to bend the flashing so it will wrap around the end of the subfascia board by about 1 in. **1** Slip the flashing under the drip edge and snug it to the subfascia. **2** Nail the bent end in place with 1-in. painted aluminum nails. **3** Then nail along the length of the aluminum about every 2 ft. Don't use stainless-steel nails—they'll corrode the aluminum coil stock. Lap neighboring panels by about 2 in., and consider the direction from which they'll be viewed as you did with drip edge.

➜ See "Drip Edge, Ice Barrier, and Underlayment," p. 152.

I treat the rake trim similarly, although in this case I lap the upper pieces over the lower ones to better drain water, even though that makes the seams more visible viewed from below—durability trumps aesthetics.

Bend a custom piece to fit around the cornice return or pork chop, wide enough that its upper edge will lap the gable subfascia by about 1 in. Snip the side corner of this piece to create a small tab that will bend on the gable subfascia. Nail your custom piece to the cornice return. **4**

Cut and bend the rake fascia, if you haven't done so already. Hold the gable fascia in place and mark the points where it meets both the gable return and the eaves fascia. **5** Cut away the bottom of the bend at your marks, leaving a tab of flashing that you'll bend and nail on the end of the pork chop. You can cut the rake fascia about 1 in. long and bend it around the face of the eaves fascia as you install it or trim it flush with the eaves fascia—that's an aesthetic choice I swing back and forth on. **6**

5 Bend the rake fascia to fit. Hold it roughly in place and mark its bottom fold where it meets both sides of the cornice return.

6 Cut the bottom fold of the rake fascia on the marks you made and the fold line between them. Fit and nail the rake fascia.

7 Snap chalklines on the outside corners to mark the edges of the vinyl cornerpieces.

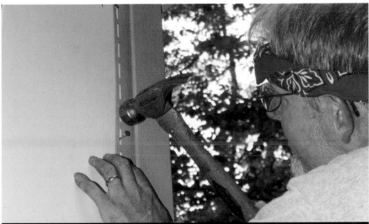

8 Butt the corner to the soffit. Set the uppermost nails at the tops of their slots and succeeding nails in the middle of the slots.

Installing outside corners

Vinyl-siding installations start at the corners. On each wall, top and bottom, mark the width of the cornerpiece. Then snap vertical chalklines between these marks. **7** On a miter-saw, cut the corners about 1/2 in. longer than the wall height.

Nail the cornerpiece to the line with roofing nails, butted tightly to the soffit. Keeping the joint between the corner and the soffit tight will force any expansion to take place at the bottom. Set the nails in the top of the cornerpiece at the top of their slots. **8** Loosely nail the rest of the corner about every 12 in., in the center of the slots.

>> >> >>

INSTALLING VINYL SIDING (CONTINUED)

Installing J-channel

Inside corners get backed up with rigid flashing, then trimmed with J-channel, or "J," that receives the cut ends of vinyl panels. A common practice is to nail a piece of J to each side of the corner, but that uses twice as much as you need. Even then, you'll use a lot of the stuff. Simply nail a piece of J to one wall, spaced 3/4 in. away from the intersecting wall. ❶ The siding on one side slips into the recess of the J-channel, the siding on the other side slips behind it.

Next, fit J from corner to corner, just below the soffit. ❷ Space nails in J about 12 in. apart, and again, nail loosely. The recess in the J will capture the top of the vinyl siding, as well as hide the cut ends of the soffit panels. If more than one piece of J is needed to span the length, lap the pieces by 3/4 in.

Setting the starter strip

The last piece I run before starting the siding is the starter strip. Measure the width of the starter strip, mark both ends of the wall at this measurement, and snap a chalkline to locate its top. This way, when the siding clicks in, it will align with the bottom of the corners. ❸ Nail the starter strip in place with 1 1/4-in. roofing nails about every foot. The bottom edge of vinyl siding, the buttlock, is hook-shaped, and engages in the starter strip. ❹

Starting the siding

Cut the first piece of siding to length (remember to leave it short for expansion) with a miter saw. It's much faster if you can stack up a bunch of pieces of siding of the same length and gang-cut them. ❺

Holding the first panel above the starter strip, slip it into the J-channel at the corner. Push the siding's bottom edge over the starter strip, then snap the hook on the siding into the starter strip. You'll feel it engage. ❻

Before you nail them, the first panel and all succeeding panels are held in place by their engagement along the bottom edge. As you install each panel, make sure it's engaged along its entire length, then nail it with 1 1/2-in. roofing nails about every 16 in. in the center of the slots. Don't worry about hitting studs, and never set the nails fully—leave them a little loose so the siding can move. ❼ At inside corners, just slide the siding from the intersecting wall behind the J you installed for the original wall. ❽

Lap abutting panels by about 1 in. ❾ Pay attention to the direction of the lap, as well. At obvious viewing points, such as the front door, lap the near piece over the far piece to hide the seams. Laps should not align vertically—separate them by at least 3 courses.

>> >> >>

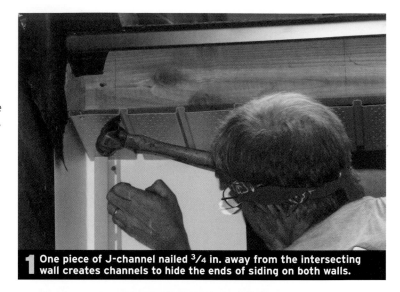

1 One piece of J-channel nailed 3/4 in. away from the intersecting wall creates channels to hide the ends of siding on both walls.

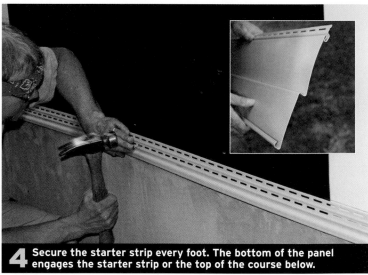

4 Secure the starter strip every foot. The bottom of the panel engages the starter strip or the top of the course below.

7 Never drive nails tight in vinyl siding. The siding should hang from the nails and be free to expand or contract side to side.

2 Nail J-channel directly below the soffit to receive the uppermost piece of siding.

3 Install starter strip so siding snapped into it will align with the bottom of the corners.

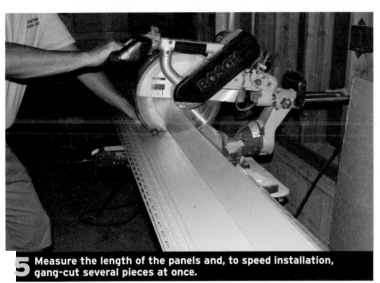

5 Measure the length of the panels and, to speed installation, gang-cut several pieces at once.

6 Bend panel to fit, slide it down over the top of the course below, engage the locking edges, and pull up to lock the courses together.

8 At inside corners, slip each siding panel behind the J-channel you previously installed.

9 Lap abutting panels. To hide the joint, make the panel closest to the usual view point the upper lap.

INSTALLING VINYL SIDING (CONTINUED)

Trimming the windows

Trim around all sides of windows and doors with J-channel. The J-channel pieces will lap each other to drain water, so add twice the width of the front of the J to each length. That's usually 2 in.

Cut the J to length with a miter saw or snips. At both ends of the top and bottom pieces, cut along the inside of the channel the width of the front of the J to create a flap. ❶ Make similar cuts to the side pieces but cut out the flaps. Nail the J in place, starting with the bottom, using roofing nails every foot. ❷ Fold the bottom-piece flaps up along the side of the window, then nail the side pieces in place, lapping the bottom flaps. Then install the top piece of J. That goes over any drip cap that's in place, and its flaps should lap into the side J-channel.

Hold the siding in place under the window to mark the width of the window. ❸ Then measure from the buttlock on the course below to the top of the J (inside the channel recess) and deduct ¼ in. for expansion. This is the depth of the cut you'll make in the siding panel. ❹ Extend the first marks to this depth and connect them using a straightedge. Using snips, make the cut on your marks. ❺

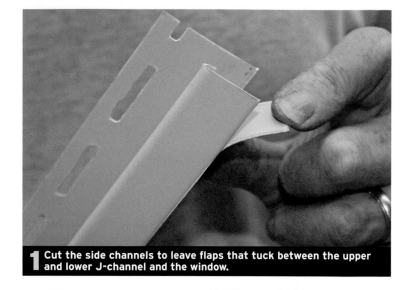

1 Cut the side channels to leave flaps that tuck between the upper and lower J-channel and the window.

INSTALLING J-CHANNEL ON WINDOWS

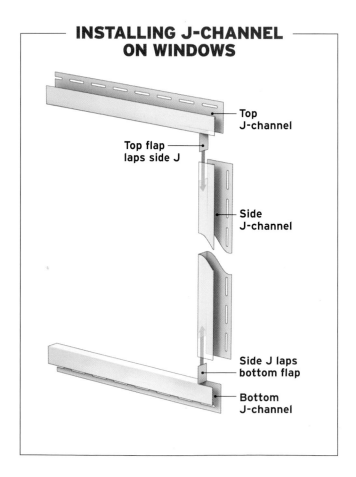

Top J-channel

Top flap laps side J

Side J-channel

Side J laps bottom flap

Bottom J-channel

3 With the J in place, hold the siding in its installed location to mark the width of the piece you'll have to cut out for the window.

5 When all your measurements are marked, use snips to cut the panel at the marks.

2 Start the J-channel installation around windows by nailing the bottom section in place with roofing nails.

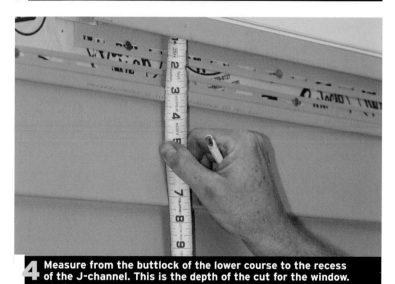

4 Measure from the buttlock of the lower course to the recess of the J-channel. This is the depth of the cut for the window.

DETAILING THE TOP PIECE

The upper piece of vinyl always has to be cut at the soffit. A lot of carpenters snap it into the piece below, and tuck the top into the J above, and call it good. I've seen a lot of pieces of siding installed that way laying on the ground after a windstorm.

Another approach is to tack the top in place with painted aluminum nails. That works, but the vinyl can buckle in the heat. I use a snap-lock punch to cut small slots in the vinyl near its top edge and use these slots for the aluminum nails driven at an angle to get past the face of the J-channel.

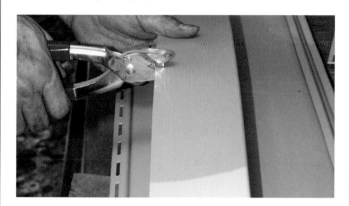

Small slots punched in the cut edge allow nailing in more visible locations (under windows or soffits) with small aluminum nails.

USING UNDERSILL

An alternative to J-channel for below windows and soffits is undersill.

Undersill is meant to grip and hold the top of vinyl siding whose nail flange has been cut off. It's a good product when it can be used, particularly under longer windows, where siding tucked into J would go without nails for a distance. But it won't keep the siding in if the siding is cut near the point where it thickens at the center or the bottom.

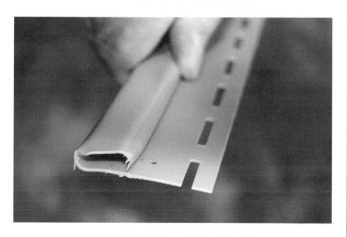

INSTALLING LIGHT BLOCKS

Light blocks are designed for mounting exterior lights. Nail the first piece through its flanges and cut the siding to fit around it. Once you've nailed the siding, snap in the trim piece.

INSTALLING TRIMWORK

ALTHOUGH TRIM GENERALLY APPLIES to doors and moldings on the inside of a house, installation is pretty much the same as for units on the exterior. Most of the techniques in this chapter apply to both basic trim styles and to more elaborate features, as well. In most cases, more complicated designs rely on the same joints and fastening methods, just in more layers.

Like all aspects of construction, trim has a definite sequence. First come doors, then the trim for the doors and windows. Next come baseboard, shoe molding, and any special trim, such as crown molding.

If closet bars and shelves are in the plans, they get tackled next. Kitchen and bathroom vanities are usually the last thing on my agenda. However, cabinets and vanities can go in any time, so if there's a pile of cabinets taking up half the garage, I'll often install them early in the sequence, just to make room.

INSTALLING A PREHUNG SINGLE DOOR

Prehung doors come hinged to their jambs and with drilled bores for the lock and latch.

1 Protect the floor with resin paper. Check the floor for level.

2 Push a shim under the level till the bubble centers. Mark the shim.

Drywall dust If you're trimming after a drywall job, first get rid of the dust. It's rough on tools, your lungs, and your throat.

Sweeping isn't enough—the exhaust from pneumatic tools kicks dust from nooks and crannies into the air. Use a vacuum. Outfit it with a crevice tool to get the dust in the crack between the floor and drywall.

The vast majority of doors you'll install will be "prehung," meaning the door comes hinged in its jamb, with stops applied and lock and latch holes bored. All you have to do is carry the unit to its opening and nail, plumb, and level it. That's a lot easier when the opening itself is plumb and level, a pretty rare condition. The craft in setting a door is knowing how to cut, shim, and tweak the unit till it's plumb and level.

Getting the framing level

First remove all the packing and shipping hardware from the unit. Then check the floor in the opening for level. Odds are, you'll have to shorten one of the side jambs so the head jamb will be level.

Use a level that's the width of the opening or longer. **1** Rest one end on the high side of the floor right next to the wall plate. On the low side of the opening, push a shim under the other end of the level until the bubble centers. Pencil a mark on the shim where it meets the level. **2**

Now, set that shim against the jamb leg that will rest on the high side of the floor, lining up your pencil mark on the outside face of the jamb. On the jamb, mark the thickness of the shim at the pencil line and extend a cut line across the jamb with a square. **3**

Shorten the jamb with a handsaw. Use a Japanese saw that cuts on the pull stroke—it won't splinter the inside face. **4**

Plumbing the framing

Check the face of the walls for plumb. If they're out, try knocking them plumb by placing a 2× block against the bottom plate and whacking it with a sledgehammer.

Use a long level to check the hinge-side jamb for plumb. Shim the stud plumb if need be, tacking a pair of shims at about the height of the top or bottom hinge, depending on which way the stud is out of plumb. **5** If it's plumb, tack the shims near the top hinge.

>> >> >>

3 Hold the shim on the high-side jamb leg, with the mark lined up on the outside corner of the jamb. Mark and extend the cut line.

4 Shorten the jamb that will rest on the high side of the opening. Using a back-cutting saw will avoid chipping the inside face.

5 Tack shims to the hinge-side stud to support the jamb plumb.

Shims Shims are simply cedar shingles split along the grain into narrow pieces. Buying a bundle of undercourse is the cheapest way to get them.

Shims are usually used in pairs with their tapers going in opposite directions. The taper angles cancel each other, and their outside faces end up parallel.

Sometimes, however, studs aren't square to the wall, and shims installed with opposing tapers can twist the door jamb. In that case, running several shims with their tapers in the same direction will put the face of the shim on the jamb square to the wall.

ORDERING TRIM

Putting together a trim order is pretty straightforward. Walk through the house measuring door openings, rooms, and windows. Door openings are usually 2 in. wider than the door itself.

Measure the windows and allow slightly more than twice the trim width extra for the miters. Order extension jambs (board stock that extends from the window frame out to the face of the drywall) and stools (the interior version of a sill) as needed.

Every room gets baseboard around its perimeter. Rooms with hard floors such as wood, tile, stone, or vinyl also get shoe molding. Simply measure the perimeter and order by the lineal foot.

Check the plans for details such as closet hardware. Order board stock for closet cleats, plywood or shelf stock for shelves, closet poles, and combination shelf/pole brackets for every closet more than about 3 ft. wide.

You'll also need nails, mostly 2½-in. and 1½-in. I usually use 15-gauge pneumatic finish nails, but 16-gauge nails are fine as well. If you're hand-nailing, use 8d finish nails for door jambs and closet cleats. Use 6d finish nails for base and for the wall side of casing. Use 4ds for the thin side of casing and for shoe molding.

Order doors specifying whether they are right-handed or left-handed. "Handing" designates where the knob is and which way the door swings. Doors are called right hand or left hand, but that designation can be confusing, referring to the hinge or the lock. There is no standard, so verify the nomenclature with the supplier. Be sure to order two sets of casing and an appropriate lockset with each door.

INSTALLING A PREHUNG SINGLE DOOR (CONTINUED)

6 With the unit in the opening, check to be sure that cutting the jamb leg resulted in a level head jamb.

7 Move the jamb in or out to bring the edge of the jamb flush with the drywall.

10 Add shims behind the other hinges as needed to make the jamb plumb.

11 Start shimming the latch side at the bottom, aiming for an even gap between the door and jamb.

Set the unit in place in the opening and check the head jamb for level. **6** Make sure the jamb is flush with the drywall on both sides of the opening. **7** Then drive 2½-in. finish nails through the center of the jamb through the shims you have already tacked to the stud (assuming there are shims there; otherwise just nail into the stud). **8** Shim the latch side of the frame to stabilize it.

Shimming the hinge side

Close the door and check the gap between the top edge of the door and the head jamb. **9** If need be, adjust the lower shims until the gap is uniform and the jamb is plumb. **10** Make sure the jamb is flush with the drywall at the lower hinge and drive two nails through the jamb and shims. Do the same through the upper set of shims.

Close the door, shim behind the center hinge, if any, or in the middle of the jamb if there is no third hinge, until the gap between the door and the jamb is even. Nail that set of shims.

Doors and humidity
Wooden doors expand as the ambient humidity increases and shrink as it decreases. In areas with large seasonal changes in humidity, good carpenters take this into account to avoid sticking doors or overly large gaps.

If it's been very humid when you're installing a door, the door is likely as wide as it will get. Make the gap at the latch side relatively small in this circumstance, say ¹⁄₁₆ in., so that when the door shrinks, the gap won't be too big. If it's very dry when you're hanging the door, make a larger gap, about ³⁄₁₆ in.

You might have to disassemble the jamb to cut a little from the head, or to open up the joint between the head and the leg.

8 Begin securing the unit by nailing into the set of shims you previously tacked to the stud.

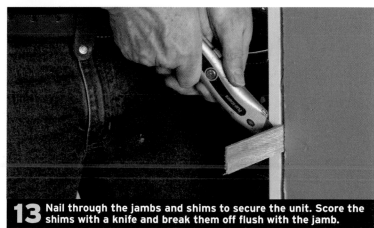

9 If the hinge-side jamb is plumb and the head jamb is level, the gap between the door and the head should be even.

12 Shim the latch-side jamb in at least four spots to ensure its straightness.

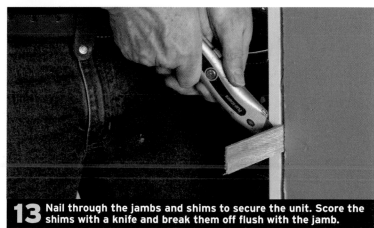

13 Nail through the jambs and shims to secure the unit. Score the shims with a knife and break them off flush with the jamb.

Shimming the latch side

Move to the latch side and shim low on the jamb to get an even gap between it and the door. **11** Close the door to be sure it's hitting the latch-side stop evenly along its length. Adjust the bottom of the jamb in or out of the opening until the door hits the stop correctly, then set the first nail through the middle of the jamb and shim.

The jamb may not end up flush with the drywall because of this adjustment, but the casing at the bottom doesn't require a miter joint, so it's easy to hide this flaw.

With the door closed, shim behind the latch-side jamb in one or two additional places as needed to make the gap between it and the edge of the door even. **12** Drive two nails through each set of shims, and the door is hung. The last step is to score the shims with a sharp knife and snap them off flush with the jamb. **13**

Plumb and level in an old house

Plumb, level, and square are ideals, but it's not always possible to achieve them. In an older house, it's likely nothing has been plumb, level, or square for decades, maybe centuries. (I've found the same thing in more than one new house I've trimmed.)

In these situations, ideals can get in the way. If, for example, you insist on hanging a door perfectly plumb close to an intersecting wall that's out of plumb, the space between them can taper obviously. No one looking at that mess will think the wall is out of plumb. They'll think the trim carpenter screwed up. Often, parallel is more important than plumb or level.

INSTALLING LOCKSETS

Although there are some differences between manufacturers, most locks are basi-
cally the same. The hardest part of installation is
usually getting them out of the blister pack.

Install the latch first, with the tapered portion of the latchbolt facing the jamb. ❶ The
flange should be flush with the edge of the
door. Sometimes you'll need to deepen the gain
(a shallow mortise for seating hardware, such
as this flange or a hinge) or square its corners
using a chisel. ❷ (I can't stress enough the
importance of knowing how to sharpen chisels
and planes, and of actually applying that knowledge.) Drill pilot holes, and screw the latch into
place. ❸

Insert the handle halves into the lock bore,
making sure the axle goes through the right
part of the latch and into the corresponding
hole in the second half. ❹ Screw the halves
together, taking care not to damage the knobs
with your screwdriver. ❺

With locking locks, which half goes on which
side of the door is obvious—locking lever inside,
keyhole outside. Passage locks (used on closet
and basement doors) don't come with the same
obvious clues. With passage locks, I assemble
the halves so their screws are on the inside of
the closet or basement, solely for looks.

Set the strikeplate in its gain in the jamb. As
with the latch flange, there may be some chisel
work involved. Always drill pilot holes in the
jamb for the strikeplate screws—otherwise you
will split the jamb. ❻ Set the screws, check the
operation, and you're done.

1 Start your installation of a lockset by test-fitting the latch
in the hole prebored in the edge of the door.

4 Install the halves of the handle, threading the axle through
the latch and into its hole in the second knob.

TRADE SECRET

Most residential doors come with the center of the lock bore
$2^3/8$ in. from the edge of the door. That's the backset. The
backset on commercial doors, and often on residential fire doors,
is $2^3/4$ in. You may have to specify this when ordering locks,
but many models allow you to adjust them to either backset.

2 Chisel the latch gain deeper if needed to make the latch flange flush with the edge of the door.

3 Insert the latch and mark the position of the holes in the flange. Withdraw the latch, drill pilot holes, and screw the latch.

5 Screw the handle together, being careful not to scratch the knob with the screwdriver.

6 Hold the strikeplate in place and mark the location of the hole. Then drill pilot holes and screw it home.

Buying interior locks Interior locksets that lock are called privacy locks. They're generally used on bedrooms only. Bath locks are pretty much the same as privacy locks, but the inside will have a chrome or nickel finish. Both types can be unlocked from the outside with a key that resembles a thin, flat-bladed screwdriver, which, by the way, also works should you lose the key. Passage locks install the same way as privacy or bath locks, but they don't lock. Dummy locks don't have a mechanism—they're just handles that fasten to twin or bifold doors.

Locks come in a variety of quality levels. Weight and cost are two signs of a lock's quality. The greater each one is, the better chance you've got a high-quality product.

HANGING TWIN DOORS

You can hang a single door slightly out of plumb and level. As long as the gaps are even, no one will ever know. You can't get away with that with a twin door, however, because the doors themselves won't meet in a straight line across the top. That's an obvious error.

Checking for level

Use a long level to check the floor. If the level is longer than the opening, place blocks under it near the jack studs, and shims on top of them. ❶ That way, you're checking for level where the jambs will rest. Trim the jamb legs if need be, shim one side of the opening plumb, and set the unit in place. Check the head jamb not only for level but also to be sure it's straight. ❷

Treat the gap between the doors as you would the gap between a single door and its latch-side jamb. It should be even, top to bottom.

Keeping the doors in plane

The head jamb will keep the tops of twin doors in plane with each other, but any twist in the doors or in the lower jambs will show up in the doors being out of plane at the bottom. ❸ Make sure the walls on both sides of the opening are plumb across their face. Make small adjustments by moving one or the other jamb out of plane with the wall. Split the difference by moving one jamb in and one out until the doors are in plane.

Twisted jack studs can also cause out-of-plane doors. Fix this by building the shims up thicker on one side of the jack than the other. ❹ Getting the twins both evenly gapped and in plane can take some fiddling around.

Installing the catches

Magnet catches hold most twins shut. Screw the metal plate to the back of the door, just below where it hits the stop. ❺ Set the magnet on the plate with the door closed and mark on the stop where the catch will go. ❻ Open the door, remove the magnet from the metal plate, and screw it in place on its marks. You might think it would be easier to screw the magnet to the stop while the door is closed and the magnet is stuck to the plate, but there isn't enough clearance for a cordless screwdriver.

If twin doors aren't plumb, their tops won't meet in a straight horizontal line, and the center gap won't be even from top to bottom.

Wide openings Once in a while, you'll find an opening that creates gaps at the jambs much wider than a couple of shims will fill. If the casing you're using will cover the gap, just nail a length of 1×4 to one or both jack studs before shimming. If the opening is much bigger than that, the casing may not cover the gap. The best solution, if possible, is to get a set of bigger doors. Otherwise, you'll have to re-frame and re-drywall the opening.

TRADE SECRET

For the miter on the casing to fit easily, the casing has to lie flat, and that means the jamb has to be flush with the wall. Walls aren't always uniformly thick, however, and it may not be possible to set the jamb flush with the drywall on both sides. In most cases, I split the difference and make minor adjustments to the miter. If the jamb is proud of the wall, it's easy to plane flush. And if the drywall is proud of the jamb, I beat it down with my hammer.

For a closet door, I'll flush the jamb with the drywall on the outside to ease fitting the visible casing miter. The fit on the inside isn't as important. No one is likely to see the miter inside a closet.

1 When hanging twins, carefully check the floor for level. Cut the high-side jamb by the thickness of the shim at the low end.

2 Make sure the head jamb is level, shim it to keep it that way and nail it straight.

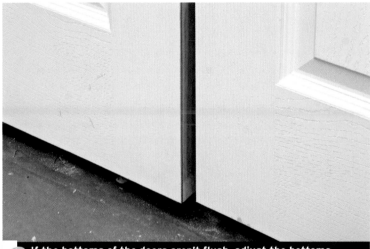

3 If the bottoms of the doors aren't flush, adjust the bottoms of the jambs in and out slightly until the doors are even.

4 If the jack stud is twisted, build up the shims thicker on one edge so the jamb sits square to the wall.

5 Screw the steel plate for the magnet catch to the back of the door, a little lower than where the door hits the stop.

6 Mark the location of the magnet, then open the door for clearance and screw the magnet in place.

SHORTENING A DOOR

Prehung doors are 1 in. shorter than their jambs (except for sliders and bifolds, which are 2 in. shorter). That 1-in. gap provides desirable clearance for air flow, but not necessarily for carpet. If you're going to carpet the floor, you have two choices to create a 1-in. gap. The easiest thing to do is rip 1/2-in.- or 3/4-in.-thick plywood blocks to the width of your jambs. Glue them to the floor (nailing or screwing might split them) directly under the jamb legs. The carpet hides the edges of the blocks, and the blocks raise the unit higher.

This solution, however, doesn't always work with thick carpet and then you have to cut the door. But that's pretty simple.

Making the cut

Mark the desired height on the bottom of the door on each side. ❶ It's best to line up a shooting board on the marks to get a straight cut with a circular saw. ❷ The shooting board also supports the fibers on the good side of the cut, preventing tearout from the sawblade.

➜ See "Making Clean Cuts," p. 15.

Once you've made the cut, chamfer the edges with a block plane or sanding block. ❸

On hollow-core doors, your cut will sometimes end up above the bottom core block, leaving the bottom of the door with a hollow recess. The fix is to rip a scrap of wood to fit snugly between the door skins and glue it in place. ❹ Use lots of clamps and place boards or cauls on both sides to distribute the force of the clamps and to keep them from marring the surface of the door. ❺

1 To cut a door shorter, first mark its length by measuring from the top.

2 Clamp a shooting board to the door on your marks and cut with a circular saw.

3 Smooth and chamfer the edges with a block plane.

4 When replacing a core in a shortened door, cut an insert to fit snugly in the bottom recess and use plenty of glue.

5 Use scrap boards as cauls to distribute clamping pressure and keep the clamps from marring the surface of the door.

SETTING JAMBS WITHOUT DOORS

There are several instances when jambs are installed without prehung doors. The first is a trimmed opening, usually between public areas such as a hall and a living room. The other two are for sliding and bifold doors.

➤ See "Installing Sliders," p. 216, and "Installing Bifolds," p. 218.

In all cases, the first step is to check the floor for level and trim one jamb leg as needed to level the head.

➤ See "Installing a Prehung Single Door," steps 1-4, pp. 206-207.

Assemble the jambs by nailing or screwing through the leg into the head and set the jamb in the opening. ❶

Shim the top of the jamb legs, as you would a prehung door jamb.

➤ See "Installing a Prehung Single Door," steps 5-9, pp. 207-209.

Without a door to help you shim the jamb legs straight and plumb, you need to use a level. ❷ I have a 78-in. door-hanger's level, and it's a pricey tool if you aren't a pro. A straight piece of 1×4 or the like combined with a shorter level gets the job done as well, if not as conveniently. Shim the legs at the top and bottom, then in one or two spots in the middle as needed.

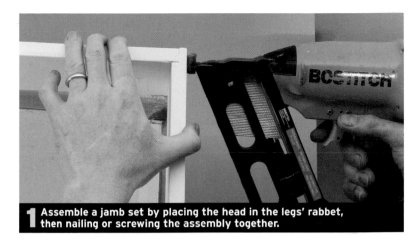

1 Assemble a jamb set by placing the head in the legs' rabbet, then nailing or screwing the assembly together.

2 Shim and nail the jamb legs in place, keeping the jamb straight and plumb.

FINISHED OPENING SIZES

The finished opening, or distance between the jambs, on a trimmed opening can be whatever you want. Trimmed openings are often fairly wide. I generally trim the jamb head so the opening is that of a standard-size door. That way, if I ever decide to add a door, I don't have to go to a lot of extra trouble.

The finished opening for bifolds is usually a standard size such as 24 in., 30 in., 36 in., 48 in., 60 in., or 72 in. Slider openings are always twice a standard door width less 1 in., so the doors overlap when closed. Slider openings are usually 47 in., 59 in., or 71 in.

For any opening more than 3 ft., I shim and nail the jamb head as well as the legs. Fasten the jamb heads for sliders in several places, as the head jamb bears the weight of the doors.

INSTALLING SLIDERS

The first step in slider installation is setting the jambs, and you can use the steps described on the previous pages for that. Once you set the jambs, sliders go up easy and quick.

➡ See "Setting Jambs Without Doors," p. 215.

Screw the track to the jamb head, typically 1 in. back from the jamb's front edge. ❶ Separate the front-door hangers from the rear-door hangers. There are always two sets. The top of the hanger (where the roller is) on the ones for the rear door extend farther in so they're over the center of the door. Those for the front door are straighter. The difference in the hangers provides clearance for the doors to pass each other. Following the manufacturer's directions for spacing, screw the hanging hardware to the back face of each door but don't set the screws fully yet. ❷

Installing the doors

Install the rear door first, easing it up and angling it backward till you can get the hanger wheels in the track. When the wheels are engaged, lower the door and give it a test slide to make sure both wheels are riding in the track. ❸ Repeat with the front door. Close each door, and check how it fits against its jamb leg. Adjust the hangers until the doors hit flush to the jambs down their length, with their tops at the same height. ❹ Once the doors are properly set, tighten the hanger screws.

Installing the floor guides and pulls

Next comes the floor-guide hardware that separates the doors and keeps them from banging into or rubbing against each other. Close the front door and eyeball it to be sure it's hanging parallel to the front edge of its jamb. Holding the door in that position, screw the guide to the floor in the middle of the opening. ❺

Then for the door pulls, drill a shallow hole in the side of each door that will meet the jambs, and insert the pulls. ❻ Finally, cut and nail a piece of $3/4$-in. quarter-round molding to the head jamb in front of the track.

1 Use the manufacturer's screws to attach the slider track to the jamb head, usually about an inch back from the front edge.

4 Use the adjuster on the hangers to fit the doors properly, then set them by snugging the attachment screws.

2 Fasten the hangers to the rear surfaces of the doors but don't snug the screws all the way.

3 Holding the rear door at an angle, ease it up until you can engage the rollers in the rear track.

5 With the doors tight to one jamb, center the bottom guide on the doors and screw it to the floor.

6 Slider pulls stay in place by friction only, so use a sharp bit to drill clean holes for them.

What to do when there's carpet

As with other doors, carpet adds some work to installing sliders. You may have to add blocks under the jambs or shorten the doors. You'll also have to add a plywood block below the center guides, or they won't stick up high enough to do their job.

Use the same-thickness plywood here as under the jambs and cut the piece so it's just big enough for the guides to sit on. Use long-enough screws on the guides to penetrate the block and at least 1 in. into the subfloor.

INSTALLING BIFOLDS

Although bifolds are typically sold in kits where the doors are already hinged together, they're a little fussier than sliders or twins. Bifolds open by rotating on top and bottom pivot pins at the jamb side. There's a third pin, or guide, at the top of the outer door that rides in a track.

Also, they have multiple adjustment points that control height, spacing from the jamb and from each other, as well as whether they're plumb. Don't be intimidated though—just take one step at a time.

Screw the track to the head jamb, typically keeping it 1 in. back from the front edge of the jamb. ❶ Insert the snubber spring into the track—in the center if there are two pairs of bifolds, at the end opposite the pivot if it's a single pair. The snubber spring jams against the upper pivot pin to hold the door closed.

Hanging the doors

Drive the pivot pin into the predrilled hole in the bottom of the door on the side that will go against the jamb. ❷ On the top of the door, drive the spring-loaded pivot and guide pins into their holes. In some cases, the pivot and guide pins are identical, but with other manufacturers they differ. In the latter case, set the pivot pin on the jamb side. ❸ Screw the L-brackets to the floor and the jamb so their centerline is plumb with that of the track. ❹ This is a simple matter of centering the track and the L-bracket the same distance from the face of the jamb. Usually, that's 1 in., but it can be farther back.

Set the doors in place, with the pivot pin going into the hole in the adjustable pivot block (that's set within the track) and the guide pin simply riding free in the track. ❺ Push up to compress the springs on the pivot and guide pins, raising the door high enough so the bottom pivot clears the L-bracket, then lower the door so the pin drops into the bracket.

Adjusting a single pair

Now comes the fussy part—adjusting the doors. First, you'll have to adjust them side-to-side so they're parallel with the jambs and far enough from them so the doors don't bind.

You'll accomplish this by adjusting the location of the upper pivot block in the track. Loosen the pivot-block screw and slide the block till there's about $1/8$-in. clearance between the edge of the door stile and the jamb when the door is closed. ❻ You may have to open and close the door a couple of times, adjusting the block till you get the spacing right. When that looks OK tighten the screw.

Now, raise the door and move the bottom pivot in the L-bracket until the gap between the door and the jamb is even. Test the operation and repeat as needed. Perform the same steps on the second pair of doors if you have them.

1 Using the manufacturer's screws, fasten the bifold track to the head jamb about 1 in. from the front edge of the jamb.

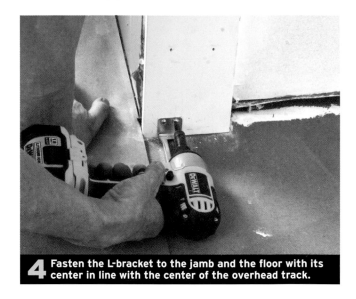

4 Fasten the L-bracket to the jamb and the floor with its center in line with the center of the overhead track.

Adjusting a double pair

With a double pair of bifolds, there are two more steps. Once the doors operate well, take a look at their tops. If they don't meet evenly in the center, adjust the bottom pivots. Lift the door so the pivot clears the L-bracket and turn it in or out to lower or raise the door. This is a trial-and-error process that you may need to repeat a couple of times. Then pick a spot about 1 ft. above the floor and attach the pair of alignment clips to the back of the doors—they keep the doors in plane with each other. ❼

Finally, attach the knobs. ❽ They go on the hinged stiles of each pair—either door is fine—so that pulling on them moves the doors outward, toward a folded position against the jamb.

2 Set the bottom pivot pin in the side of the door that will be next to the jamb.

3 Tap the two spring-loaded pins in the top of the doors. One is a pivot pin, the other a guide pin.

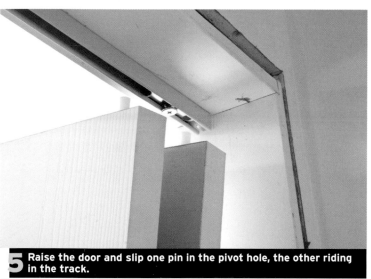

5 Raise the door and slip one pin in the pivot hole, the other riding in the track.

6 Adjust the top of the bifold by loosening the pivot block and moving it. Retighten the screw when you've adjusted the doors.

7 On a pair of bifold doors, fasten the alignment clips to their backs to keep the doors in plane when they're closed.

8 Predrill holes for the knobs if necessary and install each at the same height and centered on the hinged stiles.

INSTALLING EXTENSION JAMBS AND STOOLS

When ordering windows, it's a good idea to have them made so the frames are deep enough to extend flush with the face of the drywall. That's not always possible, though, particularly with lower-cost vinyl windows. In order to trim such a window and hide the jack stud, extension jambs are used. Extension jambs are simply pieces of 1× ripped to the span from the inside edge of the window frame to the face of the drywall, and there are usually two legs and a head.

Install extension jambs so there's about a 1/8-in. reveal where they meet the window frame, because it's practically impossible to make a flush joint that will stay flush. The reveal avoids this problem and creates a shadow line that adds interest.

Window stools, which are often mistakenly called sills (sills are on the outside), run across the bottom of the window to create a ledge for cats and plants. Stools are sometimes omitted as a cost-saving measure or to create a picture-frame design, replaced with an extension jamb across the bottom and finished with a simple picture-frame casing. I prefer the traditional look of a window stool, which references the classical Greek element of base and plinth.

The installation shown here includes a stool, but for a picture-frame design, you'll cut an extension length for the bottom of the window, assemble all four sides of the jamb, and install it as a unit. For either style, it's easier to assemble all the pieces (stool included) into a frame and install the whole shebang at once.

Cutting extension jambs

Creating extension jambs is simple. First, measure from the face of the window frame out to the drywall surface, taking measurements in several places to account for variations. Then rip the extension stock to the largest measurement. When you get the extension frame installed, it will be a lot easier to plane the jambs flush to the wall (which is usually only necessary behind mitered casing corners) than to tilt the trim inward to fit a short extension jamb.

Measure the window frame across the top and sides and cut these pieces to length. If you're not making a stool, cut a section of ripped jamb stock equal to the width of the window and assemble the sections. If your frame includes a stool, make the stool, then assemble the sections.

Making window stools

Stools need to be notched to fit inside the opening, and they need to be long enough to extend past the casing—both its front and side edges. I usually extend them about 3/4 in. to 1 in. past the sides of the casing—much more than that and you lose the effect of the base and plinth. At the front edge, I extend them at least 3/4 in. beyond the face of the casing.

Measure the width of the window and rough-cut the stool to length—the width of the window opening plus the width of the two

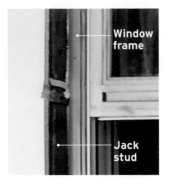
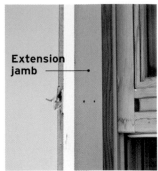

Often, a window frame will not be as deep as the thickness of the wall. Extension jambs fill in that empty space and hide the jack stud.

A reveal is a narrow area not covered by abutting trim, such as the edge of the unpainted window frame exposed by the extension jamb.

Window stools are traditional design elements. They are notched, extend past the casing, and return to the wall in a mitered block.

pieces of side casing, plus 1 1/2 in. for the extensions. Subtract the width of the window from the rough-cut length. ❶ Divide the result by two, measure in from each end that amount, and mark the stool. Those points are where the notches will begin. Measure from the face of the drywall to the window with a combination square and set it to that dimension. ❷   >> >> >>

1 Measure the width of the window; add the casing width and combined width of the extensions past the casing.

2 Measure the depth of the space between the window frame and the face of the drywall. This is the depth of the stool notch.

EXTENSION JAMBS

Drywall

Casing

Rough framing

Extension jamb

Window stool

REVEALS

Casing

Reveal between extension jamb and window frame

Window frame

Drywall

Extension jamb

Reveal between casing and extension jamb

TRADE SECRET

Because the window casing is nailed to the extension jambs, you'll want the extension-jamb material to match the trim.

If you're using stain-grade trim, then use the same species of wood in the extensions. For painted trim, make the extension from primed finger-joint pine—there are no knots to bleed through the paint.

INSTALLING EXTENSION JAMBS AND STOOLS (CONTINUED)

3 Mark the window width on the stool and lay out the notch with the square.

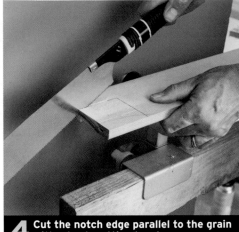

4 Cut the notch edge parallel to the grain with a back-cutting handsaw.

5 Crosscut the inside edge of the notch on a miter saw.

Use the square to mark the notch on the stool. **3** Then make the rip cut on the stool with a handsaw and the cross-cut on a miter saw. **4**, **5**

Attaching stool returns

The stool still needs to be cut to its finished length, and a simple square cut at the end of a molded stool looks cheesy and leaves end grain exposed. To avoid that, I return the stool to the wall.

In essence, returning means turning the corner by mitering the ends of the stool and gluing in a small mitered return, or block, that continues the profile to the wall. Returning is usually the best way to end any molding that doesn't end at a perpendicular wall.

Mark the ends of the stool and miter them. **6** Rip a piece of stool as wide as the depth of the section forward of the notch, square-cut the ends and then cut them off at 45 degrees so the cutoffs come to a point at the back edge of the square cut. **7** Glue the returns to the notched stool. You can clamp the joint with masking tape, but spring clamps work better. **8** Once the glue has set (overnight is safest), level the joint with sandpaper.

Assembling the frame

Gather the extension-jamb sections you cut earlier and lay them out on the floor. Fasten the legs to the head jamb and the stool to the legs with 2½-in. nails. **9** Make sure to space the extension jambs to provide the desired reveal.

8 Glue the returns to the stool and secure them with tape or spring clamps overnight.

Slide the assembly into the window opening, butting it tightly to the window frame. **10** Space the extension jambs at the desired reveal. Shim below the stool in several places and between the extension jambs and the stud—in at least two places on each side for small windows and three or four places for most others. Once you've shimmed every-thing straight and with even reveals, nail it in place with 2-in. or 2½-in. finish nails. **11**

TRADE SECRET

One difference between extension jambs and door jambs is that you can't worry about extension jambs being plumb or level. That all depends on how the window was installed. The best you can do is shim exten-sion jambs straight.

6 To prepare the corner for the return, use a miter saw to cut the ends of the stool.

7 Cut returns for each end of the stool from stool stock ripped to width.

9 Lay out the sections of the frame and assemble the jamb extensions and stool.

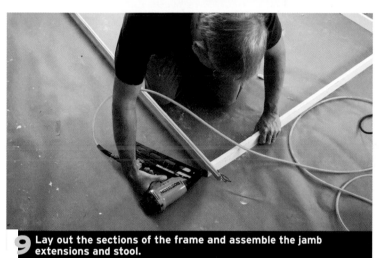

10 Lift the frame in place and seat it solidly in the recess, flush with the face of the drywall.

11 As with door jambs, shim and nail extension jambs straight. Then score the shims and break them at the edge of the jamb.

INSTALLING DOOR AND WINDOW CASING

Casing is usually a relatively thin ($^{11}/_{16}$ in. is typical) molding that joins in miters at the corners of a door or window frame. In some interior styles, however, such as contemporary or Arts-and-Crafts designs, it might be a simple piece of 4/4 stock that meets with butt joints. Here, I'll focus on miters.

Casings should leave a small reveal along the interior edge of the jamb. So first set a combination square to the desired reveal (I usually go with $^1/_8$ in.), and pencil the edge of the reveal in a few spots on the jamb, particularly the corners. ❶

Marking the cuts

Before you begin marking the casing for cuts, make sure the bottoms of the casing legs are square so they sit on the floor or window stool without a gap. Then hold an unmitered length of casing on one side of the frame and mark it where it intersects the reveal line for the head casing. ❷ Then mark the casing leg for the other side in the same fashion.

Making the cuts

Set the miter saw to 45 degrees and, with the casing tight to the bed and fence of the saw, cut to the mark. ❸ Nail one leg to the jamb using $1^1/_4$-in. or $1^1/_2$-in. finish nails. ❹ Then take the head casing and miter the edge that will adjoin the installed leg.

Hold the head casing against the installed leg and, on the bottom edge of the opposite end, mark where it intersects the vertical reveal on that side. ❺ Miter the head casing at this mark and then mark and miter the other leg as you did the first one. Check the fit. If there's a gap, using a block plane to relieve the back of the miter usually takes care of it.   >> >> >>

1 Lightly mark the reveal on the jamb with a pencil and combination square.

Most casing meets in a mitered joint (left), hiding the gap between the framing and the jamb, but some styles require butt joints (right).

2 Mark the location of the intersecting head-jamb reveal on the casing. Miter the casing leg at this mark.

3 Set the miter saw to 45 degrees and cut the miter. Aim to split the pencil mark with the sawblade.

4 Nail the first piece of casing to the jamb. Don't nail the casing to the wall at this time.

5 Miter one side of the head casing and hold it firmly against the installed leg. Mark the intersection of the side reveal.

WHAT CAN GO WRONG

Don't nail the head casing to the wall—only to the head jamb. Nailing the casing head to the wall attaches it to the header. Headers are typically large enough to change dimension by $1/4$ in. to $1/2$ in. with changes in seasonal humidity. This movement will pull the nailed casing head upward as well, which opens a big crack in the miter.

INSTALLING DOOR AND WINDOW CASING (CONTINUED)

Installing the casing

Once the dry-fit is good, spread some carpenter's glue on the miter and nail the head and second leg to the jamb. **6** Shoot a nail into the miter to hold it until the glue dries. **7** Don't be tempted to use one nail from the top and one from the side—the second nail can deflect off the first and pierce the face of the casing.

Use longer nails—generally 2 in.—to secure the casing to the walls. To avoid having to change nails in the nailer all the time, I don't nail it to the wall at the same time I'm nailing it to the jambs. Since I'll use the same nails for the base molding, I nail the casing legs to the wall when I'm back there nailing down base.

Returning the apron

The casing below a window stool, the apron, should have its ends returned to the wall. Hold the apron against the fence of the miter saw and miter one end. **8** Carry that to the window, lay it on the stool, and align the cut end with the outside of one casing leg. Mark the final length on the apron at the opposite casing leg. **9** You'll need a left and a right return, so miter both ends of a scrap of casing.

Cut the returns off by aligning the blade with the line where the miter meets the back of the casing. **10** Expect to cut extras—the sawblade tends to fling these small pieces around. Don't try to cut returns from too short a piece of scrap—you don't want your fingers too close to the blade. Nail the apron to the wall, tight under the stool. Spread a little glue on the return and push it into place. **11** There's usually enough pressure to hold it until the glue dries, or you can secure it with a headless pinner.

> **(i) TRADE SECRET**
> Occasionally, you'll have to case around an octagon or some other unusual shape. All you need to do to figure those miter angles is measure the angle with a protractor and divide it in half.

6 Spread a little glue in the miter joints to help them stay together.

9 Miter one end of the apron, then with that end lined up with the outside edge of the casing, mark the length of the apron.

7 Keep the miter face aligned with a nail driven in from the top or side.

8 Miter the ends of the apron returns with the molding standing up and tight against the fence.

10 After cutting the miter on the apron returns, crosscut them to length.

11 Glue the return behind the installed apron. The glue is usually tacky enough to keep the return in place till dry.

RUNNING BASEBOARD AND SHOE MOLDING

Running base and shoe molding (or just base and shoe, for short) goes fast, especially if you build efficiencies into your approach. Here's an outline of the method I use, one that saves both time and materials. It's especially practical for large jobs, such as whole-house renovations or new construction, but scaled down for smaller jobs it's a good way to maximize the use of your time and materials.

Working from a base station

I usually work an entire floor at once, setting up my miter saw in a central location on that floor where there's a long, clear distance to either side. That can mean setting the saw next to an openable window, so long pieces hang outside while being cut.

Making a cut list

To minimize waste, I make a cut list for all the pieces in each room. I walk around the floor, measuring the bottom of each wall. Then on the cut list, I note the room with an abbreviation (such as MBR for master bedroom), the number assigned to it, the length of the piece, and abbreviations that designate any end treatments specific to that piece (see "End treatments," at right). I also write the cut-list number on the floor with a lumber crayon next to where the piece will go. Then I do all the cutting at once, working from the cut list.

Cutting from the cut list

I start with the longest pieces and cut each piece from the shortest stock that will work. I measure the offcut and find a length on the cut list that uses it with the least amount left over. Because there are always many more short pieces than long ones, working this way ensures that you have enough long lengths of stock. Typically, the final pieces I'll cut for a floor will be only a couple of inches long, and most scrap will be 6 in. or less.

Once I cut a piece of base, I note on its back what room it belongs in and its cut-list number—in a big house, the numbers can approach 200. Each piece of cut base gets stacked with the others for its room. When I'm done cutting base for an entire floor, I distribute the pieces to the rooms they belong in.   >> >> >>

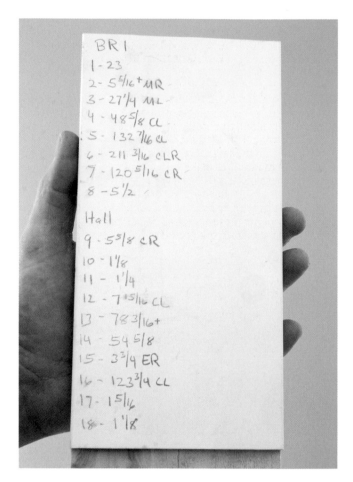

Create a cut list for each room that includes the name of the room, a sequence number, the length of each piece, and any end treatments.

TRADE SECRET

Try to avoid adding special treatments to both ends of a piece of base. Leaving one end square lets you shorten a piece that's maybe a little long with a cross-cut, as opposed to trying to take a little off a cope or a miter.

End treatments

When noting information about each base piece on my cut list, I include a code that indicates any end treatment the piece will require. The code always has an R or an L for right and left, and sometimes it has both. If the right-hand end will turn a corner with a miter, I write MR (Miter, Right). Another might need its left side coped, so the code would be CL (Cope, Left). Another might need its left end returned to the wall, so I'd note EL (End, Left).

COPING BASEBOARD

Coping results in an inside corner joint where the edge of one piece seamlessly follows the profile of the other it joins. A square-cut piece butts into an inside corner, and the coped end of the second piece fits at right angles to it.

A coped joint starts with a normal 45-degree miter cut in the end of the piece. Next, using a coping saw at an angle, cut exactly along the profile of the baseboard, leaving a beveled cut that follows the profile on the face of the base. Some turns are too tight to make with a coping saw. In these cases, start a new cut from an angle that will allow you to continue.

Test-fit the cut by holding the coped piece at right angles to a scrap piece. The coped end should fit the profile of the intersecting piece exactly. If necessary, rasp or plane away material from the back surface to perfect the fit.

There are many reasons to cope rather than miter baseboard. If a mitered corner gaps, anyone standing in the center of the room will be looking right into the crack. If a coped corner gaps, the crack will be hard to see unless you happen to be looking parallel to the uncoped piece of trim. For this reason, it pays to consider from where the corner will most often be viewed when deciding which piece to cope.

If the uncoped piece happens to be a little short, that's okay—the coped piece will hide it. That can allow for some adjustment in fitting, say, an outside miter on the other end of the uncoped piece. Finally, if the coped piece ends up a little long, you can usually spring it into place and you'll get a good looking joint. Try that with an inside miter and one side will bypass the other for an amateurish joint.

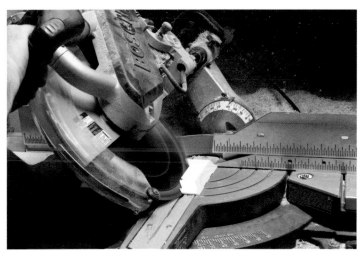

❶ The first step in coping is to cut the stock as if it were joining in an inside miter.

❷ To make the cope, cut along the profile, right up to the face of the molding.

❸ Break away pieces as needed to change the saw's approach.

❹ Test fit the cope on scrap. The pieces should fit with no light showing through the joint.

RUNNING BASEBOARD AND SHOE MOLDING (CONTINUED)

1 Drive a screw into the plate, its head flush with the drywall. The head will support the base, keeping it from tilting into any gap.

2 Verify stud locations by driving a nail in the wall at a spot that the baseboard will cover.

Floor-covering considerations

With all the base in its room, lay it out, matching the markings on the back of each piece with the location code you wrote on the floor. Now it's time to consider floor coverings. If you're planning hardwood or tile, they should be installed before the base. If they aren't, raise the base up on blocks just slightly higher than the thickness of the finished floor so the flooring can go under the base. If carpet's going in, raise the base up on $1/2$-in. blocks to keep the carpet from riding that high on the molding.

Fixing the drywall gap

Take a look at the bottom of the drywall. It usually doesn't go all the way to the floor, but gaps above it by about $3/4$ in. Even if there isn't a gap, it's likely the bottom edge tapers. (The long edges of drywall are thinner so the tape and drywall mud won't create a bulge.) The problem is that when you nail the bottom of the base, it wants to tilt into the recess, throwing off the joint. It's the biggest cause for poor joints in base molding.

To fix this potential problem, drive a drywall screw into the bottom plate at the location of baseboard joints—leave the screw head flush with the face of the drywall. The back of the base will bear on the head of the screw and not kick inward. **❶**

3 Stretch out a tape with a layout dimension under a verified stud location. Nail off the base by following the layout.

> ### TRADE SECRET
> You can always find the studs in a wall using "treasure hunt" methods, but a stud finder makes the job a whole lot easier and accurate. Stud finders are relatively cheap and a great investment, considering the time they save you and the mistakes they keep you from making.

CUTTING MITERS

Cut wide-base miters with the baseboard stock lying flat on the table of a compound miter saw.

Cut narrow base molding standing up on a regular miter saw, keeping it tight against the fence.

Finding the studs

The nails you drive at the bottom of the base will enter the wall plate, of course, but those you drive on top need to hit studs. Thus you'll have to find the studs before you install the base.

How do you find them? There are always studs in the corners and next to doors and windows. If the wall hasn't been painted, it's easy to spot the drywall screws, which go into studs. If the wall has been painted, sometimes you can still spot the drywall screws, especially in raking light. If you can't, look for electrical boxes. Most electricians, like most people, are right handed. It's easiest for right-handed electricians to nail boxes to the right side of studs, so consequently, most electrical boxes have a stud to their left. Verify this by driving a nail or screw into the wall where the base will hide the hole. ❷

Once you've found a stud (corner, door, and window studs don't count because their location won't necessarily be on the wall's layout), mark it on the floor. Then find another to determine their spacing. Put the base in place, then stretch out a tape on the floor with a 16-in. layout number on the stud mark (or use the 24-in. or 19½-in. marks, depending on the stud spacing). Then nail the bottom and top of the base at each layout mark. ❸   >> >> >>

CLOSING OUTSIDE CORNERS

Miters on outside corners can be the most difficult kind to manage. If a miter is open at the front, the fix is relieving the back with a rasp or plane. Remove just a little wood at a time and test-fit often until the edges of the corner close.

RUNNING BASEBOARD AND SHOE MOLDING (CONTINUED)

In situations where the base ends in the middle of wall, complete the piece with a return.

In a coped corner, install the unmitered piece first, running it all the way to the wall.

BUILT-UP BASE

Fancier houses sometimes get a two-piece base. Typically this will consist of a 1×6 or 1×8 bottom piece and a cap molding.

The same techniques apply as for single-piece base, except that simple butt joints replace copes in the 1× portion.

The important thing to remember is to allow twice as much time for the base.

Installing the base

Start installing base at an outside miter, if there are any. Test-fit the pieces, and if the joint opens to the front, ease off a bit from the back with a rasp or plane. Outside corners are the trickiest joints to get right, and a good fit often requires some patience. Don't worry if you end up shortening the piece a little—odds are there's a cope that will hide that at the other end.

See "Closing Outside Corners," p. 231.

There will usually be a couple of spots where the base has to end without joining another piece of base. This happens at stair landings and in bathrooms where the base abuts wall tile. Simply return it to the wall as you would on a window apron.

See "Returning the Apron," p. 226.

When two pieces need to be joined in the center of a long wall, it creates an awkward situation. The solution I'm most comfortable with is simply a butt joint. (See "Joining Baseboard in the Middle of a Wall," facing page.)

Installing shoe molding

Most floors aren't perfectly flat, and most base isn't perfectly straight. Consequently, there will be a gap between the base and finished floors such as hardwood, tile, stone, and vinyl. That's where shoe molding comes in. It's not generally used with carpet, although it can be.

Cut shoe the same way you do base. A lot of carpenters don't bother to cope shoe, but I do. It just makes a better job for a small time investment, and the more coping you do, the faster you become.

The one critical thing with shoe molding is where you nail it. It is always nailed to the wall and the base, never the floor. Of course, you couldn't nail it to stone or tile, anyway, but you could nail it to hardwood, and that would be a mistake. Hardwood floors exhibit considerable cross-grain seasonal movement—as much as $3/4$ in. Shoe hides this movement, while allowing it to happen. If you nail shoe to a hardwood floor, it will move with the hardwood.

JOINING BASEBOARD IN THE MIDDLE OF A WALL

When two pieces need to be joined in the center of a long wall, it presents you with a confusing situation. Carpenters obsess over the best way to solve this. I've tried several over the years and have concluded that, no matter what, the joint will most likely end up being visible. Because of this, its location matters.

The joint does have to be over a stud, but it rarely has to be centered on the wall–usually, you have some latitude.

Think about where there will likely be a couch or a bed, and put the joint there, or where it will usually be hidden by an opened door. Cut the second piece a little long to force a tight joint, and install it by pushing in on the bow created in the center. Align the pieces and nail. It ends up looking fine.

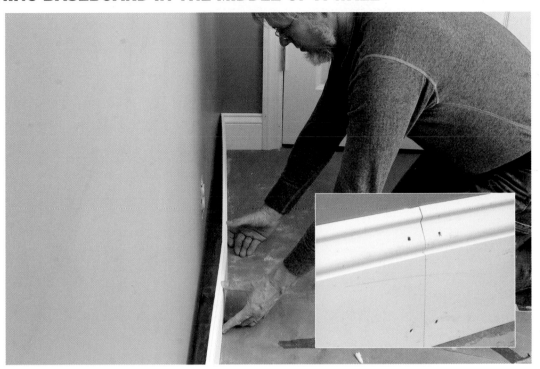

INSTALLING SHOE MOLDING

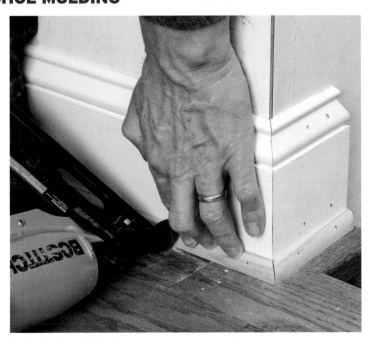

Baseboard will conform to the floor in some places, but will rarely fit tight against the entire floor. Shoe molding conforms to the surface of the floor, following any irregularities. Be sure to nail the shoe to the baseboard, not to the floor.

INSTALLING CROWN MOLDING

Crown molding stymies a lot of people–the molding sits on the wall at an angle, and that means its miters and copes are compound angles.

You can cut the compound angles with the crown laying flat on a compound miter saw by using specific bevel and tilt angles, but I've run miles of crown and never bothered with that. I simply hold the crown upside down in the miter saw, as if the saw bed is the ceiling and the fence is the wall. Then I miter the piece at 45 degrees. ❶ You have to hold the crown so the two flats on its back seat fully on the saw. Some carpenters clamp a fence to their saws to ensure this, others draw a pencil line. I go by feel.

Crown gets nailed to the double top plate (wider crown to the wall studs) and to the ceiling joists. That's a problem–on the walls to which the ceiling joists run parallel, there might be a joist where you need it, but probably not. For those walls, I rip triangular crown backer from 2×4, and screw it to the double top plate. ❷ Stop the backer a couple of inches from the corners so it won't keep the un-coped ends of intersecting crown on the adjoining from running all the way to the corner. Size the backer so there's about ¼-in. clearance between it and the back of the crown. This leaves a little wiggle room to adjust the crown when fitting a joint. Nail through the face of the crown into the backer.

Measure for crown as you would base, and think about where to place the copes just as you would for base.

➔ See "Coping Baseboard," p. 229.

Cut pieces you'll cope for inside corners a little long to ensure a tight fit. Shorter pieces, say up to about 8 ft. long, should be cut about ¹⁄₁₆ in. long. Longer pieces might be as much as ⅛ in. long.

Even more so than with base, outside miters are the hardest thing to get right. They should be your starting point, and you should avoid where possible having to cope the other end of these pieces. Hold, mark, and cut one piece, then the other. ❸ Dry-fit the joint before nailing either piece. ❹

When installing crown, make sure both flats sit flat on the wall and ceiling. It may be impossible to get a perfect fit to a wavy ceiling without scribing or caulking. Nail every 16 in. with 2-in. nails, but stop about two studs away from the corner when installing the uncoped side of an inside corner. Snap the coped piece into place. ❺

Most gaps in coped crown come from one or both pieces not sitting at the proper angle to the wall. Adjust them as needed until the joint is tight by tapping on a block of scrap material. ❻ Once you like the joint, nail both pieces.   >> >> >>

COPING CROWN

Coping crown usually requires starting the cuts in several places. It always requires back-cutting severely. When you've completed a cope, tilt the crown on the bench as it will be on the wall. Test fit your cope on a scrap and remove more material as needed. Most of the time, what causes gaps in a coped joint is material in the back of the cut, so begin adjusting the fit there rather than cutting into the face.

Angle the coping saw at about 45 degrees to the rear when coping crown.

Reinsert the saw at as many places as needed to complete the cut, keeping the cut line on the front edge of the profile.

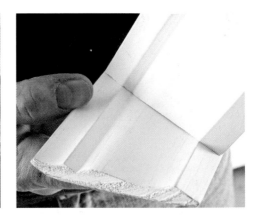

When you've finished the cut, test-fit the coped edge against a piece of scrap. Remove material from the back of the cope as needed.

1 Miter crown upside down in a standard miter saw. Orient yourself by thinking of the saw's bed as the ceiling and the fence as the wall.

2 Install crown backer to provide a nailing surface for walls that are parallel to the joists above.

3 Hold the first piece of crown stock firmly against the wall and ceiling and mark the reverse side where it intersects the wall.

4 Cut the first piece and mark the second one. Then dry-fit the joint to check it before nailing either side.

5 Cut coped pieces a little long and snap them into place.

6 With scrap, tap a piece of crown up or in to change its angle and tighten the joint.

INSTALLING CROWN MOLDING (CONTINUED)

It's common to have to end a run of crown with a return, usually where a foyer ceiling intersects the wall of a stairwell above. Miter the end of the crown and cut a return on the miter saw. ❼ Glue the return to the long piece before installing it, securing the return with spring clamps. ❽ Let it dry overnight, then nail the entire assembly up as one. ❾

The second hardest joint in crown is usually the last one. The last piece usually ends up being coped on both ends, and there's little room for adjustment nailing the last joint. Place that joint in the least visible corner of the room.

7 Cut crown returns by mitering them, then lay the stock flat to square it.

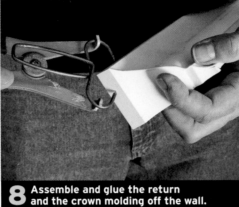

8 Assemble and glue the return and the crown molding off the wall.

9 When the glue has dried, install the returned piece as one assembly.

CLOSETS

For years, I set the height of the shelf in clothes closets at 72 in. I'm 6 ft. 2 in. tall, and it seemed natural. Then I trimmed a closet for a customer who stood 5 ft. tall (I think she was being generous at that), and she made me come back and lower the shelf and bar. Point is, closets are personal things, and it pays to tailor their details to the main user.

My current default shelf height is now 66 in., with the rod ending up about 2 in. lower. The exception is for a closet with a double clothes rod. Then I set the center of the top rod at 78 in. and the bottom rod at 40 in.

You can buy wood closet rod or adjustable metal ones. Both work fine. Wood rod requires sockets on each end, and either type needs rod and shelf brackets for spans over 3 ft. The rods and the closet shelf rest on 1× cleats fastened to studs. Wider closets end up with rod and shelf brackets every 32 in. To support closet rods, use 1×4. If you just need to support a shelf, 1×2 works fine.

1 Fasten the end cleats to the corner studs and any you find in the middle of the wall.

2 Fasten vertical cleats over studs where there will be a rod and shelf bracket.

TRADE SECRET
Pantry-shelf installation is similar to that for closet shelves, but the shelf height is different. For pantries, I usually set the bottom shelf at 24 in. and the rest at 36 in., 48 in., 60 in., and 68 in.

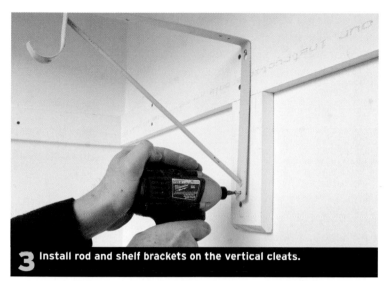

3 Install rod and shelf brackets on the vertical cleats.

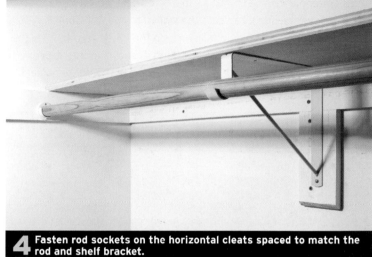

4 Fasten rod sockets on the horizontal cleats spaced to match the rod and shelf bracket.

5 Add double bars to the closet installation to double its shirt/blouse capacity.

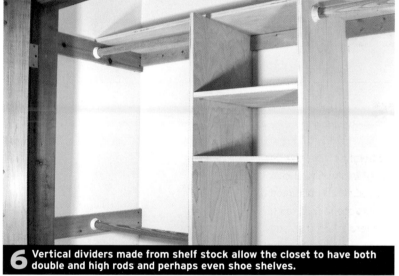

6 Vertical dividers made from shelf stock allow the closet to have both double and high rods and perhaps even shoe shelves.

Speaking of shelves, don't use particleboard or MDF. It will sag. The best material I've found is 3/4-in. hardwood plywood—birch or luaun. Rip it to $11^{7}/_{8}$ in. for clothes closets and $15^{7}/_{8}$ in. (or as works with the closet depth) for pantries. Before ripping, it's a good idea to sand the sheet on both sides with 100-grit paper and roll fast-drying water-borne varnish on both sides to mini-

mize splintering. Rip it, sand and ease the edges, then let paint do the rest.

In clothes closets, most of the weight is borne by the cleats on the end. Cut and install them first, using hammer-driven 8d finish nails or $2^{1}/_{2}$-in. cabinet screws in every stud. (Don't use drywall screws—they won't take the shear load.) ❶

When using screws, predrill to avoid cracking the cleats. The reason to run the end cleats first is to be sure you can catch the corner stud with fasteners. Run the back cleat, and vertical cleats as needed for the rod and shelf brackets. ❷ Then install the

brackets and rod sockets and hang the rod. Cut the shelf stock 1/8 in. short so you don't beat up the walls installing it. ❸, ❹ Using the same techniques, install double bars in a locations that makes access convenient. ❺

One way to increase the capacity of a closet is to divide it vertically with a piece of shelf plywood. Nail this to the floor and into the ends of the back cleats. On one side, install a closet bar at 66 in. for hanging pants and dresses. On the other side, install a double closet rod for shirts. You can even use two vertical dividers to make shoe shelves. ❻

INSTALLING CABINETS

1 Mark a point 34½ in. above the high spot on the floor and extend a level line at that point across any wall that will support cabinets.

2 Measure and mark the desired height for the bottom of the upper cabinets and extend a second level line from this point.

5 Shim the unit plumb, then drive the screws home.

6 Clamp the next cabinet to the first unit and adjust the cabinets to bring the faces of their stiles flush.

The following pages illustrate basic kitchen cabinet installation, but these methods apply to bathroom vanities and most other built-ins, as well. The dimensions used here are standard, but individual installations may vary from these. I install the uppers first, but there's no hard and fast rule. Installing the uppers first lets me get right underneath them for lifting, and prevents me beating up base cabinets with my tool belt as I lean in to screw the uppers to the wall. Speaking of screws, I use 2½-in. cabinet screws with broad heads.

Cabinets are square and precisely dimensioned. Walls, however, rarely meet that standard. Nevertheless, because of their unvarying squareness, cabinets have to be installed plumb and level, so your first step is to assess the kitchen.

Measure and mark

Compare the actual measurements of the space with those on the cabinet plan. If there's a discrepancy, figure out what to do about it before you open a cabinet box. If the cabinets end up shorter than the space, it's likely you can make it up with a manufacturer-supplied filler strip. If the cabinets are bigger than the space, then you'll need to swap a cabinet or two for smaller ones.

Next check the walls for plumb. Walls that lean out generally don't create a big problem, but ones that lean in might mean the space you thought was available is really smaller.

Finally, check the floor for level. A rotating laser works best for this. Walk around measuring between the laser beam and the floor, and find the high spot. Note that point and mark the base cabinet height (usually 34½ in.) above it on the wall. Mark a level line from this point across the main cabinet wall and extend it across any wall that will support cabinets. **❶**

From the level line that represents the location of the top of the base cabinets, measure up 19½ in. That's the standard separation between the base and upper cabinets (18 in., plus 1½ in. for a laminate countertop). Mark a parallel level line representing the bottom of the upper cabinets. **❷**

3 Mark cabinet backs with stud locations and drill pilot holes for the screws. Remove the doorstop.

4 Raise the first cabinet to the level line, and drive a few screws to secure it.

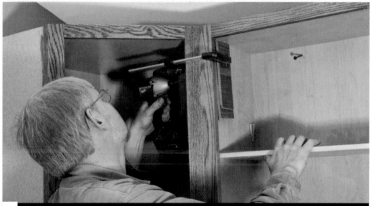

7 Drill pilot holes through the cabinet stiles, lubricate the screws with wax or paraffin, then screw the stiles together.

TRADE SECRET
If you're working alone, screw a cleat to the wall at the line representing the bottom of the upper cabinets. You can rest the cabinet there while screwing it to the wall.

TRADE SECRET
Never install cabinets with drywall screws. Drywall screws are not meant to handle shear loads across their shanks, and they can break.

Installing the upper cabinets

Remove the cabinet doors, shelves, and drawers. This lightens the units and makes clamping easier.

Before you start installing upper cabinets, find the stud locations as you did for base molding. Then measure the distance from the corner to the first stud.

➡ See "Finding the Studs," p. 231.

Measure from the corner of the first cabinet and mark the stud locations on its back along the hanger rails. Drill pilot holes. **3** Start a couple of screws in these holes and, with a helper, raise the cabinet into place and drive the screws loosely. **4** Shim the cabinet plumb and drive the screws home. Score the shims with a knife and snap them off at the cabinet edge. **5**

Once the first cabinet is installed, measure from it to the studs you've marked, subtracting any amount the stiles overhang the cabinet box. Mark these dimensions on the back of the next cabinet box

and drill pilot holes. Clamp the second cabinet to the first, making sure the faces of the cabinets are flush (sometimes you need to back out some of the screws in the previous cabinet to tweak it). Then repeat the installation steps on the second cabinet. **6**

With a drill bit equal in diameter to the cabinet-screw shank, drill three pilot holes (two in short cabinets) through one cabinet's stile (the vertical member of the face frame) and screw the two together. **7** In most cases, $2\frac{1}{2}$-in. screws are perfect for this, but that depends on the stile width. You want the screws to penetrate at least 1 in. into the receiving stile, without sticking out. Because the stiles are usually hardwood, lubricating the screws makes a big difference. I use beeswax, but paraffin or any wax will do.   >> >> >>

INSTALLING CABINETS (CONTINUED)

8 Blocks screwed to the floor provide a method for attaching base cabinets that don't fit all the way to a wall.

9 Screw 2×4 cleats to the wall on the level line behind cabinets that don't extend to the wall. The cleats will support the countertop.

12 Start holes for pipes in sink bases from the rear and finish them from the inside to avoid tearout.

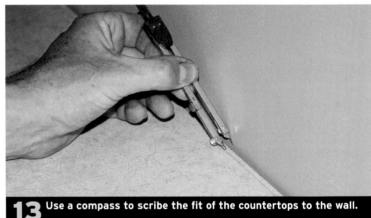

13 Use a compass to scribe the fit of the countertops to the wall.

Installing base cabinets

Base cabinets are easier to install than uppers, although most of the techniques are the same. They have to be shimmed plumb and level, and the stiles clamped and screwed before fastening them to the wall. Unlike uppers, most base cabinets get screws only through a top rail and to the stiles of any abutting cabinets.

You will need to leave openings for dishwashers and stoves. Get these dimensions right. Most dishwashers are 24 in. wide, and most stoves are 30 in. or 36 in. Be sure the cabinets to either side are plumb, and you should err on the side of making the opening 1/8 in. larger. Never make it so much as 1/16 in. smaller.

Start in a corner. Many times, the first cabinet to go in is a lazy Susan. Most lazy Susans don't go all the way to the wall, so you have to draw the cabinet location on the floor and screw blocks down along a line coinciding with the back face of the toekick. **8**

Screw cleats to the wall to support the countertop behind the lazy Susan. Then install such cleats behind any base cabinet that doesn't go all the way to the wall. **9**

Shim the cabinet level and to the height of the line on the wall. Glue these shims together and to the floor so they stay put. (Island and peninsula cabinets get affixed to the floor in the same way.) **10** Set the cabinet in place and push it to contact the face of the blocks. Anchor the cabinet by screwing through the toekick and into the blocks (you'll finish the toekick later, as you would a cabinet side).

Once the first cabinet is installed, proceed with the remaining cabinets using the same procedures: Predrill the hanger rail at stud locations and start the hanger screws, predrill one of the stiles, set the second cabinet in place, clamp the faces flush, screw the stiles together, and then shim and screw the unit to the wall.

Dealing with pipes

Before you can install the sink cabinet, you have to drill holes in the back for the plumbing. Measure carefully from the edge of the adjoining cabinet to the centers of the pipes and mark the sink cabinet for drilling. **11** Using a sharp holesaw, drill holes about 1/2 in. oversized. For pipes coming in from the wall, lay out the holes and start drill-

10 Shim base cabinets plumb and level and to the height of the level line on the wall representing the base cabinet height.

11 Measure the distance from the edge of the adjoining cabinet and the center of the pipe. Mark the pipe center on the sink cabinet.

14 Belt-sand the edge of the countertop to the scribe line.

15 Screw the countertop from below, through the cabinet corner brackets.

ing from the back. When the point of the bit penetrates the inside of the cabinet, finish drilling the hole from the inside. **12** This minimizes tearout where it shows. Lift the cabinet over pipes entering from the floor, and drop it into place with any wall pipes coming through the holes in the back. You may need to push the pipes one way or the other to align them with the holes.

Installing the countertop

Once the base cabinets are in, install the countertop. With a helper, slide the countertop in place. If necessary, scribe it to conform to any irregularities in the surface of the wall. To accomplish this, fit the countertop as well as you can, and set a compass to the widest remaining gap. Slide that compass along the wall, marking the countertop. **13** Remove the countertop and belt-sand the edge to your scribed line. **14** Use a coarse belt—60-grit or so. Reposition the countertop and screw it from below, being very careful to use screws short enough not to come through the top. **15** >> >> >>

Measuring for pipes

Pipes are rarely square to the wall or floor. Consequently, if you measure to the end of the pipe to figure out where to drill the holes in the cabinets, those holes won't be in the right place.

Measure to the center of the pipe at about the point where it will penetrate the cabinet. You might have to muscle the pipe to the side to fit it in the hole initially, but as the cabinet drops into place, the pipes and the holes will align.

INSTALLING CABINETS (CONTINUED)

Finishing up

Sometimes there's a tall pantry or oven cabinet at the end of a countertop. Such cabinets are installed last. Then, of course, you need to install all of the drawers, doors, and shelves. Installing doors is pretty simple—just use the existing screws and screw holes.

Check to be sure the door tops are at a consistent height and adjust as needed. You can use a level for this, but eyeballing them works in most cases. And don't forget, you have to cut out the countertop for the sink. (See "The Sink Cutout," facing page.)

If the cabinets run all the way to the ceiling or to a soffit, there will probably be a scribe molding to hide the joint. Scribe molding is thin and flexible, and installs with brads or headless pins. Other times, the upper cabinets get finished off with a crown molding. Cutting and joining this is the same as on a wall, except this crown is only affixed to the cabinets.

Stock cabinets often come with unfinished sides. If the cabinet is at the end of a run, you'll be staring at particleboard unless you add an end panel. (See "Finishing End Panels," right.)

Reinstall the doors using the existing screw holes. Control the speed of the drill so the tip doesn't slip from the screw, marring the door.

WHAT CAN GO WRONG

When disaster strikes and you make a small chip in a laminate countertop, don't panic. Laminate manufacturers make repair putties in many of the colors they sell. These putties dry hard and permanently. They have saved me from replacing an entire top.

FINISHING END PANELS

Cabinet manufacturers sell finished plywood end panels. Coat the back with glue and drive a few brads to hold the panel until the glue sets. When starting short brads, hold them with diagonal cutters.

Be sure the brads you're using won't stick through inside the cabinet. With very thin cabinet sides, nail near the edge of the panel so the brads go into the cabinet back. At the front, angle the brads into the stile.

Spread glue on the back of finished end panels.

Hold short brads with diagonal cutters when starting to drive them.

THE SINK CUTOUT

A task that most carpenters dread is cutting out the countertop for a sink. You have to be very careful not to chip the laminate.

Center the supplied sink template over the sink base and draw the cut line. Verify that there's enough clearance at the rear line for your jigsaw to make the cut. Use a sharp 3/4-in. spade bit to drill holes in the corners, and make the cut using a downcutting blade (one whose teeth face down, not up) in a jigsaw.

Before cutting the last side, screw a scrap to the center of the cutout that's long enough to bear on the remaining countertop. That controls the cutout's drop, reducing the risk of damaging the laminate. When done, pull the cutout up using the cleat.

❶ Outline the sink cutouts using the template supplied by the sink manufacturer.

❷ Drill holes at the corners for starting the cut and easing the turns.

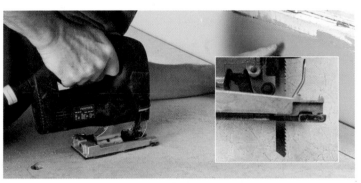

❸ Cut out the opening for the sink using a jigsaw with a downcutting blade.

❹ Before the last cut, screw down a cleat to keep the scrap from falling into the cabinet upon completion of the cut.

❺ For the last cut, reinsert the jigsaw blade in the hole. Remove the cutout by pulling up on the cleat.

TRADE SECRET

How do you draw visible lines to cut out for a sink in a dark-colored countertop? Center wide masking tape where the cut lines will go and draw the lines on the tape.

STAIRS

THERE'S SO MUCH TO SAY ABOUT building stairs that I've actually written a book on that topic alone. Here, there's only space for the basics—but the basics are the same for every straight stair. I'll start with the theory behind design and layout. Then, I'll lead you through a basic set of stairs such as one from a garage to a house, or to a basement, or from a deck. I'll also show the basics of installing finish treads and risers on a main stair.

Along with stairs come railings. Handrailing provides something to hold onto while you're using a stair. Guardrails are used alongside stairs and in level applications such as balconies or decks. They reduce the chance of falling off to a lower area. Although similar, the codes governing them differ considerably. Codes regarding tread width and riser height vary regionally, but no matter what, count on the stairs being one spot the building inspector scrutinizes.

STAIR THEORY

Stairs break big vertical rises, such as those between floors, into a series of smaller, uniform steps spaced horizontally by treads. The risers and treads are supported by hefty diagonal members called stringers, which are typically notched to receive the treads and risers. It's also possible to support the treads with cleats nailed to the stringers, or to mortise the stringers to receive the treads and risers. Both latter techniques are outside the scope of this book. The risers on a set of stairs all have to be the same height, and the treads all have to be the same depth (within 3/8 in.). That's because people quickly develop a rhythm on stairs, and breaking that rhythm leads to trips and falls.

Calculating rise and riser height

Rise, the vertical component of stairs, is pretty easy to understand, and the first thing you'll compute when designing stairs. Begin your computation by measuring the distance between floors (the overall rise). Then find the number of risers by dividing that measurement by a trial rise of 7½ in.–a comfortable rise and one that's within the maximum 7¾ in. permitted by code.

For example, let's say the distance between floors is 28⅝ in. Dividing that measurement by 7½ results in an individual rise of 3.81. Round 3.81 up to 4, and you have the number of risers.

Then, to make the numbers fit your stair location exactly, find the individual riser height–divide the overall rise (28⅝ in.) by 4. In this case, the risers will all be 7 5/32 in., which I'd round down to 7⅛ in. You can always use a rise that's shorter than the code maximum, which may result in an easier climb but also adds steps. Those added steps mean the set of stairs will extend farther into the lower room, which is OK if you have enough room and can leave at least 3 ft. of clear landing space at the bottom, as required by code. (More on figuring this later.)

Tread depth and run

Next is tread depth. There are two components to tread depth–the theoretical run (from the front of one riser to the front of the next, which I'll refer to simply as "run"), and the tread overhang (from the front of a riser to the front edge of the tread). For now, you can ignore tread overhang because what you want to know first is the measurement for the cuts in the stringers. Most stairs use the code-minimum run of 10 in. (9 in. in some states). Using the code-minimum run creates stairs that take up less floor space, and it makes good use of nominal 12-in. tread stock. Add 1¼ in. to the run for an overhang, and the actual 11¼ in. dimension of the tread stock is perfect. So in general you can use a run of 10 in.

STAIR ANATOMY AND DIMENSIONS

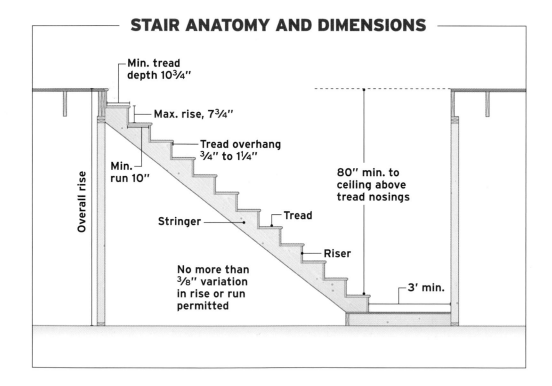

- Min. tread depth 10¾"
- Max. rise, 7¾"
- Tread overhang ¾" to 1¼"
- Min. run 10"
- Overall rise
- 80" min. to ceiling above tread nosings
- Stringer
- Tread
- Riser
- No more than ⅜" variation in rise or run permitted
- 3' min.

TRADE SECRET

If possible, measure the overall rise between the finished floors at both the top and bottom of the stairs. If the finished floors aren't installed yet, find out their thicknesses before calculating the overall stair rise. Subtract the thickness of the lower floor from the overall rise and add that of the upper floor. If the stair tops out at a door, count the highest part of the threshold as the finished floor elevation.

Find the overall rise of a stair by measuring between the two levels it will connect.

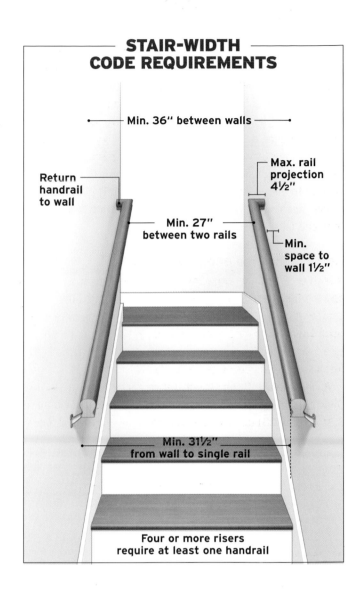

STAIR-WIDTH CODE REQUIREMENTS

Min. 36" between walls

Return handrail to wall

Max. rail projection 4½"

Min. 27" between two rails

Min. space to wall 1½"

Min. 31½" from wall to single rail

Four or more risers require at least one handrail

Using a deeper run makes a more comfortable stair, but the stairs will take up more floor space. A deeper run also means a deeper cut in the stringer, which might mean the use of wider stringer stock.

➡ See "Leave Enough Meat," p. 249.

Thus, a key design decision related to the individual run is the resulting floor space you'll need. To find that, multiply the number of treads (always one less than the number of risers) by the run. To this product, add 1¼ in. to allow for the bottom tread overhang. In our example, this would be 3 × 10 = 30 in. + 11¼ in. or 31¼ in. Measure this distance out from the wall where the stairs begin, and make sure there's at least 3 ft. clear to any obstruction such as a wall.

If there's less than 3 ft., use a shallower run if you can. Or, try a larger rise, within code requirements, which may eliminate a tread and shorten the stair. Finally, if the traffic flow at the bottom of the stair is to one of the sides, not directly forward, you can add a landing with one or more steps down to that side to eliminate some length in the main stair. If none of these approaches work, you need to move a wall or throw yourself on the mercy of the code official. Additionally, there are width and railing requirements for stairs.

⚠ ACCORDING TO CODE

In many Northeastern states, the maximum individual rise is 8¼ in. If that's the case in your jurisdiction, you may be able to decrease the number of risers.

ⓘ WHAT CAN GO WRONG

When a part of a stair is within 36 in. horizontally and 60 in. vertically of a window, the glass in the window must be safety glazing. Usually, the inspector will look for an etching in the glass indicating it's tempered.

LAYING OUT BASIC STAIRS

To speed layout, clamp a straight stick so it crosses the edges of a framing square at the rise and run dimensions.

2 Lay out each notch so the rise starts at the run of the previous one.

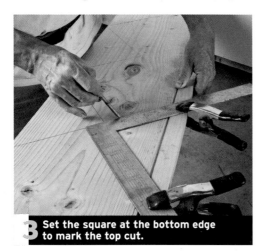

3 Set the square at the bottom edge to mark the top cut.

4 Mark the bottom riser line one tread thickness shorter than the other risers.

5 Mark the bottom level cut between the bottom of the stringer and bottom riser.

Once you've figured out the rise and run of the stairs, you have to transfer that information to the stringers, then notch them. The most accurate way to do this is to lay out, cut, and test the first stringer, then use that one as a template for the remaining stringers. Set the stringer stock on your work surface with the crown at what will be the top edge of the stringer.

Marking the notches

Lay out the stringer with a framing square. **1** Think of the square as a template for the notch—one leg of the square represents the run (tread) and the other represents the rise. Hold the square so both the run dimension on one leg and the rise dimension on the other leg intersect the top edge of the stringer, mark the points and lines with a pencil, and you've laid out one notch.

Move the square up the stringer and repeat so the end of the rise you just laid out meets the end of the run you're about to lay out. **2** Clamping a straight stick to the square at the rise and run dimen-

sions both aids in maintaining a consistent angle and speeds the process along.

Marking the top cut and bottom riser

After marking the top tread and riser, move the square to the bottom edge of the stringer and mark the top cut, which continues the line of the riser to the bottom of the stringer. **3**

The bottom riser is a little different. It has to be one tread thickness shorter than all the others. Mark the bottom riser line at that point. **4** Flip the square around, and mark the level cut where the stringer will meet the floor so it intersects the bottom rise at the point you marked. **5** If you didn't do this, when you added the first tread, that step would be too tall by the tread thickness. Lowering the stringer the thickness of the tread makes the step perfect. Of course, this also lowers all the tread cuts, including the top one. However, installing the treads brings that back up to the perfect height.

STAIR STOCK

For strictly utilitarian stairs, such as a run from a garage to the house, dry 2×12 stock is fine for stringers. If the stairs are out-doors, use pressure-treated 2×12s, and apply end-cut preservative to the cuts to prevent rot. Pressure treatment does not always reach the center of wide stock, and cuts can expose untreated wood. Figure 14 in. of stock length for each riser in the stair. Don't use green lumber for interior stringers. Because wood shrinks significantly more across the grain than parallel to the grain, the notches will go out of square as the wood dries out.

For long runs, particularly for main stairs where creaking would be unacceptable, I prefer to use nominal 12-in. engineered lumber—either 1³⁄₄-in. LVL beam material or 1¹⁄₄-in. OSB rimboard. Both are stable and strong.

Since the stairs shown in this project are utilitarian, I used 2×12 for the treads and 1×10 ripped to size for the risers, leaving the sides of the steps open. You could easily transform this basic design into a more formal stair by using 5/4×12 hardwood treads (available at home centers and lumberyards), covering the sides with 1×12 or 5/4×12, and replacing the 4×4 newel with a turned one. Always select dry, flat, straight, good-looking stock for the treads.

Engineered lumber is a more stable material for stringers than sawn lumber.

LEAVE ENOUGH MEAT

Once you lay out the first notch, measure between the back of rise/run intersection and the bottom of the stringer. There must be at least 5 in. of stock left. If there isn't, stop. Code requires at least 5 in. of a 2×12 below the notch. Either use a smaller run or deeper stringer stock—LVL or rimboard.

This is one reason to avoid the precut stringers. The ones I've seen are 2×10 stock, leaving only about 3 in. below the notch. Additionally, they're cut to an arbitrary rise, which might work for you, or might not. Better to cut stringers that fit your design perfectly.

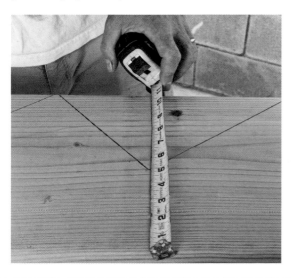

RISER ADJUSTMENTS

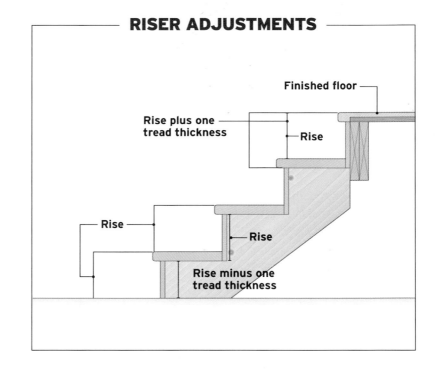

CUTTING STRINGERS

After all the math and layout, cutting the notches in the stringers is simple. **①** Start with the first stringer and once you've cut it, set it in place for a trial fit. If everything's OK, use the cut stringer as a pattern for those remaining.

Cutting the first stringer

Use a circular saw, take your time, and try to split the layout line with the blade. Stop the front edge of the sawblade just short of the intersecting line and finish the cut with a handsaw or jigsaw. **②** Overcutting the notch with the circular saw is fast, and some production carpenters do this, but it weakens the stringer. If an overcut comes closer than 5 in. to the bottom of the stringer, it's technically a code violation.

➡ **See "Leave Enough Meat," p. 249.**

Checking the fit

Check the fit of the first stringer. Measure down from the finished floor (use shims as a substitute for the thickness of the finished flooring if it's not in place yet). The top tread cut should be at the riser height plus one tread thickness from the top of the finished floor (or in this case, the top of the threshold). Check the stringer for level. **③** It should be dead-on level. If it isn't, check your measurements, calculations, and cuts until you find the source of the error. You can cheat the stringer up or down by ⅜ in. and still meet code, but I don't like to cobble my work together like that.

Cutting the remaining stringers

If the fit is good, take the cut stringer back to each of the remaining lengths of the stringer stock and lay them out using the first stringer as a pattern. **④** Use a sharp pencil. When you cut these stringers, try to completely remove the pencil line with the sawblade. **⑤**

ⓘ **TRADE SECRET**
Don't pitch the pitch block. After you've notched the stringers, save at least one of the triangular pieces. You'll need to use it as a "pitch block" to set the saw angle for cutting the end of the guardrail.

Stop sawblade just short of the intersecting line.

1 When cutting stringer notches, stop the saw cut just at the back of the notch. Don't overcut.

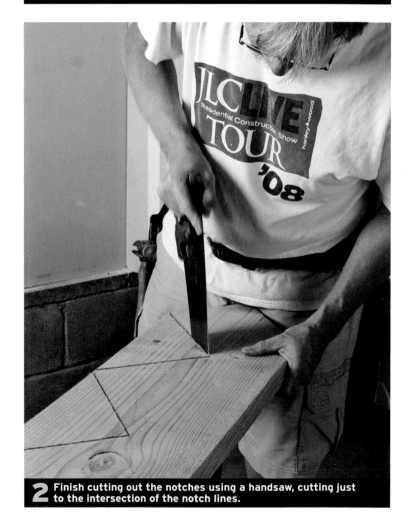

2 Finish cutting out the notches using a handsaw, cutting just to the intersection of the notch lines.

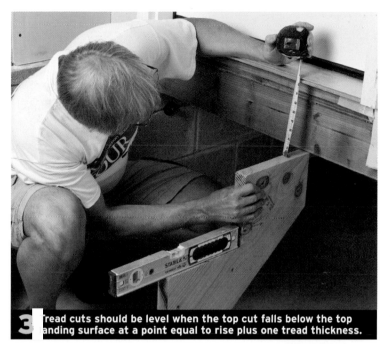

3 Tread cuts should be level when the top cut falls below the top landing surface at a point equal to rise plus one tread thickness.

5 When cutting the remaining stringers, try to remove the pencil line with the saw so these stringers match the original exactly.

4 Use the first stringer as a pattern for the rest.

How many stringers?

The answer to this question depends on several factors, including the width and length of the stairs and the tread material.

The stairs shown here are only about 3 ft. wide and can be done with three stringers, assuming you're using either 2× material or 5/4 hardwood for treads. If the stairs are on a deck and the treads are synthetic decking, check with the decking manufacturer for the maximum span between stringers—it can be as small as 12 in. Generally, I don't like to exceed 18 in. between notched stringers.

When the overall run exceeds 7 ft., you may need to add either additional stringers (at no more than 12 in. apart) or install mid-span support in the form of a header and posts leading down to solid bearing. If you have any doubts, check with a code official or a structural engineer.

INSTALLING STRINGERS AND A NEWEL POST

The most important thing about installing stringers is to prevent them from sliding forward—if they can't slide forward, they can't drop down, unless the stringer itself breaks. There are several ways to accomplish this, including notching the bottom of the stringer to hook on a 2×4 fastened to the floor, or screwing or nailing the stringers to enclosing stud walls. (See "Anchoring the Stringers," below)

Anchoring stringers to walls

If I'm fastening the stringers to the walls at the head of the stair, I'll use a 24-in. hardware strap fastened to the stringer with Simpson Strong-Tie® structural screws. Use screws here because the fasteners are subject to withdrawal, and it's a code-violation to load nails in this manner.

Fasten the strap to the bottom of the stringer, ❶ then place the stringer and screw the strap to the framing. ❷ Additional lateral support is needed with this connection to prevent the stringers from rolling sideways. This will be provided by the risers.

➡ **See "Installing Handrails," p. 258.**

Because this stair requires a guardrail, it also needs something to support the guardrail: a newel post at the bottom. Here, I used a fir 4×4.

Planning the newel post

The newel height is a function of the guardrail height, which will be at least 34 in. above the line of the tread nosings. A guardrail height of 36 in. is better (and is also the minimum required guardrail height on a balcony), but there is no code-prescribed maximum. However, at this stage of the installation, the treads aren't on, so how do you know how tall to make the newel? Forty-eight inches usually works, if you align the front of a nominal 4-in. newel with the front of the bottom riser. Here's why—it's about 7½ in. to the top of the first tread. From there, it's about 4 in. to the line of the nosings. That total is 11½ in. If the guardrail hits the newel at 35 in. above the nosing line, the total height is now 46½ in. Drawing out the newel-stair-rail assembly full scale and measuring that before cutting anything is a good idea.

Mounting the newel

Cut the newel to length and use a miter saw to chamfer its top on all four sides for looks and safety—a ½-in. cut at 45 degrees. ❸

Mounting the newel requires a stout connection. If this stair were on a framed floor with access from below, I'd open up the floor sheathing and tie a longer newel into the joists below with blocking. However, this stair is on a slab, so I'm handling the side load from the newel with a Simpson-Strong-Tie DTT2 connector.

Clamp the newel plumb to the stringer so it extends beyond the stringer by the thickness of the riser. Drill the center of the newel for the DTT2 connector—as close to the top of the stringer's tread cut as the width of the hardware allows. ❹ Use ½-in. bolts to affix the newel to the side of the stringer and to the connector. ❺

Cut and nail or screw (with structural screws) solid blocking between the stringers. Then fasten the DTT2 to the blocking. ❻ Install a second DTT2 at the bottom of the blocking to secure it to the center stringer. ❼

ANCHORING THE STRINGERS

A A 2×4 screwed to the floor and fit in notches in the stringers keeps them from sliding out.

B Fasten stringers to surrounding walls to provide mid-span support.

1 Fasten straps to the bottom of the stringer with structural screws.

2 Then screw the straps from the stringers to the framing.

3 Using a miter saw, chamfer the top of the newel to soften its sharp edges.

4 Plumb and clamp the newel to the stringer before drilling hardware holes.

5 Tighten the nut that fastens the hardware to the newel and stringer.

6 Fasten the DTT2 and blocking between the risers with structural screws.

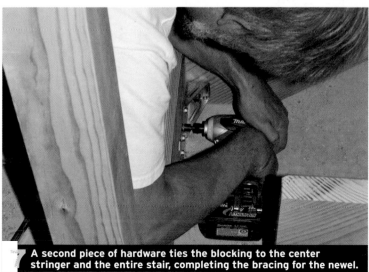

7 A second piece of hardware ties the blocking to the center stringer and the entire stair, completing the bracing for the newel.

INSTALLING A GUARDRAIL

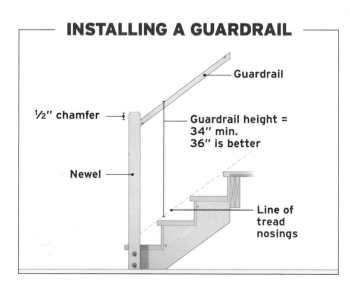

Guardrail

½" chamfer

Guardrail height = 34" min. 36" is better

Newel

Line of tread nosings

TREADS AND RISERS

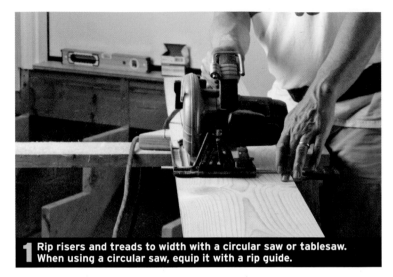

1 Rip risers and treads to width with a circular saw or tablesaw. When using a circular saw, equip it with a rip guide.

2 Cut treads and risers to a consistent length with a miter saw on a stand equipped with adjustable stops.

5 Screw the tread to the stringers through its face, then fasten it to the riser above with screws from behind.

6 Preassemble the top tread and riser as a unit, then install the assembly with screws driven into the risers and wall framing.

Except for the top and bottom risers, rip all the riser stock so its vertical dimension equals the stair's rise. Use a circular saw or a tablesaw for ripping both the risers and the treads. **1** The bottom riser will be one tread thickness narrower than the others. The vertical dimension of the top riser may also differ from the others. In this case, because the stairs start below a door, the top riser has to meet the bottom of the threshold.

Cutting the stock

When cutting tread and riser stock to length, use a circular saw, or better, a slide-miter saw. **2** Because of how I intend to make the railing, the ends of the treads and risers will be flush with the edge of the outside stringers. This way, the 2×4s I'll use for balusters can simply run up the side of the stringers. You could also configure the treads to overhang the side of the stringer like they do the risers, depending on the baluster configuration.

Installing treads and risers

At each step except the top one, install the riser first, then the tread. Use nails or 2-in. deck screws to fasten the riser to the stringers. **3** Predrill for the screws to avoid cracking the stock, particularly near the ends of the pieces.

Then place and fasten the tread. Using screws that are at least twice as long as the thickness of the tread stock, screw the tread to the stringers and to the riser below. **4** Then screw through the back of the risers into the edge of the treads. **5**

At the top step, you won't have access from behind to make the connection between the top tread and riser, so preassemble these pieces and install them as a unit. Screw the tread to the stringers and the risers to the wall framing. **6**

3 Predrill at the edges and fasten the risers to the stringers with 2-in. deck screws or the equivalent.

4 After cutting the treads to a consistent length, set them in place, starting with the bottom tread.

INSTALLING A GUARDRAIL AND BALUSTERS

Since a guardrail has to follow the diagonal plane of the stairs, you'll need to mark its location at both top and bottom. Lay a level or other straightedge across the tread nosings. Make light pencil marks both where the bottom edge of the straightedge intersects the back of the newel and where it touches the wall. **1** Measure up from these points and mark the guardrail height on the newel and the wall. **2**   >> >> >>

1 Use a level to mark the point at which the line of the treads intersects the wall and the newel.

2 From the marks of the tread line, mark the guardrail height on both the wall and the newel.

INSTALLING A GUARDRAIL AND BALUSTERS (CONTINUED)

3 Set the saw to cut the guardrail using one of the stringer cutouts.

4 Cut one end of the guardrail and pencil a line for the second cut location.

5 Assemble both pieces of the guardrail with screws.

Cutting the guardrail

Use a pitch block to set up a miter saw at the proper angle to cut the guardrail. **3** (Here, my guardrail will be assembled from two lengths of 2×4–a flat member fastened to an "on edge" apron.)

Cut one end of the guardrail flat to this angle, lay it flat in place on the stair, and mark the location and angle of the bottom cut at the point it intersects the face of the newel post. **4** Cut the guardrail apron to the same length but with the angles oriented vertically. Screw the two members together with 3-in. deck screws so the angles of both pieces are flush and the apron is inset 1½ in. from the stair side of the flat member. **5** At the top, fasten the guardrail to the wall framing with more 3-in. screws.

Installing the rail

Now place the guardrail between the wall and the newel. Support the bottom of the guardrail with a clamp, predrill the bottom edge of the apron at an angle, and fasten the guardrail to the newel with several 3-in. deck or cabinet screws. **6**

Laying out balusters

With the guardrail in place, the next step is installing some sort of infill or balusters between it and the stringer. For this utilitarian stair, I'll use 2×4s as balusters. Measure horizontally from the newel to the wall. **7** This example measures 26½ in. Figuring baluster spacing takes math, and there are as many ways to do it as there are carpenters. Here's my approach.

Add together the width of a baluster (here, a 2×4) and the code-specified maximum spacing (4 in.) = 7½ in. Divide the horizontal distance by this number: $26½ ÷ 7½ = 3.533$. Round this up to find the number of balusters; in this case, 4. Multiply the baluster width by the number of balusters: $3½ × 4 = 14$. Subtract this number from the horizontal measurement: $26½ - 14 = 12½$. Find the spacing by dividing this number by the number of spaces, which is one more than the number of balusters: $12½ ÷ 5 = 2½$.

Lay out the edge of the first 2×4 baluster 2½ in. from the newel. Lay out the second baluster by adding 6 in. (one 2×4 + one 2½-in. space) to the first dimension. **8** Add another 6 in. for the third baluster, and so on.

Installing balusters

These balusters worked out to be 48 in. long. I angled their tops to meet the guardrail (use the pitch block to set the angle on the saw). I like to bevel three of the bottom edges of the balusters ½ in. to ¾ in. like I did the newel (but make sure you don't chamfer the edge that attaches to the stringer). Screw the balusters plumb to the guardrail and the stringer with 2½-in. deck screws. **9**

TRADE SECRET

Do not use drywall screws for any structural connections, such as in a guardrail. Drywall screws are weak in side, or shear, loading strength. Use cabinet screws, structural screws, or deck screws instead.

6 Clamp the guardrail in place and screw it to the newel through predrilled holes in the bottoms of both pieces of the guardrail.

7 Measure between the newel and the wall to help compute the baluster location.

8 Lay out the baluster locations on the stringer by measuring over from the newel and marking the successive spacings.

9 Secure the balusters to the guardrail and stringer with 2½-in. deck screws.

INSTALLING HANDRAILS

Handrails must either die into a perpendicular wall or newel, or be returned as shown here.

Mark and cut the top end of the handrail the same way as the guardrail, then hold it in place and mark its bottom cut.

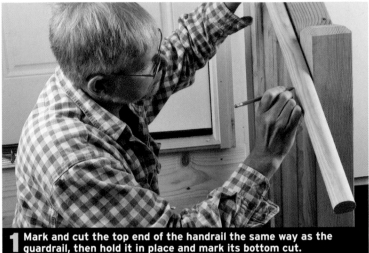

4 Nail or screw the top of the rail to a secure location. Support the bottom of the handrail temporarily as you complete the next step.

As I said earlier, guardrails are not handrails. They serve different functions, although in some cases, particularly with formal hardwood rails, such as one on a main stair, one rail can do both.

Cutting the handrail components

Mark the location of the handrail, set the saw to the proper angle, and make the first cut as you would for a guardrail.

→ See steps 1-3, "Installing a Guardrail and Balusters," pp. 255-256.

Cut the top of the handrail to that angle, and hold it in place with its top resting on the wall at the proper height (between 34 in. and 38 in., measured up plumb from the line of the tread nosings). Mark the lower end of the handrail end flush with the face of the newel. **1** Miter-cut this end of the railing at 45 degrees for the return. Figure the length of the return piece by laying the railing on the bed of your miter saw and holding a handrail bracket against the saw's fence. **2** Cut the return to length, and screw it to the main rail through pre-drilled holes with 2-in. screws. **3** Screw the top of the rail to the wall or, in this case, the door casing. **4**

Installing the rail

Hold the railing-return assembly in place and mark the location of the lowest bracket. **5** Screw or nail the bracket to the newel post with 2½-in. or longer screws and then to the bottom of the railing **6** Install the bracket within about 6 in. of the top and at the bottom of the rail. **7** Longer rails require brackets in the middle, as well. I don't space brackets more than 4 ft. apart.

ACCORDING TO CODE

Handrails are required by the IRC on at least one side of a stair with four or more risers. At the bottom, the handrail must die into or return to the newel or wall. If they return to the wall or newel, they must extend at least as far as a plumb line drawn up from the faces of the top and bottom risers. Typical round utility handrails must be no smaller than a diameter of 1¼ in. and no larger than 2 in. in diameter. There's more to the code than that, but it applies more to formal hardwood railings than we can cover here.

2 Find the length of the return piece by seeing how far out from a perpendicular surface the bracket puts the handrail.

3 Miter-cut the rail, and before installation, assemble the return to the handrail with 2-in. screws.

5 Hold the handrail and bracket in place to mark the location of the screw holes.

6 Fasten the bottom of the railing to its bracket.

7 Always use at least two brackets, even on short railings.

TRADE SECRET
Most stores still sell both heavy and light-weight handrail brackets. Buy the heaviest brackets you can. The difference in cost is minimal, and it's worth every penny if the bracket doesn't break when someone falls on the railing.

WARNING
Always attach handrail brackets to solid framing. When attaching them to a wall, find the studs and never attach brackets using drywall anchors. If you encounter a wall framed with steel studs, be sure there's solid-wood blocking installed between the studs for attaching handrail brackets.

BUILDING MAIN STAIRS

Main stairs, such as those between the first and second floor, lay out and install pretty much like utility stairs, with a few exceptions. In a new-construction project of more than one floor, I build main stairs early in the process so I can use them as soon as possible—they're both safer and more convenient than ladders.

I don't want to put the finish treads and risers in place though. Instead, I install subtreads and subrisers of ¾-in. plywood. These serve as the treads and risers during construction and form the base for finish treads and risers. The effect this has on layout is that I need to add the ¾-in. thickness of the subtread to the tread thickness when calculating how much shorter to cut the bottom riser.

➡ See "Stair Theory," p. 246.

To leave room to the side of the stringers for drywall and a finish skirtboard, I space the stringers from the sidewalls with a 2×4.

➡ See "Finish Skirtboards, Treads, and Risers," p. 262.

Installing main stringers on a wall

First, cut the stringers, place them in the stairwell location, and pencil a line on the studs at the bottom edge of the stringer. ❶ Cut a 2×4 so its bottom aligns with these marks, using the lower portion of the stringer as a pattern to lay out the length and cuts on this 2×4. Nail the 2×4 across the studs, just above the pencil line, with at least two 16d nails per stud. ❷ Now, permanently install the side stringers, fastening them to the 2×4 at least every foot with 16d nails or 3-in. structural screws. ❸ Also install the center stringer(s), fastened at the top with a strap, as described earlier.

Installing subtreads and subrisers

Using a circular saw or tablesaw, cut the subtreads and subrisers from ¾-in. plywood to the run and rise dimensions and to a length equal to the total width of the staircase. That way, they will sit flush to the outside edges of the stringers.

Working from the bottom up and one step at a time, install the subriser first, then the subtread as follows:

- Spread construction adhesive on the stringer edge.

- Set the subriser in place.

- Screw the subriser to the stringer. ❹

- Spread construction adhesive on the back edge of the subtread.

- Set the subtread in place and screw it to the stringer and the subriser below. ❺, ❻

1 Lay out the location of the 2×4 spacer by holding the stringer in place and marking its bottom on the studs.

4 Install the subriser to the stringers with construction adhesive and screws.

Finally, reach behind the subriser and predrill through it into the back edge of the subtread about every foot. ❼ Screw through the subriser into the rear edge of the subtread with 2-in. deck screws. Repeat this as you go, all the way to the top of the stair. The screws and the adhesive help considerably in stiffening both subtreads and subrisers.

2 Cut the 2×4 spacer, using the bottom of the stringer as a template for the bottom cuts. Nail the 2×4 spacer to the wall.

3 Fasten the stringer to the 2×4 spacer with 16d nails or 3-in. structural screws.

5 Spread a wide bead of construction adhesive on the top edge of the stringer.

6 Screw the subtread to the subriser below, as well as to the stringers.

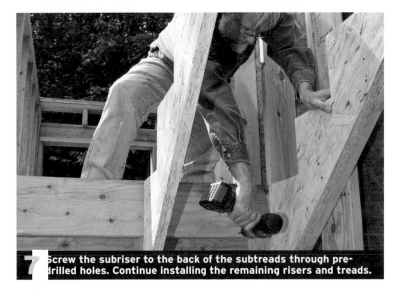

7 Screw the subriser to the back of the subtreads through pre-drilled holes. Continue installing the remaining risers and treads.

FINISH SKIRTBOARDS, TREADS, AND RISERS

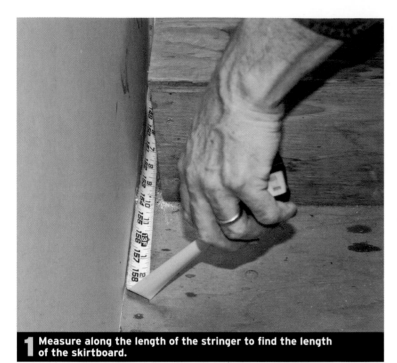

1 Measure along the length of the stringer to find the length of the skirtboard.

2 Using a framing square set to the rise and run of your stairs, lay out the ends of a skirtboard.

Finishing main stairs is a task left until the drywall is up and includes the installation of 1×10 skirtboards along the sides of the stairs and covering the subtreads and subrisers with finish-grade stock.

Installing the skirtboards

First, sweep the dirt off the stairs. After months of construction, they'll be covered with all sorts of crud. Next, use a sharp chisel to pare away any hardened construction adhesive that oozed out when you fastened the subtreads and subrisers.

With a helper, measure the stringer from where the bottom subriser meets the floor to where the back of the top subtread meets the floor framing. Stretch the tape tight to measure the stringer, reading the measurement where the bottom subriser meets the floor. **1** Use that as the bottom dimension of the skirtboard. Use a framing square and the rise and run dimensions of the stair to lay out a plumb cut at the top of the skirtboard. **2** Clamp a square to the skirtboard at the short end of this plumb cut. **3** Pull a

tape from here and mark the length of the stringer that you just measured on the bottom of the skirtboard. At the bottom of the skirtboard, use a square to lay out a level cut extending 6 in. or so beyond the length you just marked. Flip the square around and lay out a plumb cut to the end of this level cut. Cut the skirtboard's ends with a circular saw. **4** There will be two skirtboards, and they'll be mirror images of each other. Test fit the first, then lay it face to face with the stock to lay out the second.

Drop the skirtboard down alongside the stringer. **5** I like to shim the skirtboards away from the wall and tight to the stringer. That makes the 1×10 skirtboard look like heavier stock after I trim the gap between it and the wall with a piece of cove or quarter round. You can, however, simply fasten the skirtboards directly against the drywall, letting the ends of the finish treads and risers cover the gap between the skirtboards and the edges of the subtreads and risers.

Shim at each stud, inserting the first shim

of each pair butt end first and the second one thin end first. **6** Screw the skirtboard to each stud, close enough to the subtreads so the finish tread will cover the screw. **7** Score and snap off the shims. >> >> >>

3 Clamp a layout square to the skirtboard at the bottom corner to anchor a tape to lay out the length.

4 Make careful circular saw cuts on the ends of a skirtboard.

5 Place the cut skirtboard in the gap between the stringer and the drywall.

6 To keep the skirtboard plumb, shim the skirtboard tight to the stringer.

7 Fasten the skirtboard to studs through the shims. Use screws in spots that will be covered by the treads.

TRADE SECRET

I usually use 1×10 primed pine or hardwood, such as oak, for the skirtboards. Finish treads are readily available in home centers. Most are oak- or pine-veneered 5/4×12. Through online sources, they can also be had prefinished and in a wide variety of wood species. The risers are typically made from 1×8 primed pine.

FINISH SKIRTBOARDS, TREADS, AND RISERS (CONTINUED)

8 Measure the cutting angles and the length of the risers or treads using a tread template.

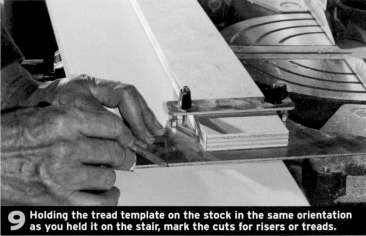

9 Holding the tread template on the stock in the same orientation as you held it on the stair, mark the cuts for risers or treads.

11 Prevent squeaky treads by using lots of construction adhesive.

12 Set the tread in, slide in the riser behind it, and move the tread in tight.

13 From below, screw the treads and risers for a fastener-free look.

Cutting treads and risers

You may need to rip the tread stock on a tablesaw to the specific run of your stairs, but add 1 in. to 1¼ in. to the run for the overhang beyond the front edge of the finished riser. When there are skirt-boards on both sides of the stair, as here, the finish risers don't need to extend the full height of the subrisers. They should come flush with the top of the subtreads, but they can hang above the subtread below as long as the finish treads will hide the gap.

You might think you could measure between the skirtboards and cut the tread and riser stock square, but that rarely works. If the cut is off half a degree from the skirtboard, it makes a noticeable gap.

I measure both the width and the edge angles of each tread and riser using a tread template. **8** The one I use is made by the Collins Tool Company, and it is slick. The ends fit on a 1×4. Align them on the subtread or subriser, tighten the nuts, and you have an exact template of the workpiece. You can do pretty much the same thing with two pieces of plywood, each the width of the tread and a little

more than half its length. Hold the pieces in place, with their ends tight to the skirtboards, then screw them together. If you're doing more than one stair, buy the template.

Installing the treads and risers

Beginning with the bottom step, work up one step at a time, cutting and fitting each pair of treads and risers as you go.

Transfer the length and cut angle from the template to the tread—use a sharp pencil. **9** If you're cutting with a sliding miter saw—the best tool for the job—check that the saw is set at the correct angle by making a test cut ⅛ in. or so beyond the line. Any discrepancy will be apparent, and you can then make whatever slight adjustments are called for. **10** Whatever you use to cut the tread, remove the line, but no more, with your cut.

Spread construction adhesive on the subtread **11**, then set the finish tread in place leaving enough space to let the riser slip in behind it. **12** Set the riser next, tapping it flush with the top of the

10 Make a test cut next to your mark to graphically illustrate any angle adjustment you may need to make. Cut the stock.

14 Measure precisely for the molding between the skirtboards with pinch sticks made from scrap and a spring clamp.

Trim below the tread nosings with cove molding to hide the gap between the riser and the tread above it.

subtread above, then push the finish tread tight to the face of the riser. Treads and risers should seat with just a little hand pressure.

If there's no access to the bottom of the stair, then shoot a few finish nails into the tread and riser to hold them until the glue sets. If, as in this case, there's access from below, have a helper keep the tread and riser from moving, and screw them in from below. **13** This takes a lot of moving from the top to the bottom of the stairs, but it's worth it to achieve a no-fastener look. Be sure your screws don't penetrate the face of the tread or riser.

Use pinch sticks—a pair of sticks with their corners mitered to points—to measure for cove or scotia molding. Hold them so the ends contact both skirtboards and clamp them together with a spring clamp. **14** Use the clamped pinch sticks to mark the length of the molding and tack it in place.

GLOSSARY

APRON The bottom piece of an interior window casing, below the stool.

BALUSTER Closely spaced vertical member in a railing system.

BASE MOLDING Trim piece installed where a wall meets a floor.

BEAM Horizontal structural member, often supporting other members.

BUTT JOINT Joint created when two members meet at 90 degrees.

CASING Molding used to transition between a door or window jamb and the wall.

CLAPBOARD Horizontally applied siding, each upper member lapping the lower.

COLUMN Vertical structural member.

COPED JOINT Joint created by cutting the end of a piece of molding to fit the profile of the intersecting piece.

CRICKET A pitched section of roof intended to divert water from an assembly such as a chimney.

CROSSCUT To cut perpendicular to the grain of the wood.

CROWN The convex edge of a piece of lumber.

CROWN MOLDING Trim piece installed where a wall meets a ceiling.

CUP A lumber defect characterized by turned-up edges.

DEAD LOAD The weight of a structure itself, without a live load. See Live Load.

EAVE The overhang at the bottom edge of a roof.

ELEVATION Height relative to a benchmark; blueprint view of a building as if viewed from the front, side, or rear.

END GRAIN Wood at the end of a board exposed by a crosscut.

FASCIA Trim board run along the ends of rafters or roof trusses.

FLASHING Metal, plastic, or membrane used to divert water in roofing or siding.

FLUSH A condition created when the edges of two surfaces lie exactly in the same plane.

FLUSH BEAM, FLUSH GIRDER A beam or girder whose top is at the same level as the tops of the joists it supports.

GABLE The triangular end of a roof.

GIRDER See Beam.

GUARDRAIL A railing intended to prevent one from falling past an edge.

HANDRAIL A railing intended to provide a steadying grasp along a stair.

HEADER A short beam, typically above a door or window opening.

HIP The intersection on a roof where two pitched planes meet at an external angle.

IRC International Residential Code, the most common American building code.

JAMB The edge pieces from which a door hangs, or which contain window sashes.

JOIST The principal horizontal load-carrying member of a floor or ceiling system.

LEDGER Horizontal framing member attached to a wall and supporting a joist system or shed roof rafters.

LEVEL Perpendicular to Earth's axis, 90 degrees from plumb.

LIVE LOAD The expected weight of a structure's furnishings and occupants.

MITER Joint created when each member is cut at half the angle of the intersection.

MUDSILL Flat, horizontal structural member joining wood framing to the foundation.

NEWEL Post supporting a railing.

OSB Oriented strand board, a type of structural panel made from wood chips.

PITCH The measure of an angle relative to the horizontal.

PLAN VIEW Blueprint drawn from a viewpoint directly above.

PLATE Flat, horizontal structural member, typically at the top and bottom of walls.

PLUMB Parallel with Earth's axis, 90 degrees from level.

PLYWOOD Wooden panels composed of laminated veneer layers, typically used as sheathing or subfloor.

RAFTER The principal carrying member of a traditional roof system.

RAKE The gable edge of a roof, or its angle.

RIDGE The uppermost member of a roof, which provides a nailing point for the tops of the rafters.

RIP To cut in the direction of the grain of wood.

RISE A measure of elevation.

RISER The vertical component of a stair, interspersed between treads.

RUN A horizontal measurement.

SASH The glass of a window and its frame.

SEISMIC LOAD Stresses placed upon a building by an earthquake.

SHEAR Loads parallel to a plane such as a wall, floor, or roof.

SHEATHING Structural panels used to cover floors, walls, and roofs.

SHOE MOLDING Small trim piece used where base molding meets the floor.

SILL The pitched member at the exterior bottom of a door or window.

SOFFIT The underside of eaves assemblies.

STOOL Interior shelf-like molding at the bottom of a window.

STUD A vertical member of a wall assembly.

SUBFLOOR Structural floor sheathing applied directly to the joists.

TREAD Portion of a stair upon which one walks.

TRUSS An engineered-lumber assembly used in place of rafters or floor joists.

UNDERLAYMENT Panels applied between subflooring and finish floors.

VALLEY The exterior surface of a roof created at the intersection of two pitched roof planes meeting at an interior angle.

WANE Rounded edge on a board, left from where the bark attached to the tree.

WIND LOAD The force applied to a structure by wind.

INDEX

INDEX